Deny, dismiss, dehumanise

MINISTER-PRESIDENT

Mr P. Cluskey
Veurseweg 20
2252 AG VOORSCHOTEN

Binnenhof 19
2513 AA Den Haag
Postbus 20001
2500 EA Den Haag
www.rijksoverheid.nl

T 070 356 44 50

Our reference
4046221

Date 31 January 2019

Dear Mr Cluskey,

Let me begin by expressing my sincere condolences on the death of your wife. I can scarcely imagine what you and Adrienne went through in recent years.

I have great respect for Adrienne's tireless efforts to achieve official acknowledgement and increase transparency in cases of medical errors. I am also terribly sorry that you feel you and your wife did not receive the support to which you were entitled from the organisations involved. I can fully understand your desire to draw attention to this situation.

In your letter to me, you enclosed the letter that you sent to the Ministry of Health, Welfare and Sport. It has been agreed with that ministry that you will receive a detailed response from, or on behalf of, the Minister for Medical Care as soon as possible.

What happened to your wife is indescribably tragic, and I wish that circumstances were otherwise. May you find the strength to cope with this immense loss.

Yours sincerely,

Prime Minister of the Netherlands,

Mark Rutte

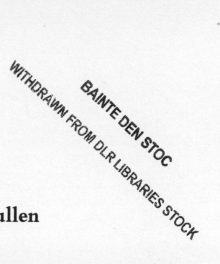

Adrienne Cullen

DENY, DISMISS, DEHUMANISE

What happened when I went to hospital

Index

The Scale of the Problem

23% of EU citizens claim to have been directly affected by medical error. Strategies to reduce the rate of adverse events would lead to the prevention each year of more than
- *750,000 harm-inflicting medical errors*
- *3.2 million days of hospitalization*
- *260,000 incidents of permanent disability*
- 95,000 deaths

WHO[1]

In 2003, I became involved in setting up the patient safety programme within the UMC Utrecht. We started from scratch – the Dutch word for patient safety at that time literally did not exist.
Ian Leistikow[2]

"Medical error – the third leading cause of death in the US"
BMJ, 2016[3]

---

1   A World Health Organization report from Regional Office for Europe.
2   Ian Leistikow was co-ordinator of UMC Utrecht's patient safety programme from 2003 to 2011. He is now a senior inspector at the Dutch Healthcare Inspectorate. Quote is fromLeistikow, I. (2017) Prevention is better than Cure: Learning from Adverse Events in Healthcare. CRC Press: Boca Raton, Florida.
3   *British Medical Journal.* (May 2016) A report by Martin Makary and Michael Daniel, Department of Surgery at Johns Hopkins University School of Medicine.

Preface to Adrienne Cullen's book

You are about to read an extraordinary story ...

Adrienne Cullen's cancer diagnosis was delayed for two years when a pathology test result went "missing" in 2011 in the hospital where she was being treated, UMC (University Medical Centre) Utrecht. This delay allowed Adrienne's cancer to advance undetected to the stage where it became incurable, meaning that Adrienne would die unnecessarily as a result of that missed diagnosis. This was inescapable. To make matters even worse, if that were possible, her hospital fell severely short in giving her appropriate support after the medical negligence was discovered. For a long time, there was no apology despite the scale of the negligence, and, despite multiple requests to the hospital's board, no investigation into what had caused it.

After a considerable battle, Adrienne and her husband, Peter, received financial compensation that was unprecedented in the Netherlands (though small in comparison with many other EU countries, including Ireland and the UK). However, communication between the hospital and the patient it had harmed was now through their lawyers only. Her doctor tried to maintain contact and ensure there was adequate follow-up

Deny, dismiss, dehumanise

care, but he himself was, in effect, also a victim of the hospital's inadequate systems and traumatized by what had happened. He received very little support from his peers. That is perhaps because of the culture in medicine: doctors see themselves as people who provide care, and all too often find it difficult to ask for care and support themselves.

I was, at that time, one of the medical managers in this hospital and belonged to the leadership of the department that Adrienne had trusted to treat her. Only when I met Adrienne and her husband for the first time, 16 months after the discovery of the missed diagnosis, did I realize that we had failed spectacularly to provide the care that was needed by both Adrienne and her doctor when the hospital system failed them both. After 25 years in clinical practice, I finally understood the true meaning of the term 'a just culture' after medical error, and saw first-hand why it is so essential – to both patients and doctors.

Medical error occurs, unfortunately. But Adrienne tells a story that is about much more than human error by doctors. It goes further and uncovers the systemic and cultural issues that allow health providers to fail their patients. Adrienne's perseverance in excavating these complex multi-faceted issues was clear-eyed, quite exceptional, and very courageous. Not many people could have achieved it. In spite of being very ill and a foreigner here in the Netherlands, Adrienne fought for years to get the care she was entitled to, and kept pointing out the many lessons to be learnt from her story, not just by doctors and hospitals, but by patients themselves, by healthcare regulators, and by legislators. She died at Antoni van Leeuwenhoek hospital in Amsterdam on December 31, 2018, but those hard-won lessons live on here in the pages of this book, completed just two days before she passed away.

Adrienne was adamant about one thing in particular, and having been part of her tragic story, I agree with her totally: Patients are the co-owners of the healthcare system and the partners of the medical professionals entrusted to run it. Without acknowledging this and acting in a manner which makes that partnership real and meaningful, will we never succeed in improving the services on which countless people – our families, our friends and our fellow citizens – depend every day. In an era when we strive constantly for value and frequently speak about patient-centered healthcare in that context, we need to think again about what we actually mean. As doctors, we must empower patients, use our skills to explain, counsel and recommend, ask what they need, and then listen to them. Adrienne contributes enormously to this notion by telling her own story in such detailed and uncompromising terms. Although she is gone, her words will continue to create a new awareness.

Adrienne has forgiven and, remarkably, sometimes even protected, the doctors who treated her at UMC Utrecht and who subsequently apologized to her. In the following pages she shows huge generosity of spirit, respect for human rights, and belief in her own core values of empathy, compassion and honesty. To quote the 18th century English poet, Alexander Pope, "To err is human, to forgive divine". Perhaps that is the most compelling aspect of Adrienne Cullen's terrible story: her extraordinary capacity for forgiveness and her belief that, in the end, it is forgiveness and not conflict that breaks down barriers and leads to lasting change.

Arie Franx
Utrecht, January 2019

1 | June 2013 … UMC, Utrecht

It is much easier patiently – and tolerantly – to avoid the person you have injured than to approach him as a friend.
You need courage for that.
Ludwig Wittgenstein

I knew something was wrong the moment I saw the doctor arrive. I could tell by the half-smile he gave without true eye-contact, by his tentative body language as each of us stood back to allow the other enter the consulting room first – a hesitancy that had us both colliding idiotically with a pot plant strangely placed right outside the door. I knew this man well, and I knew with certainty what was about to happen next. But when he said "I have bad news", I still flinched and looked away to the other side of the room asking, "How bad is it?"

The answer was that it was very bad. A cone biopsy performed a few weeks previously on my cervix had contained a one-centimetre chunk of an adenocarcinoma. Worse still, the margins weren't clean. That meant that while the biopsy had removed some of the tumour, the rest of it was still inside me. I had cancer, and I had had it for a long time.

Let's roll back a little to two years earlier, May 2011. I was in the same room. I was with the same doctor, Huub van der Vaart. I knew him quite well as we had been trying to figure out for nearly a year why I had a strange vaginal discharge. Tests had been carried out, but no answers had emerged. So in that consulting room in the gynaecology department of the University Medical Centre in Utrecht in the Netherlands, I was told, gently but insistently, that my vaginal discharge was "idiosyncratic", that all the tests showed nothing abnormal, nothing worrying. I was told that whatever was causing the discharge, it was not gynaecological in origin. The doctor and the department could do nothing further to help me. And so I went away and tried to learn to live with it. That's what patients with "idiosyncratic" symptoms do.

But something had been forgotten. Something had been overlooked. Something was sitting in my file unseen by my doctor that day in May 2011 – something that had not been flagged by UMC Utrecht pathologists. That something shouted loud and clear that I had cervical cancer.

A sample of my cervical tissue had been taken a month earlier, on 13 April 2011, while I was under general anaesthetic for cryosurgery, a small, unrelated gynaecological procedure. I didn't know this tissue sample had been taken and sent to the lab – so I didn't ask about it when I saw the doctor in May. And because the taking of this sample was secondary to the procedure being done that day, he didn't remember he had carried out this curettage (scraping of the lining of the cervix) and had sent some of the tissue to the lab. And so he didn't notice when he received no notification about it from pathology. As a result, the test result that shouted loud and clear that I had cervical cancer remained unheard and unseen. And it stayed that way for two years.

Back to 2013 again, 3 April, almost two years after the cancer-positive result slipped into my file unseen by everyone, a research student came across it. He saw result indicating suspected adenocarcinoma ... but no mention of follow-up. He was puzzled. Why had nothing been done? He brought it to the attention of Van der Vaart.

Let's just imagine for a minute what that feels like. You're a kind doctor. You've always cared for your patients and always treated them with respect. You're hard-working, you're good at your job, and you're dedicated. You're at the top of your field of specialization – in fact, you made professor last year. You're liked and held in high esteem by your colleagues, your students and your patients. You're a good physician. And then you see that your patient – you remember her well – has a two-year-old cancer warning in her file. You ordered that test, you never saw that result, and now some research fellow is standing in front of you. Can you feel the blood draining from your face and the sweat starting to prickle cold around your hairline? Can you feel the urge to sit down quickly because you're afraid your legs are going to stop holding you up? Can you hear the voice saying, "This can't be happening", but knowing it is? What do you do?

Professor Van der Vaart did the right thing. On 3 April, 2013, he phoned me. In my ignorance, I didn't fully grasp what he was telling me and thought it was simply a routine follow-up from the cryosurgery two years earlier. He asked me if I still had the vaginal discharge. Of course I had. He asked to see me at my earliest convenience. I still didn't really get it – not on that day.

Van der Vaart did the next thing right too. A few days after the discovery, he knocked on the door of his line manager, Professor Bart Fauser. He told him what had happened, that a cancer diagnosis had appeared in a patient's file in April 2011 without him ever having seen it or signing off on it and it had only been brought to his attention, almost two years later. Van der Vaart speculated that the transition from paper-based patient files to electronic files that had been taking place at the time might have been responsible. Fauser looked up from his research just long enough to tell him to inform the hospital lawyers. That was the extent of the peer support, counselling and human concern my doctor received from his bosses at UMCU. And it was pretty much on a par with the support, understanding and humanity they showed to me and my devastated husband, Peter.

Better late than never, I underwent various tests to try to put together a picture of what had been happening inside my cervix. The worst fears, shared by Peter, Van der Vaart and myself, turned out to be true. I had a chunky, barrel-shaped adenocarcinoma measuring some 4.7 centimetres long and about three centimetres in diameter. On 13 June 2013, I was diagnosed with cervical cancer.

Strangely, I could come to terms with this. Although it was deadly serious, I was coping, after a fashion. And so was Peter. But what neither of us could come to terms with was the way I was being treated by UMCU. To me, it was central to my treatment that everybody who came into contact with me should know what had happened. They needed to understand why I felt betrayed, terrified, alienated and confused. I had become a hypervigilant patient, watching what was happening to me at every moment, querying every decision. I was traumatized by events, and the fact that I spoke no Dutch was making the alienation unbearable.

But healthcare workers, professional doctors and nurses, would be able to understand this, right? Apparently not. They neither understood nor saw why there was any need to understand. Van der Vaart was no longer in charge of my care. He wasn't an oncologist, so he had no further role in looking after me. I was almost as devastated by what had happened to him as by what had happened to me, and it was a further distress for me that I had no way of knowing how he was coping. To my mind, he too had become a patient. Paradoxically, although he was the person at the centre of the terrible fiasco that had caused two years to pass before I was given any cancer treatment, he was the only person in the hospital I trusted.

Deny, dismiss, dehumanise

My new doctor, Dr Brouwer, a gynaecological oncologist at UMCU knew what had happened, but didn't see any particular need to address it, beyond an initial acknowledgement that he was aware of it. Nor did he see any need to take it into consideration during my ongoing treatment. Both he and the department's other gynaecological oncologist were adamant that the vaginal discharge I had had when I was sent away from the hospital in 2011 had nothing whatsoever to do with cervical cancer. "It's not a symptom", they declared.

My tumour was too big to be removed by robotic surgery – UMCU's preferred method for dealing with early cervical cancers. So the protocol dictated radiotherapy with adjuvant chemotherapy. I was asked if I'd take part in a Europe-wide clinical trial in which half the patients with my stage of the disease underwent surgery after their radiotherapy and chemo. I wanted to know which was better – to have surgery afterwards or not, or indeed if conventional surgery on its own would be better, or surgery and then radio-chemo. I was told it didn't work that way. I had to choose whether to go on the clinical trial or not and then it was the luck of the draw whether I'd be in the surgery group or not after my radio-chemo, and if I wasn't, they wouldn't operate. I didn't want to be experimented on. I wanted to know which was the best option for me and to have that option made available. Peter agreed with me. The doctors apparently didn't see it that way. The conversation went nowhere. I asked for something to help me sleep as I hadn't slept since I was first given the diagnosis the previous week. I was asked why I couldn't sleep. I thought the reason was obvious.

At the MRI suite, I joined the queue with all the other patients. I was reprimanded for not alerting them in advance that it was difficult to insert a cannula in my veins. I had apparently delayed their morning's schedule because they needed to call an anaesthetist to insert a cannula for the contrast dye. Stupidly, I apologized and said I'd remember to tell them in future. No one there knew or cared that UMCU had made a serious error that would ultimately cost me my life. I was just another patient getting in the way of an otherwise smooth-running system.

In the operating theatre, where I had to have a gynaecological examination under anaesthetic, a well-meaning staff member asked me why I was there. I told her I had cervical cancer. She replied, "Never mind. I'm sure they have caught it very early". I burst into uncontrollable tears. I wanted to scream, "No! This hospital lost my cancer diagnosis for two years and there's a good chance I'm going to die!" But I said nothing. The woman had intended to be kind. I just cried and cried and no one had any idea why. No one knew I was a victim of medical negligence at their hospital. The anaesthetist didn't know either. "Think of something nice", he encouraged. That made me cry even more. He didn't have time for this unreasonable display of emotion, so he just knocked me out anyway. Where was my doctor during all this? Who was there to support this totally traumatized patient? No one. The fact that I was the victim of medical negligence at UMCU wasn't known. No one told any of the staff who were looking after me in the theatre, post-operatively or in the wards what had happened. So they must have decided it wasn't relevant.

When I came around from the anaesthetic, I was still crying. I was very distressed and shivering uncontrollably. The nurse looking after me kept saying, "Stop shivering. I can't get proper readings because you keep shivering". So she didn't know anything either. She was just looking after an emotional foreign patient who was causing a fuss for some reason.

I remembered TV ads about MacMillan Nurses who specialized in supporting cancer patients, so we asked in UMCU about an equivalent service here in the Netherlands. We were told there was nothing like that here. So we asked for a psychologist in the hospital who specialized in looking after patients who had just had a cancer diagnosis. Again, we were told, "No, there are no cancer-specialist psychologists in the hospital and we are unaware of any such speciality anywhere in the country."

We were puzzled, hurt and disbelieving that there was no specialist help on offer for me. Why was UMCU not stepping in to help? Everyone was treating me as though nothing unusual had happened, and I needed to just get on with it and stop making a fuss. We asked about making a complaint. We were given a brochure in Dutch about the hospital complaints procedure and a form to fill in. For us, the situation had gone way beyond filling in a complaints form.

We discovered later, much later, that apart from Fauser, the hospital lawyers and a few members of the gynaecology team, no one in the hospital knew that they had lost my cancer diagnosis, not the patient safety officer, not the hospital board and not the CEO, Professor Jan Kimpen – and it was nobody's job to offer help to patients damaged by hospital errors and medical negligence. "Second harm" was a concept they had apparently never heard of. UMCU had no policies for dealing with the consequences that medical errors and negligence have for patients and their families. The hospital had no "sentinel events" policy that included any form of specialized care for patients, for their families or for the physicians involved. Apart from Van der Vaart, who was devastated, no one at the hospital apologized to me. It never occurred to them that this would be the appropriate thing to do. There wasn't even enough common decency or compassion at UMCU to realize that they should have been actively helping us, not looking at my tears with incomprehension and tight-lipped disapproval.

Van der Vaart asked a particularly kind and able nurse, Claire, to look after me when I was at the hospital – and without her kindness, Peter and I would have been in a very bad place. But Van der Vaart and Claire were the only ones helping us. It wasn't enough. We spoke to Van der Vaart twice in the days after the cancer diagnosis to see if we could learn more about what had happened. He told us again that he believed that somehow the transition to electronic patient files had caused the test results to slip into my file without him seeing them. But this was only speculation on his part. He had no answer as to why the pathologist had not contacted him directly by phone to notify him that his patient had a suspected cancer, especially since the finding was so much at odds with the procedure being performed by him in theatre that day. It was an unexpected finding that he would have expected the pathologist to have flagged. But that didn't happen. And no one from hospital management was stepping forward to explain. We were so sure that an investigation was being carried out that we didn't even question it. We were waiting for those investigating the errors to talk to us.

Each time we went to UMCU, we expected someone to find us and say, "We heard what happened to you at our hospital and we'd just like to say how sorry we are and to assure you that we are doing everything in our power to find out what went wrong". We also expected them to say, "We realize that getting a cancer diagnosis in these circumstances is doubly traumatic for you both. What we can do to make this easier? We want you to know we are here for you". But no one said any of those things. In fact, UMCU had absolutely nothing whatsoever to say to a patient who now had a potentially terminal cancer as a result of their negligence.

So we went to a lawyer, and there we found compassion. She asked UMCU's legal department to report the incident to the Dutch health inspectorate (IGZ).[4] They declined on the grounds that whatever had happened had occurred two years ago, so in their opinion, it was too long ago for the inspectorate to be interested in it. And anyway, the specific circumstances of what

---

4   IGZ stands for Inspectie voor de Gezondheidszorg. Since 2017, it has become known as the Inspectie voor de Gezondheidszorg en Jeugd (IGJ).

Deny, dismiss, dehumanise

happened to me would not be repeated because they did things differently now. So UMCU's lawyers told no one. We were also assured that there had been no similar incidents involving other patients as UMCU moved from paper-based files to electronic files.

Our lawyer encouraged us to ask for a second opinion – fast.

2 | July 2013 … AMC, Amsterdam

There should be no discrimination against languages people speak, skin colour, or religion.
Malala Yousefzai

D r Ko van der Velden at the Academic Medical Centre (AMC) in Amsterdam was a breath of fresh air. This unpretentious man disarmed me with his common-sense kindness and insight. And he had read my file. That might sound obvious, but I have discovered over the past five years, in almost every hospital I have visited, no one reads the patient's file. No one knows the patient's history. It was clear to me after talking to Dr Van der Velden for five minutes that he was "my man". Whatever it took, this was the doctor I wanted to be sitting across from as I went on the cancer journey. He spent the first ten minutes of our meeting recounting my own story to me in English tinged with an Australian accent. He had worked in Sydney for a while in the 1990s during his training and some of the Aussie tones had stuck. Listening to him tell my story to me was both shocking (because it externalized the harsh facts) and reassuring (because it was a comfort to see that someone understood the catastrophe that had

Deny, dismiss, dehumanise

befallen me). Not given to commenting on the mistakes of others, he nevertheless found the details of my story hard to fathom. On the matter of my vaginal discharge, which UMC Utrecht had been adamant was "not a symptom of cervical cancer", Van der Velden merely observed, "Oh, I think it is. Don't you?" And he was correct. Staining tests carried out on the tumour later revealed that my adenocarcinoma was mucinous, and a vaginal discharge such as I had was indeed a symptom. But I'm getting ahead of myself a bit here.

After what had happened to me in Utrecht, it was going to be very unlikely that I would ever again trust another doctor or another hospital. In fact, it seemed to me then – and I still believe this – to be a dereliction of my duty to myself ever again to place my fate blindly in the hands of others. But I couldn't treat myself. I needed the help of doctors, nurses and hospitals. So in so far as I was ever going to trust another doctor again, I decided to trust Van der Velden. That afternoon, I asked him if he would agree to take me as a patient, and by close of business I had informed UMCU that I would not be back. Within days, I was booked in for a gynaecological examination under anaesthetic. Afterwards Van der Velden told me that he and the radiologist who performed the examination with him had reached a different conclusion from UMCU about my cancer staging, and so about my treatment options.

The new plan was to operate to remove the tumour. This would entail a Wertheim Okabayashi radical hysterectomy. Anyone interested in the gory details, feel free to Google it, but all you really need to know was that the cervix, the uterus, lots of lymph nodes and as much of the surrounding tissue as the surgeons dared to take would be removed. One of the big downsides was that it was hard to perform this operation without damaging at least some of the nerves to the bladder. I might wake up from the surgery not able to empty my bladder normally, and whether this would be permanent or temporary, only time would tell. But the major advantage was that I had about a 50/50 chance of needing no further treatment – so no radiotherapy and no chemo.

I was admitted to the gynaecology ward of AMC on 22 July 2013 for surgery the following day. The nurse who admitted me was very "curious" that I was living and working in the Netherlands and didn't speak Dutch. "But you are planning to learn, right? If you're living here, you should speak Dutch", she admonished. "The law says you must." Idiotically, I tried to justify myself. My explanations about working for an international company where English was the common language sounded lame, as did excuses that a long daily commute and working 40-hours-a-week in a dynamic new job while trying to deal with an undiagnosed cancer left little energy for anything except sleep. But I was getting nowhere. This nurse made it clear that trying to live in the Netherlands without speaking Dutch was, in her opinion, bad-mannered and impractical. She told me that I could get a better job if I spoke Dutch, that staff were not allowed to treat patients in any language except Dutch, and that it was not fair to expect staff to have the same empathy with patients who didn't speak their language. I felt very unwelcome, but tried my best not to let this nurse upset me. Curiously, I don't think she had any idea that she was being unkind. She thought she was helping me by setting me straight. She knew what was best for me. I fought back the tears and waited for someone else to come on shift.

The surgery went well. The tumour was gone, as were my uterus, cervix and 36 lymph nodes. It was too soon yet to tell if my bladder was still functioning.

The day after surgery, I started to feel itchy all over and very unwell. Sensitivity to one of the painkillers was suspected, and I was wheeled back to post-operative recovery to have the offending drug stopped. They gave me OxyContin instead. That made matters worse. For the next 12 hours, I was on the scariest of "bad trips" – hallucinations, feelings of dread and terror, heart racing, dry mouth, inability to sleep or even remotely relax. Luke was the nurse on shift that night. He explained to me what was happening. He told me how long it was likely to last. He held my hand. Somehow, knowing what was happening and that it would end by the following morning made it more manageable. I could bear it, even though some of the hallucinations were overwhelming, repulsive and very dark.

I had been aware that I was sensitive to the benzodiazepine family of drugs (tranquilizers such as diazepam and temazepam) after suffering an extreme paradoxical reaction to midazolam a few years earlier. Now it was starting to look as though I was sensitive to some painkillers too. Luke checked on me regularly to make sure I was alright and to reassure me it would eventually stop. I started to tell him what had happened to me in UMCU. Actually, I had assumed he already knew. I thought everyone knew. I was still a "hospital innocent" at that stage and believed that important information about patients was communicated from department to department with the patient's file and from shift to shift. I thought it was in some obvious place in my file – the first thing anyone looking at it would see. But even in my OxyContin-induced horror, I realized that Luke knew nothing of my background. Neither he nor any of the staff looking after me had any idea that my cancer was as advanced as it was because of serious medical negligence at another hospital.

Over the years, Peter and I have told many people in several hospitals about my medical background and the proven negligence at UMCU. In every instance, the person we told has agreed that it is vital for nurses and doctors to have this information in order to understand fully how best to care for me. But in every instance, the only way they have ever found out was if Peter or I told them. On that night, Luke listened patiently and with full understanding of the impact this must have had on me as a patient. He is a good nurse and a good listener, but it is not easy to tell my story to strangers.

As promised, the OxyContin worked its way out of my system shortly after sunrise and I started to doze. Nurses came and went. I was cleaned up and, feeling more comfortable, I started to relax.

Mid-morning, the door to my room opened and a woman came in. She started speaking to me. I caught that her name was Anoeska (the same name as one of my friends) and that she was a physiotherapist. I held out my hand to her and said, "I'm Adrienne, and I'm very sorry, Anoeska, but I don't speak Dutch". She drew back from me, put her hands on her hips and shouted at me, "Why don't you speak Dutch? You *live* in the Netherlands!"

I asked her to stop shouting at me and said I couldn't believe that she had just said that to a patient in a hospital bed. She shouted back that she wasn't shouting at me. I put my head in my hands and asked her to leave.

"Do you want pelvic physiotherapy or not?" she demanded.

"Just leave me alone."

"Whatever you want", she said as she flounced out the door. She wrote in the ward's day book that the patient had "refused treatment". But, of course, she didn't say why.

Some time later, a kind nurse, Anna, came in to see how I was. She didn't say anything about my morning visitor, so I told her that a very unpleasant woman had been in earlier. A physiotherapist.

"She shouted at me because I can't speak Dutch", I told Anna.

"I heard", she replied.

I thought she meant she had heard her shouting at me, but all she meant was that she had heard that the physiotherapist had been turned away by me and that I had refused treatment. No one had asked her why. And to this day, although I have told numerous people at AMC what Anoeska did and said, no one has ever approached her to ask her what she was thinking of shouting at a vulnerable, post-op patient about not speaking Dutch. Most people prefer to believe it never happened.

The reason, it transpired, that a physiotherapist had come to see me was that I needed to learn a new technique for emptying my bladder, in case the surgery had damaged the nerves to my bladder too much. If I didn't succeed in mastering the physiotherapy technique, or if there was too much nerve damage, I would have to learn how to self-catheterize and would have to do so five or six times a day for the rest of my life. Visions of trying to insert catheters while balancing precariously in smelly, cramped public toilets flashed across my mind, as did hiding catheters in my locker at work and figuring out how to get them to the toilets without causing curiosity. Learning this physiotherapy technique was going to be important to my quality of life from now on.

A few days later, Anoeska's physiotherapist colleague, a woman around my own age whose name I mercifully can't remember, came to show me how it was done. Anna promised she would stay with me throughout and assured me that this lady had no problem with English speakers as some member of her family was married to someone from England. The physiotherapist arrived and immediately started speaking Dutch and continued for some long sentences. I didn't understand any of it. After half a minute or so, I apologized and told her that I really didn't understand Dutch. She smiled and said, "I know, but I like to start every session with a few words of Dutch, just so we all remember what country we're in".

Anna was very embarrassed and didn't know where to look. I had a choice. I could take exception to this nasty little speech and ask the woman to leave (furtively concealed catheters, smelly public toilets, disposing of bags of my own urine all danced across my mind again), or I could submit and let her have this petty and mean-spirited power over me. So I laughed as though

I too thought this was a good-humoured observation and the appropriate way to deal with a foreign patient's lack of Dutch. I still haven't forgiven myself for doing so.

This "treatment" for not speaking Dutch continued intermittently for the rest of my stay. The kind nurses, the majority, were always caring, careful and concerned for me, but two or three others continued to bring up the language issue every time they were on shift. Sometimes, it was just some pursed lips when I responded to something with a polite, "I'm sorry, I don't understand". Other times, it was disapproval disguised as well-meaning advice, and with one nurse, it was disbelief that I couldn't understand what was being said to me, so the sentences were repeated, still in Dutch, but louder. The only person on the ward who really couldn't speak English was the most compassionate and most patient person. With gestures, smiles, humanity and patience, we communicated just fine.

But as time and the hour always run through even the roughest days, I was discharged back into the real world. I tried to forget the unkindness and focus on the fact that I had a doctor I liked, that the majority of the nurses had been kind, that this hospital had not lost any of my test results, and that soon I could get back to my husband, my home, my cat and the job I loved.

Deny, dismiss, dehumanise

3 | August to October 2013 ... AMC, Amsterdam

Recompense injury with justice, and recompense unkindness with kindness.
Forget injuries. Never forget kindness.
Confucius

The feeling of well-being I had when I was discharged from AMC on 30 July was tremendous. I was up and about. They'd found a painkiller that was strong enough to take the edge off the post-operative pain without causing hallucinations, and I was raring to go. I read books and went online to find the best ways of adapting my lifestyle to combat cancer. I was already relatively fit and cooked most meals from scratch using fresh ingredients, but I felt there was room for improvement. I bought more organic vegetables, fruit, meat, pasta, bread and rice. My neighbour practised Traditional Chinese Medicine and I started taking herbal supplements to boost my immune system and, allegedly, fight against the formation of tumours. There was no western style "proof" that any of this worked, but there could certainly be no harm in switching to more organic products. I had it all figured out. I'd take a month or so to recuperate, and then start working part time from home, and by mid-September I'd be back in the office. Easy-peasy. I'd even come to an arrangement with my bladder – if I took my time and used the delightful physiotherapist's technique, my bladder would co-operate and I could keep AMC's takeaway self-catheterization kits in their box.

Within a week of going home, I was taking short walks, digging the garden (when Peter wasn't watching) and feeling on top form. The wound was healing fast. Van der Velden mentioned that he once had a patient who was a long-distance truck driver and she was back behind the wheel three weeks after her radical hysterectomy. He wasn't advocating this, but my competitive soul rose to the challenge and said, "I bet I could do that too".

Early August, and it was time for my post-op checkup at AMC. It took us both by surprise that the pathology results were not good, and my chances of survival had dropped. One of the 36 lymph nodes removed during surgery had two millimetres of cancerous growth. The hospital protocol was that if any cancer-positive lymph nodes popped up, the patient should be treated with radiotherapy and adjuvant chemotherapy (cisplatin). This is the protocol in almost all hospitals in the world.

I considered asking for just chemo, which is the protocol in Germany and Japan. I figured that while chemo is poisonous and kills even harmless cells, at least I would be spared the effects of radiotherapy, which often delivers nasty surprises years after treatment. But really my problem was there had been just one tiny lymph node with a tiny growth on it – and it had been removed. Was there a need for treatment at all?

No one could answer that question for me. It was quite possible that I could decline all further treatment and never have any recurrence of my cancer. The endlessly patient Van der Velden didn't push me. He answered my questions and discussed the implications – medical, emotional and philosophical. He described as much as he could the possible and probable side-effects. He offered his experience, but didn't promise his way was the best. He encouraged me to think it through.

In the end, my decision came down to one argument that turned out to be a deal-breaker. How would I feel in, say, three years' time, if I didn't go for treatment now and the cancer returned? Would I feel guilty and regretful? Would I feel I had done myself a disservice? You bet I would! I would find it very hard to live with the consequences if the cancer returned and I had not done what pretty much every hospital in almost every country in the world thought was the right thing.

The treatment would be radiotherapy every Monday to Friday for five weeks. Each Wednesday, I would stay overnight in the chemotherapy room on AMC's gynaecology ward. I was not happy to be returning to the place where I had been tormented in July for not speaking Dutch, but I tried to put my fears aside and do the right thing.

Monday, 9 September was the date for my first radiotherapy session. The hospital advised me to ask my health insurers to arrange a taxi to bring me to AMC and take me home afterwards. This is standard in the Netherlands. But like every other patient, I was asked to pay the first €90 myself. In my book, that was a good deal. The week before the treatment started, I spoke to my insurers, who referred me to the taxi company they dealt with in my area. I worked out a schedule over the phone with a taxi company based on my radiotherapy appointments for the following week.

Monday morning arrived, but the taxi didn't. My appointment was for 11:15, the taxi was due at 10:15. The drive to Amsterdam usually took about 40–45 minutes, maybe a little longer on a Monday morning. The radiotherapy schedule was tight and the machines were in full swing from early morning to late evening. Patients were slotted in at 15-minute intervals in order to get everyone treated. Late arrivals would mess up the day's schedule and delay other cancer patients. At 10:25, I rang the taxi company. A woman answered giving her name as Monique. I asked if it was okay if we spoke in English. She replied in Dutch that was clear enough and slow enough for me to understand: "Madam, this is the Netherlands. Here, we do our business in Dutch". Despite my previous experiences, I was shocked.

"Can you put me on to one of your colleagues who is happy to speak English?" I asked. She replied something else to me in Dutch. I didn't understand, but I judged by the tone that it was more of the same. I started babbling pathetically, "Why are you being horrible to me? I only want to know when the taxi is coming because I have my first radiotherapy treatment this morning and the taxi is late". She told me then, in perfect English, that she would ring "planning". After a few minutes, she was back and told me that they were very busy and the traffic was heavy, but that my taxi would be with me at 10:45. That would be 30 minutes late, and too late to get to radiotherapy by 11:15. I told Monique this. I started to cry. Peter took the phone and asked to speak to someone in charge. He told her that 10:45 was half an hour later than agreed. She told him in English that she didn't know what he was talking about and hung up.

I hadn't wanted either Peter or myself subjected to a stressful drive up and down one of the Netherlands' busiest motorways before and after my radiotherapy sessions. But the prospect of being late for my first appointment was even more stressful for me. We got into the car and Peter drove. I rang the taxi company again. I had to make sure no taxi showed up at the house and marked us as a "no show". And I had to do something brave to make up for my pathetic blubbing earlier. This time, I got a nicer person. I told him what had happened earlier with Monique. He was apologetic, but I could tell he didn't really believe me. I asked him whether calls to his company are recorded.

"They are", he confirmed.

Great. I told him I wanted to make a complaint and asked him who I should talk to. He promised that someone would ring me later in the day when I was home from the hospital.

Deny, dismiss, dehumanise

My next call was to my insurance company who were paying for the taxi to bring me up and down to AMC. I told them the story. I told them that I would not ever ring that company again and that I didn't want that company to be responsible for getting me to my daily appointments. They too were horrified and promised that they would make enquiries and call me in the afternoon.

The radiotherapy wasn't half as stressful as getting a taxi was. Not that week at least.

A woman from the taxi company's client services phoned me that afternoon. She was really very good at her job. She told me she had listened to the tape of my earlier phone call with Monique, and that the conversation had happened just as I described. She also admitted that she agreed with me that it sounded as though Monique made a habit of answering non-Dutch speakers in this way – it had a sort of practised fluency to it. She said she had taken her off the phones already so that she wouldn't be dealing with the public for the moment. She also said that they would listen back to recorded calls to see if she had done the same thing before. Then she tried to persuade me to give the company another chance. She promised that the schedule I had lodged with them would be adhered to without flaw and that I would not have to phone the company again – I would be collected at the house each morning and again at AMC afterwards without having to chase them. I'm such a pushover. I believed her.

Of course, it didn't happen. There was no more abuse for not speaking Dutch, but the promises made by client services never materialized and the next two days were a nightmare of long waits, repeated phone calls, breakdowns on the motorway and general unpleasantness. By Thursday, we had opted for the train instead while my insurers looked for another taxi company.

On Monday morning of week two, on the dot of the appointed hour, the doorbell rang. My new taxi driver was

Freddie from Taxi Avance – a young man in his best suit. He was a sweet guy. Every day when I was finished my radiotherapy, I texted him and he would pull up in front of the hospital in two minutes flat. He never complained if the radiotherapy ran late. He was always where he promised to be.

But as the journeys up and down became easier, the treatments became harder. By the third week, the radiotherapy had started to hurt. Lying in precisely the same position every day, face down, with a full bladder while the machine went through its radioactive routine was becoming painful. The weekly chemo was also taking its toll and I struggled with nausea interspersed with strange and acute food cravings. Cisplatin doesn't cause hair loss – but that's the only good thing I have to say about it. I hadn't realized that chemo hurts as it goes into your vein.

"That's because it's poison", explained one of the nurses.

In the chemo room, they gave us warm packs to put on our hands or arms where the cannulas were sited to make the cisplatin hurt less as it went through our veins. That helped. Unlike with some other chemotherapy drugs, they keep you in overnight when you are on cisplatin. Before they start the drug, they give you a 1.5-litre bag of fluids intravenously (IV) to reduce the impact that cisplatin has on the kidneys. Then you have 90 minutes of discomfort as you get the chemo – and then you have to have three more litres of IV fluids overnight, again to support the kidneys.

So no one in the chemo room gets much sleep on Wednesdays, cisplatin day. Each of us is up every hour wheeling our drips across the ward to the toilets. And just because it's chemo day it doesn't mean that we escape our daily trip to the radiotherapy suite. Somehow, the staff in radiotherapy manage to help patients in various stages of their illness, in various levels of pain and with a variety of drips and other impedimenta into and out of the machines. Sometimes patients throw up. Chemo does that. Sometimes people get scared or can't manage – that's cancer for you.

Deny, dismiss, dehumanise

As you sit waiting for your turn, you see one of the patients is about four years old, bald, thin and playing with a hideous orange plastic giraffe. That puts it up to you. You struggle hard to hold it together then. You glance around, pretending you're not looking. Everyone else is thinking the same. We can deal with this happening to us, but to a baby! It's hard not to cry. But no one does. What right have we to cry self-indulgent tears to comfort ourselves while the parents are smiling and chatting as if a morning in radiotherapy is as routine as a trip to see granny? So we copy the parents' "normal" faces and make believe we're waiting at the hairdressers.

In all of the 23 times I visited the radiotherapy suites at AMC in 2013, not a single person ever said an unkind word to me about not speaking Dutch. The women at reception never mentioned it, the kind and understanding technicians who spend their working lives in lead-lined rooms where no daylight is ever seen, never said a harsh word. Back up in the gynaecology ward for my weekly chemo, the story was the same. The other patients? Never has another patient been anything except helpful when they discovered I couldn't speak Dutch – regardless of how sick they were feeling themselves. When they could, the other patients included me in the conversation.

Many of the other women there were having a harder time than me. Some weeks, one or two of them were not well enough to receive chemo and had to be given extra blood. Others were traumatized to find that their first rounds of chemo and radiotherapy had not worked and they were back on the ward for more. By comparison, I did okay. The anti-emetics handled the worst of the nausea. The last week or so of the radiotherapy was hell and I was in too much pain to walk, but I was coping. Psychologically, I was discovering I was a lot tougher than I had realized. What I was going through was hard, but it was something I could deal with. I felt a lot better being in the hospital now that the nastiness about me not speaking Dutch seemed to have stopped. The chemo and the daily trips to the radiotherapy suites ended and I started planning the rest of my life.

4 | October 2013 to October 2014 … UMC, Utrecht

A person may cause evil to others not only by his actions but by his inaction, and in either case he is justly accountable to them for injury.
John Stuart Mill

When my treatments finished on 10 October I was thrilled, relieved and all set to return to my pre-diagnosis self. My plan was to start working part time from home in November, and to be back in the office in Amsterdam full time after the Christmas holidays. I missed my job. I missed the fast pace of the office, the energy, the excitement, and the delight I felt to have been hired, at the age of 51, into such a bold and dynamic company. I missed my colleagues too, exceptionally bright and gifted high-achievers hired from all parts of the world for their skills, their work ethic and their ability to think outside the box. I had been working at Booking.com in Amsterdam for a little over a year when I was first diagnosed, and I was enjoying every inspiring second of it. I couldn't wait to pick up where I had left off in July.

But I had no idea just how hard it was going to be. My get-back-to-normal plans weren't working. For week after week, all I wanted to do every time I got out of bed was to crawl back in again. The pain from the radiotherapy had gradually eased over the weeks, as had the nausea from the chemo, but the exhaustion was still grinding me to a standstill. By mid-November, I was well enough, just, to get a haircut or go out for a coffee as long as I was with someone, and invite friends over for lunch. I still hadn't been out of the house on my own. I couldn't drive, I couldn't cycle and I couldn't walk far without having to stop and rest. Where had my independence gone? I had stopped being an autonomous adult functioning in the real world and had become a patient. I was finding this intolerable – and I wasn't having it. I would try harder.

Past experience had always taught me that the secret of success lay in persistence. You just had to keep doing your best, and you'd eventually achieve your goal, right? Wrong. Apparently, after chemoradiotherapy, the old rules don't apply any more. I'd stepped into *Alice in Wonderland* and I was the White Rabbit fretting: "The hurrier I go, the behinder I get". I was exerting maximum effort, and making minimum progress.

"It's perfectly normal", explained my psychologist. "Many cancer patients experience this after treatment." I had finally found a psychologist who specialized in helping cancer patients. I wish I had found her back in July when I was first diagnosed, and when I badly needed her to help me make sense of what was happening. She explained that by pushing myself physically and mentally as hard as I could tolerate, and then some, I was stopping my body from getting the rest it needed to recover. I had to learn to stop *before* I got tired.

I heard what she was saying, but struggled to put it into practice. In December, I started travelling to Amsterdam once a week to work at the office. Everyone was delighted to see me back, and I was happy to be there. But by lunchtime I was incoherent with exhaustion. I was so tired I couldn't absorb what

Deny, dismiss, dehumanise

was being said to me. The week before Christmas, a typically dark December day, I was too tired to function, and this must have been obvious to those around me. I had just spent ten minutes talking to a colleague without having anything but the vaguest idea what we were talking about – and I wasn't even a hundred per cent certain who she was. So at three o'clock, I called it a day and started the journey home.

My commute from Amsterdam goes through Schiphol with a change to the Sprinter at Leiden. That day, I slept through Schiphol, slept through Leiden and woke only when a train guard at the terminus in The Hague started shaking me and telling me the Christmas party was over. He thought I was drunk. Okay, lesson learned. I accepted I was pushing myself too hard. I had to learn a new technique: how to succeed by not trying so hard.

Nearly five years later, as I write this, I still haven't mastered that art.

****

Christmas came and went and 2013, the year from hell, ended. The new year dawned glittering with hope. This was the year I would recover from cancer and get my life and career back. I threw every ingenuity at my recovery. Instead of the long commute to and from Amsterdam, I'd stay overnight once a week. This way, I could spend two days in the office and work from home two days. The fifth day, even I admitted, was beyond me.

****

In February, UMCU admitted legal liability for the negligence that had led to my cancer results being "unseen" in my file from April 2011 to April 2013 – resulting in an advanced and untreated tumour.

This was an important step. Our lives had already been turned upside down by the hospital, and we feared that there was a lot more trauma to come. Peter and I were still disgusted that no one from UMCU had ever approached us to say sorry, ask if we needed help or explain what had gone wrong. I had maintained contact with Van der Vaart from time to time, but this was a personal correspondence in which we did not go over the events of 2011 – and anyway, he didn't represent the hospital. It was incomprehensible to us that what had happened to me, later categorized as a "calamity" by UMC Utrecht itself, was never even acknowledged, let alone investigated by those in charge. Therefore, no report had ever been produced, and no notification had been sent to the IGZ. We had no idea whether any other patients had been put at risk during the transfer from paper to electronic records. We had asked this in June 2013, but no one had an answer. All we knew was that people were going to that hospital every day in total ignorance of what had happened to me, and perhaps to others. That wasn't right. Such information belongs in the public arena. Patients, all of us taxpayers, are entitled to know what happens in the hospitals we fund.

On a personal level, the lack of official acknowledgement that a calamity had occurred to me, and the absence of any official attempt to explain it, sent a loud and clear message that what had happened was unimportant, and UMCU had nothing to say.

Maybe we were deluded by watching too many episodes of *ER* and *Holby City* and other fictional accounts of how hospitals conduct themselves, but what we expected would happen was that someone from the hospital, the CEO or another board member, would contact us to discuss what had happened, would apologize on behalf of the hospital, would try to offer an explanation and assure us that they were doing everything in their power to find out how such a thing could happen. We had expected that the hospital would take control of the situation, explain to us what

Deny, dismiss, dehumanise

was going to happen next, involve us in the investigation into the causes of the calamity, appoint someone to act as our point of contact in the hospital, offer proper counselling, and find out what help we needed. The fact that we were foreigners who did not understand the systems and who spoke no Dutch should have alerted the hospital that we really needed their help. But it seems to have had the opposite effect – perhaps they thought our "foreignness" would make us more likely to walk away and not question what had just happened.

So we asked our new lawyer about it. He understood what we were saying, but explained that it didn't work that way in the Netherlands. No Dutch hospital that he knew of operated in the way we were describing. The only thing UMCU was obliged to do was to continue to provide medical treatment, if I wanted it, and to deal with us otherwise through their lawyers. They were under no obligation to carry out an investigation into what had happened and they had already refused to report themselves to the IGZ. Since I had moved to AMC for my treatment, they felt they had no further duty of care to me and didn't expect to hear from me or see me again.

When UMCU accepted liability in February, they appointed a loss adjuster to deal with our lawyer on their behalf. Her job was to make sure that they didn't pay a penny more compensation than they had to. Frieda de Bruin was well known in the sector to be a very shrewd negotiator. The line of communication between the hospital and their damaged patient now went like this: the hospital spoke to the loss adjuster, the loss adjuster spoke to our lawyer and our lawyer spoke to us. We were astounded. The bottom line with the legal case was that we had to show how much we were out of pocket financially as a result of UMCU's negligence, and De Bruin would try to show that UMCU wasn't liable for all of the consequences and fallout of their negligence. There's a fuller account of the legal process in Chapter 9, but at that stage, in early

2014, all we knew was that the Dutch legal system didn't really believe in paying much damages for pain and suffering – even when the injuries are severe and lead to death. Any payment we would get from UMCU would be based on what they alleged was my loss of income. There was an algorithm to work out how much their mistake was going to cost UMCU's legal department. After Frieda de Bruin was finished, it probably wouldn't be very much. Our disgust deepened.

We left our lawyer to his own devices for the time being to work on this dreadful calculation and asked him if he could arrange for us to talk to someone representing the hospital, preferably someone from the board.

"That isn't usual", he warned.

"Try anyway", we encouraged.

It took a bit of persuasion and a long wait while we accommodated summer holidays, but eventually the hospital agreed that we could meet two UMCU representatives. The only proviso was that we could not discuss anything related to liability, including what had caused my cancer results to lie unseen in my file for two years. We still had many unanswered questions, but what we wanted to discuss now was more important than the legal case, so we decided we could just about live with that condition for the duration of the meeting. What we most wanted to ask was if the hospital thought the way they had chosen to care for me, their patient, in aftermath of the calamity was appropriate, professional, or even humane.

On 10 October 2014 – a year to the day since I had my last radiotherapy treatment and 18 months since the hospital realized it had lost my results – we first met Professor Kit Roes, the hospital's director of care quality and patient safety, and Professor Arie Franx, chair of UMCU's gynaecology division. They were accompanied by one of the hospital lawyers, there presumably to ensure we played by the rules and didn't ask any questions the

Deny, dismiss, dehumanise

professors weren't allowed to answer. We met at the offices of our lawyer in Amsterdam.

Peter, who was even more exercised than I was about the way I had been treated, set the ball rolling. He asked the two professors whether they thought the way UMCU, as an institution, had handled the aftermath of my diagnosis the previous year was in any way acceptable. Specifically, he pointed out that no one representing UMCU had ever approached us to acknowledge that an error had been made; we had been informed of no investigation; no offer of help had been extended, and it was left entirely up to the medical staff treating me to handle a life-threatening error. He mentioned that we had both been astonished when no attempt was ever made by UMCU to provide any type of support or to step in and use their expertise to handle a very complex and distressing situation.

Roes replied that although he was not attempting to absolve UMCU of their responsibility or excuse what had happened, there were some partial explanations. He said that the lack of a response at board level could be partly explained by the fact that no one on the board of the hospital knew about the incident at the time it happened, or for some time afterwards.

I'm hard to surprise, but I wasn't expecting that answer. I knew that Huub Van der Vaart had informed the hospital lawyers in July 2013, and the hospital had accepted full liability in February.

"When did they find out?" I asked.

"A few months ago, during this summer", replied Roes.

That was when we had pressed our lawyer to contact the hospital and ask for this meeting.

"Do you mean that the board were first notified that there had been a calamity in their hospital more than 12 months after it occurred – and even then, only because we contacted them?" I asked.

Roes confirmed that that was the case.

"But … then the hospital admitted legal liability for medical negligence without the board knowing that any calamity had occurred?" I asked.

No one replied to that, but it was obviously the case. I was speechless, but Peter wasn't.

"That's a mind-bending admission", he said. And we all fell silent for a while.

Breaking the silence, Roes told us that he himself had not been in his care quality and patient safety role at the time that my laboratory results had gone walkabout. As a result, he could not describe what safety procedures were in place in the hospital at the time regarding the flow of information from the laboratory back to the doctors.

Franx was also not in his current position at the time of the calamity, although he had been a senior member of the gynaecology department, and was now Van der Vaart's line manager. He asked whether we had not found at the time of my diagnosis that the attention of Van der Vaart had met our needs in terms of someone senior in the hospital being involved. I explained that I had always found Van der Vaart a considerate and understanding doctor and he had helped as much as he could at the time of my diagnosis, but he had ceased to be my doctor the moment my cancer was confirmed, and I had no reason or context to have any further contact with him. I also pointed out that I had been acutely aware at the time how traumatized Van der Vaart had been by what had happened, and so to expect him to shoulder the entire burden of dealing with the practical, psychological, emotional, financial and medical fallout of an adverse event that he himself was at the centre of made no sense. Indeed, it seemed rather cruel. That was the hospital's job, not Van der Vaart's.

Both Roes and Franx were listening to what Peter and I were saying, and appeared to agree with us that, in retrospect, it

Deny, dismiss, dehumanise

did seem as though the hospital should have stepped in in 2013 and provided support for us. They explained that there was no protocol in UMCU for dealing with patients damaged by the hospital other than for the doctor involved to inform them of what had gone wrong as soon as possible. I started to say that I still didn't really know what had gone wrong or exactly how and why my test results had not been seen by my doctor– but that was in contravention of the rules. We weren't allowed to talk about the ins and outs of the calamity. So I bit my tongue and concentrated on the aftermath of the fiasco. UMCU's shrug of indifference, we explained, made it pretty clear that at an institutional level, they cared little what happened to their patients. Notwithstanding the hospital leadership's medical credentials and their ostensible commitment to patient welfare, when a mistake was made and a patient damaged, they all stepped neatly aside and that patient became a mess for the lawyers to mop up. Franx said that what he was hearing was making him realize that the damage to me had been compounded by UMCU's behaviour afterwards. He said that they had let me down twice – first by making the mistake and then by not stepping in with the correct support after the mistake had been discovered.

"I am ashamed", he said.

Peter and I looked at him closely. That had sounded genuine. And Arie Franx certainly looked as though he had meant it. I felt that for the first time, we had broken through a barrier of corporate indifference.

"I'm glad you're ashamed", said Peter. "Because you absolutely should be ashamed. You should be ashamed of the hospital and everything that happened to Adrienne there."

The room fell silent. Peter continued.

"What you just said is the first honest thing anyone has said to us since it all happened."

Roes looked horrified. I don't think he had been expecting

Franx to be quite so honest. I glanced quickly at the UMCU lawyer. His face was without expression, but he had gone very still.

There followed some pretty routine assurances that although no actual investigation had been carried out, UMCU had learned from what happened to me, had found meeting us instructive, and were determined, should similar unfortunate incidents occur in the future, to approach them differently.

What was still missing was an enquiry about what the hospital could do now to provide the support that they had neglected to provide the previous year. There was no commitment to stay in touch. There were so many ways that the hospital, with its expertise, contacts and resources could have made our lives easier, even then. But when Roes and Franx left that afternoon, they didn't look back. And so UMCU let us down a third time.

What Peter and I didn't understand that day was that Roes and Franx were not members of the UMCU board and had no authority to represent the hospital. We assumed, as so many members of the public assume, that division heads and safety officers sit on the board and have the ability to influence decisions and effect change. In the years that followed, it became clear that this was not the case, and that the hospital had a tendency to allow its senior doctors to take the flak while the board remained silent and out of sight.

5 | October 2014 to February 2015 ... AMC, Amsterdam

Wherever people feel safe, they will be indifferent.
Susan Sontag, *Regarding the pain of others*

Throughout 2014, our "unfinished business" with UMCU was not the only thing bothering Peter and me. In consultation with Van der Velden, we had decided that the best way to see if the cancer was coming back was to examine my blood for cancer markers. We knew that the primary tumour – let's call it Tumour 1 – removed in July 2013 had caused the levels of CEA[5] and CA-125[6] in my blood to rise dramatically. So, to monitor any recurrence of the specific type of mucinous tumour I had, we decided to take CEA measurements every few months. This should give us a good picture, and maybe steal a march on any metastases. The "normal" level for CEA in the blood should be below 5.5.

Early in 2014 my CEA levels rose to 9.3, and we all held our breath. But they were back to 5 at the next check, so normal

---

5   Carcinoembryonic antigen (CEA).
6   Cancer antigen 125.

breathing resumed. In the summer, they rose again to 12. That was a worry. And at the next check, they were tipping 22, so some imaging was required. Van der Velden ordered an MRI.

The letter arrived inviting me to an MRI on October 14 – four days after our appointment with Roes, Franx and UMCU's lawyer. The letter was quite long, and as I hadn't had an MRI at AMC before, I decided I'd phone and ask for help understanding it.

"Do you not have any nice Dutch neighbours who can tell you what the letter says?" asked the woman on the phone in a condescending tone. I explained that I had lovely neighbours but I didn't want to discuss my cancer or my MRI with them. Such things are private.

"I don't have time for this", she snapped impatiently and hung up.

I had a go with Google translate, typing the three pages of unfamiliar words into the Translate box.

MRI day arrived. My appointment was quite late, so I went along to *Wachtkamer 6*, Waiting Room 6, at AMC after work. The nurse who brought me into the MRI suite was kind, but not everyone was. I had no idea what was being snapped at me through my headphones during the 40-minute long procedure, and all attempts to talk back to them failed. But luckily I had had two MRIs before at other hospitals, so I just hung on in there for the claustrophobic 40 minutes or so, half remembering and half guessing what was being said to me. I told them afterwards what had happened.

"Not everyone here speaks English, you know", responded the MRI operator.

I went home.

The MRI didn't show anything amiss, but when I went for my next blood test in January 2015, the CEA levels had upped the ante again to 36.8. Van der Velden wanted a CT scan. So

Deny, dismiss, dehumanise

before long I was back in *Wachtkamer 6*. I was brought into a room where a nurse would insert a cannula for the contrast dye that's pumped into my blood to make tumours easier to see on the scan. I asked her was it okay to speak English, and she assured me it was. I was asked to remove my bra as I had to be metal-free for the CT machine. Then she started the hunt for a vein. First my left arm, then my right and then each of my hands in turn. It wasn't her fault, my veins had always been bad and chemo makes them worse.

"So, how long have you lived in the Netherlands?" she asked.

Stupidly, I told the truth: "Six years".

She glanced up briefly from her search for a co-operative vein in my right hand.

"And you still don't speak any Dutch", she said shaking her head slowly from side to side. That had been a statement, not a question.

I went into defence mode. "I don't think it's very kind, when you're treating a patient, to make comments about whether they do or don't speak Dutch", I said.

"Oh, I was just being friendly", she said. "We get it all the time – people who've lived here for years and don't speak a word of Dutch. This morning, I had a little one in here who said she worked in a company in Amsterdam where there are thousands of foreigners and they speak only English." She shrugged her shoulders and made a face.

Obviously the hundreds of thousands of foreigners living in the Netherlands and working for international companies, embassies, international tribunals and NGOs were a source of great bemusement to her. I recognized that she was probably talking about my company, and sure enough, I found out later that an Asian colleague had attended AMC for an MRI the same day as me. The woman this nurse had described as "a little one" was a professional Chinese woman in her mid-thirties who had worked at a senior level in several European and Asian countries. My company was very glad to have her expertise and she was a valued member of my department.

By now, the nurse's words had upset me. I was finding the constant reproaches about not speaking Dutch were affecting me deeply. Was I supposed to justify myself to every nurse and doctor in AMC before I received kind and professional treatment? I told her I was tired of hearing critical and unpleasant remarks at the hospital about my inability to speak Dutch. My reasons for being in the Netherlands and my inability to speak the language were my own business and not subjects for her idle curiosity.

She found a vein and I was sent outside to wait in the corridor, my bra stuffed into my shoulder bag. In due course, the receptionist came to bring me to the CT machine. To my surprise, it wasn't anywhere near *Wachtkamer 6*. We went down to the ground floor, across two wide reception areas and along a corridor to AMC's nuclear medicine department. All the while without my bra.

At the CT machine, the nurse showed me to a changing room.

"Don't forget to take off your bra", she reminded me.

I told her they had already made me remove it upstairs. "Why did they make me take it off in *Wachtkamer 6* and then walk all the way through the hospital without it?" I asked her.

"I've no idea", she replied.

Just another little indignity.

Like the MRI the previous autumn, the results of the CT didn't show a tumour either, but the blood tests were adamant that something was amiss. Van der Velden sent me for a PET-CT scan. We also discussed going for treatment in the hospital's hyperbaric oxygen chamber. The removal of 36 lymph nodes in the surgery in 2013 and the subsequent radiation had left me with lymphoedema in my mid section and in my legs. This means that my body's lymphatic system had been compromised,

Deny, dismiss, dehumanise

and the lymphatic fluid could not drain away on its own, causing painful swelling. If not managed with manual drainage, this can develop into hardening and thickening of the skin and recurrent infections. My physiotherapist had told me that many of her lymphoedema patients had benefitted from a course of treatment in the hyperbaric oxygen chamber because the high levels of oxygen make tissue able to heal better than it would in normal atmosphere. Van der Velden referred me to a doctor at AMC's hyperbaric oxygen chamber to find out more.

I turned up a few minutes early for my 10:15 appointment on 18 February. It's a small department and there didn't seem to be any particular reception area so I put my head around the door of a room where I could hear people talking. I waved my patient ID card and said, "Good morning, I have an appointment for 10:15". One of the nurses got up and came out to me. She started speaking in Dutch. I handed her my patient card and said gently, "I'm sorry, but I don't understand." She looked at the patient card and then back at me and continued speaking to me in Dutch.

"I can't speak or understand Dutch", I said.

"You don't speak Dutch?" she echoed. "But you live in the Netherlands!" She held my patient card up to prove her point.

I tried my best to hold it together. "Maybe you could ask one of your colleagues to help me instead?"

"Do you not speak *any* Dutch?" she persisted.

"Please get someone else to help me."

She didn't move.

"Get someone else", I pleaded.

She went back into the room and came back with a doctor. They had a brief conversation together which I couldn't understand. Then the doctor spoke.

"The nurse is only trying to do her job", he said. "You can't expect everyone to be able to speak to you in English", he reprimanded.

"I don't!" I exclaimed. "That isn't what happened. What did she say to you?"

There then followed a full five-minute interchange where I tried to explain to the doctor that I was constantly being reproached for not speaking Dutch and that it wasn't appropriate in a hospital. As I explained it, I lost it completely and ended up crying and trying to describe the previous encounters I had had with hospital staff making an issue of the fact that I lived in the Netherlands and couldn't speak Dutch. But he had made up his mind. The nurse was doing her job, and the patient was causing trouble. All this took place in the public corridor with me shaking and crying and the doctor looking at me with irritation. This doctor was the professor that I had an appointment to see. Either I dealt with him, or I went home.

I remember little of what happened at that appointment except that I had to remove my thick compression stockings and panties (standard issue if you have lymphoedema, and called *compressiebroekjes met pijpjes*, one of the few Dutch terms I knew). No privacy was offered and I struggled out of the constricting garments in the room alongside the doctor and his assistant. No curtain was pulled to offer privacy. At the end of the appointment, another nurse came in. He mentioned what had happened earlier and tried to excuse his colleague, saying that she hadn't meant to upset me.

"I'm sure she did", I told him. "She was pretty rude about pointing out that I lived here and couldn't speak any Dutch."

He was quiet for a moment. "I really get what you're saying", he said. "My parents came to this country from Morocco and they have often been laughed at in the street because they can't speak Dutch properly."

The image of this kind nurse's parents being ridiculed in the street was too much to bear and I felt tears threatening to return.

I never went back to AMC's hyperbaric oxygen chamber. I

Deny, dismiss, dehumanise

heard about another chamber nearer where I lived, but in the end, my health dictated that the treatment might not be suitable for me.

Shortly after my experiences at the hyperbaric oxygen chamber, a letter arrived giving me a date for the PET-CT. At the top of the letter in blue pen was written *Bel ons over deze afspraak*, "Phone us about this appointment". So I did. I had never had a PET scan before and had no clue how to prepare. This letter was way too long for even the most patient patient to type into Google Translate.

"It's no problem speaking English", reassured the woman who answered the phone. "I'll put you through to someone and they'll be able to help you."

I breathed a sigh of relief. My call was transferred and another woman answered. I explained why I was phoning. There was a sniff on the other end of the phone and the line went dead.

I phoned back immediately and spoke to the woman who had originally answered the phone. I told her what happened. This constant aggravation because I couldn't speak Dutch was too much on top of dealing with the likelihood that my cancer was back. I was crying again. The receptionist transferred me to an English doctor who was working in the department. I told my story again, telling her of the many times in AMC that not speaking Dutch had caused me to be treated so unpleasantly. Her colleague hanging up the phone on me that morning was just the latest.

"I'm really sorry", she said. "I can't imagine who here would do that. It's most unusual."

I didn't argue.

"Everyone here speaks English", she added.

She was very kind, genuinely distressed by what had happened to me and told me what I needed to do to prepare for the PET-CT. I needed to fast for six hours before the scan. I would be asked to drink a radioactive sugar solution and given an IV radiotracer. I'd also be given an IV contrast dye during the CT part of the scan. She asked me to come a little early to allow them time to find a vein. I asked her if she would be around on the day of my appointment. She worked in another part of the department she explained, so she wouldn't be there. She promised to let everyone know what had happened and said she would ask them to be understanding. She assured me there would be no problem.

But I was punch drunk. I knew that what had happened to me so many times, on the ward, as an outpatient and on the phone, was wrong. It shouldn't be happening at a major teaching hospital in the Netherlands that non-Dutch patients were being subjected to this intolerance because they couldn't speak the language. I knew from asking around a bit at work that similar things were happening to my co-workers. It infuriated me that these young colleagues, thousands of miles from home and falling ill in a foreign country, instead of being treated with additional understanding, were being routinely subjected to smart comments, hung-up telephones and low-level bullying because they couldn't speak Dutch. It was being made very clear to us by some staff members that we were not welcome in the hospital.

The Netherlands prides itself on being a tolerant place where all are welcome. Of its 17 million or so inhabitants, 1.8 million were born outside the country, giving it a sizeable expat population of over 11%. The largest group of expats in the Netherlands comes from other EU countries, and most live and work in the Randstad – the collective name given to the Netherlands' four largest cities, Amsterdam, Rotterdam, The Hague and Utrecht.[7] The country's reputation for social tolerance attracts large international conglomerates as well as organizations such as the International Criminal Court, the International Court

---

7   2010 figures from EUROSTAT, a Directorate-General of the European Commission.

Deny, dismiss, dehumanise

of Justice, Europol, Eurojust and hundreds of international NGOs and human rights bodies.

In order to staff these companies and organizations, a common world language is needed: English. "Not a problem", say the Dutch who, after the Swedes, speak the best second-language English in Europe. As a result, hundreds of thousands of people move here – some for a few months, some for a few years, and some for longer. While most don't speak Dutch, almost all speak English, and are told that that is sufficient to live and work in the Netherlands. And mostly it is. The vast majority of shops, restaurants, estate agents and private companies like to have the expat business and are happy to speak English. The Dutch State is happy enough too to have the tax euros and the spending power of these largely transient and relatively well-heeled immigrants. It's a model where everybody is happy – until one of us gets seriously ill. It then fairly quickly becomes clear that some staff, in some hospitals, such as AMC, are absolutely not happy. Their frustration at being expected to speak English in the course of their work is taken out on the person least able to do anything about it, the patient. When you have a chronic condition requiring multiple hospital visits, it happens over and over again.

AMC is located in an area of Amsterdam that has one of the most culturally diverse communities in Europe. Staff and patients come in all shades and from all sorts of cultural, religious, ethnic and linguistic backgrounds. On the face of it, it looks like one happy multicultural family. But the truth is that patients often hear in various ways that this is the Netherlands and Dutch is the language spoken here.

I resolved to contact AMC's board of management. I believed that they couldn't possibly be aware of what was happening to non-Dutch-speaking patients and I decided to tell them what had been going on.

6 | 25 March 2015 … AMC, Amsterdam

It takes two to speak the truth – one to speak and another to hear.
Henry David Thoreau, 1849

Wednesday, 25 March, was going to be a long day at AMC. In the morning, we had an appointment with Van der Velden, and in the afternoon, we were scheduled for a half-hour meeting with the hospital's CEO, Professor Marcel Levi. I had written to the hospital's executive board outlining my experiences since 2013, including a number of the hurtful and intolerant comments that had been made to me on the ward, at outpatient appointments and on the phone, in relation to my inability to speak Dutch. I pointed out that it was a problem in many of the departments I had been treated in and that friends and colleagues had also reported being treated the same way. I pleaded with them to intervene so that future appointments at the hospital would not be yet more opportunities for staff to make reproaches. I also asked the board to take action to provide training that would make staff realize they were accountable for what they said to patients. I also offered to work with them – if they were interested – to help to find possible solutions.

Deny, dismiss, dehumanise

So it was always going to be a busy day for us at AMC, but we didn't realize just how traumatic it was going to be.

I think most patients develop the ability to tell from a quick glance at their doctors when bad news is on the way. So before we even entered his office, I knew from his body language that Van der Velden wasn't happy. He had the results of the PET-CT and he showed us the two "hotspots" that the scan had revealed. Hotspots are areas of the body that light up on a PET scan. As I understand it, and put simply, the radioactive sugars and tracers that they give you before the PET scan travel to areas of the body that are very "active", or using a lot of energy. Some areas of the body use a lot of energy in the normal course of events, but when doctors see areas that shouldn't be using a lot of energy but are lighting up in the scan anyway, they know there could be a tumour there.

My two hotspots looked beautiful on the computer screen – two bright stars or fireworks against the brown fuzzy background of my pelvis. But they spelt disaster. One bright star was in my abdominal wall a few centimetres below and to the left of the navel. The other appeared to be on the wall of my sigmoid colon. While PET scans are very useful at showing the presence of tumours, they don't give a very clear picture of size or exact location. This is why most PET scans, including mine, are done alongside a CT scan, so that the CT can give more focused information about the tumours that the PET has exposed. But in my case, even the CT imaging was not 100 per cent clear. What was clear though was that the cancer was back.

I knew from reading about cervical cancer, particularly in the case of an adenocarcinoma, that once it metastasizes, survival chances plummet. We asked Van der Velden to speculate on my prognosis. That's a really tough question to ask anyone, because when a patient is in my situation, it's really anyone's guess what the prognosis is. If a doctor is too pessimistic, he removes a patient's hope; too optimistic, and he fosters unrealistic expectations.

Van der Velden had known Peter and me for almost two years at this stage, and he knew us well enough to know that we like to have as much information as possible in order to make the right decisions about my ongoing care. Like most cancer patients, I had researched online and I knew that patients with metastatic cervical cancer were considered incurable and rarely survive more than a couple of years. So I had no illusions about what today's news meant. When pushed a little, Van der Velden confirmed that the average survival for patients with recurrent cervical cancer was between 11 and 18 months. He drew a bell curve to illustrate it. The majority of patients fit into the middle of the bell – the 11-18-month period.

"But that doesn't mean *you* only have 11 to 18 months", he emphasized.

I could be anywhere on the bell curve, a few years beyond the 18-month, high-end of average survival, or conceivably, in the less than 11-month thin edge of the bell curve. With a bit of luck, I could live for years yet – but although Van der Velden didn't say so, we all knew that wasn't very likely. The arrival of these first two metastases were probably, we were told, just "the tip of the iceberg".

"What are the options for treatment?" Peter asked. We needed to gather more information, but just judging by the imaging, the tumour that appeared to be on my sigmoid colon was likely to make surgical removal undesirable, if not impossible. Operating on a bowel that had previously been irradiated, as mine had, was not an inviting prospect. Irradiated tissue is compromised and post-operative healing is slow, or sometimes doesn't happen at all, leaving a leaky bowel – which is not tenable, and even a colostomy is very often problematic after radiotherapy. Further radiation to treat the new tumours was also ruled out as you can't give new radiation to previously irradiated areas, and my whole pelvis had been irradiated in 2013. More chemo (not cisplatin this time but another chemo combination that would be much stronger) was a possibility, but no one treating metastasized cervical cancer had any illusions about the effectiveness of chemo in cases like mine. About half the time, it doesn't work at all, and the rest of the time, it can prolong life by several months – but it never "cures" it. Even the medical oncologists weren't really pushing more chemo as a solution, although I did speak to them about it. They had no way of knowing who would react well and be given a few more months, and who would not benefit at all. The only certainty, as far as I could see, was that chemo would make me desperately sick with only a forlorn chance that it would buy me more time, time during which I would be miserably ill. It was too soon for decisions that day, but I knew then that quality of life was more important for me now, and that chemo and operating on a bowel already compromised by radiotherapy were both options that I would ultimately turn down.

But I'm jumping ahead. First, we needed to establish whether that rather inaccessible tumour (let's call it Tumour 2) was inside the colon (indicating a totally new cancer) or on the outside (indicating a metastasis). We also wanted to biopsy the more accessible Tumour 3 in the abdominal wall – if pathology confirmed that was a metastasis of the original cancer, the overwhelming probability was that the Tumour 2 was also a metastasis. Two new tests awaited me, a colonoscopy and a biopsy.

★★★★★★★★

But before any of that could be arranged, Peter and I had our appointment in the hospital's executive wing with Professor Levi. I was raw and shell-shocked after the trauma of the morning's news, and I was tempted to cancel the meeting. But I felt that I might not get another chance – and as I was now all set to have a lot more interaction with various AMC departments, I resolved to try my best to stop the language harassment continuing to make my life a misery.

The meeting didn't get off to a good start. Levi opened by saying that he had heard that I had an issue with AMC staff not speaking good enough English. I nearly hit the roof.

"No!" I exclaimed in horror. "I would never complain about such a thing – and anyway that's not the case. Most people's English is very good. My problem is that I am routinely being reproached and subjected to unpleasant comments when I say I don't speak Dutch."

Levi seemed surprised. "What do you mean by 'routinely'?" he asked.

"I mean that it is happening to me all the time … on visits to the hospital … on the phone … and even when I'm a patient on the ward."

"But not everyone is able to speak in fluent English", he said.

"I don't expect them to", I replied. "I fully appreciate how difficult it must be to have to switch to English in the middle of your working day and I am very grateful that people do this at all."

Levi seemed more puzzled. "So what's the problem then?" he asked.

"It's not about staff speaking English", I explained. "It's about me getting grief for not speaking Dutch. Some staff are constantly disapproving and making unhelpful and hurtful comments about the fact that I live in the Netherlands and can't speak Dutch."

His face reflected that he didn't believe me, and he was obviously still puzzled. "What people?", he asked. "And when was this?"

Now I was puzzled. "Did you read my emails?" I asked.

He prevaricated for a while saying that he had seen that there was some email correspondence from me, but eventually admitted that he hadn't read the two emails I had sent to the hospital board.

Someone else had read them and reported to him what they believed the issue was. To me it was the essence of rudeness and arrogance to arrange a meeting with someone to discuss an issue they had raised without ever having read what the issue was about. It was clear that Levi knew nothing of any of the incidents I had described. There was silence.

Peter broke the silence by asking what we were all doing in Levi's office.

"Why did you not think it was important to read her emails before asking to meet Adrienne?" he asked.

"Do you know how many emails I get every day?" was his reply.

"And as a result we are here wasting your time, and more importantly, wasting our own time turning up to a meeting where we're the only ones who know what that meeting is about. That's not very respectful, is it?" Peter asked.

After that, it was an uphill struggle to try to tell Levi all over again and as quickly as possible about the unsolicited advice, the accusation that I was breaking the law, the cruel shouting at me and the nasty comments while I was an inpatient in 2013; the hurtful comments on several occasions in the radiology department; the public reprimanding in the hyperbaric oxygen chamber; the "go ask the neighbours" comment when I asked for help understanding my MRI letter, and the hung up telephone when I asked if I could speak English when enquiring about a PET scan. It all came out in a bit of a rush (we only had a 30-minute meeting) and I'm not sure how coherent I was being. It might have been hard to follow, and Levi had been totally blindsided by whoever had allegedly "read" my letters to the board and reported the contents misleadingly to him. Peter, who usually loses his cool long before I do, was holding the meeting together and had stepped in to take over when my rope had all but run out.

Towards the end of the meeting (I think it ran over by 15

minutes), I felt we had made some headway in explaining the situation, but we were also aware of a determined resistance to believing the substance of the experiences I had reported. Levi did, however insist that the hospital board would – although he didn't accept that any such thing was happening – find mistreatment of non-Dutch-speakers totally unacceptable. He also denied that the hospital demanded that staff must speak only in Dutch to patients. Most importantly, he agreed that issues to do with ethnicity, nationality, religion, language ability, and whether or for how long patients have lived in the Netherlands are not acceptable or appropriate areas for staff to inquire about – even in what they feel may be a "friendly" manner. When pressed, he agreed that political views about immigrants and whether or not they are welcome in the Netherlands, and in what circumstances, had no place in AMC. He promised he would discuss what we had said to him with the board and try to find a way of reiterating such matters in a way that all staff could be aware of them. When we asked how he proposed to do this, he suggested that he might write something in the monthly magazine. I asked if we could be kept informed of what actions would be taken by the hospital, and he promised to get back to me.

When we left Levi's office, Peter and I were both drained. I wasn't even thinking about our morning meeting with Van der Velden and the consequences of my cancer returning. I was totally focused on stopping the bullying being dished out by some members of AMC staff and I was optimistic that if the CEO initiated a dialogue somewhere in the hospital on the matter of not intimidating patients for not speaking Dutch, then the situation would surely improve. But I was also acutely aware that Levi had not believed that I had been telling him the truth.

A few days after the meeting, I wrote him an email recapping on what had been discussed and agreed. He wrote back a few days later promising that he would, "convene with our Communications

Deny, dismiss, dehumanise

department to plan the most suitable way to explain to our staff that patients who do not speak Dutch (for any reason) [should not be] quizzed or even reprimanded about this". He also undertook to keep me posted on what they proposed to do, and encouraged me to let him know directly should I, "encounter these difficulties again at our hospital".

I was optimistic that the message had got through, and that the bullying would be brought out into the open – and so stopped. I didn't hear from Marcel Levi again until I wrote to him again almost a year later.

7 | April 2015 ... AMC, Amsterdam

When you come to the end of your rope, tie a knot and hang on.
Franklin D Roosevelt

After the stressful meeting with Levi, I shifted my attention back to my own health and the news that the cancer had returned. I asked for information about medical trials that used immunotherapy. It transpired that I was not a suitable candidate as I didn't have HPV high-risk Type 16 or Type 18 (which are responsible for 70% of cervical cancers) and the immunotherapy being trialled focused on these two strains of the virus.

Maybe now is a good time to take a very quick look at why women get cervical cancer, and, more specifically, some of the reasons why it wasn't diagnosed in my case. Briefly and simply, virtually all cervical cancers (over 95%) are caused by the human papilloma virus (HPV). According to the US Department of Health and Human services, almost all men and women will be infected with HPV at some point in their lives. Usually, it has no symptoms, so people don't know when they are infected. It's spread easily through sexual contact, causing no harm in the

Deny, dismiss, dehumanise

vast majority of people. In most cases, our immune systems deal with it swiftly and easily. Some common strains of the virus, specifically Type 16 and Type 18, are particularly nasty, or "high-risk", and are more likely to cause the development of cancers when someone's immune system fails to fight back successfully. Often, cancers don't develop until years, even decades, after the original HPV infection. When women go for routine Pap smear tests, the idea is that atypical or pre-cancerous cells will be spotted before they can develop into nasty tumours.

However, the Pap smear test is not an accurate test and not a diagnostic test. Sometimes, it throws out false positives, and at other times, it doesn't catch situations where a cancer is developing. And that is what happened to me. From my twenties to my fifties I had had regular Pap smears in all the countries I lived in, including when I first came to the Netherlands in 2009. When I presented with a vaginal discharge (for a long time, misdiagnosed as urinary incontinence), I was given a Pap smear, which came back clear. This test was repeated several times in different hospitals and clinics, including by Van der Vaart in UMC Utrecht, but the results continued to come back normal. When I eventually got a result in 2011 that showed there was inflammation on the tip of the cervix, I went for cryosurgery, but no one was alarmed because such inflammatory cells are very routine, and all my other tests indicated nothing was seriously amiss. (Apart that is from the sample taken deep inside the cervix during the cryosurgery in 2011, which flagged "adenocarcinoma of the cervix" – and that was the test that lay somewhere unseen for two years.)

Because Pap smear tests are known to be unreliable, with some sources suggesting that as many as 35% of cancers are "missed",[8] some countries have started to perform HPV tests on patients along with smears. But this is not routine and often patients are

8   Jane Harrison-Hohner (June 2011) 'How Accurate is My Pap Smear Result?' WebMD.

asked to pay if they want an HPV test. This is absolutely *not* an instruction not to bother with Pap smears. They are the best defence you have and you should go regularly. But if you are worried, or if something seems amiss, ask your doctor for further investigations and ask if you can have an HPV test.

Over the past ten years or so, many countries started giving HPV vaccines to teenage girls. A number of countries are now offering it to teenage boys too. Many feel that this, along with regular Pap smears, has effectively dealt with cervical cancer. But such a view is complacent. The vaccine delivered in most countries protects only against HPV Type 16 and Type 18 – leaving the 30% or so of cervical cancers caused by other high-risk strains of the virus free to develop. There are now HPV vaccines that protect against up to nine types of HPV.

The more I was learning about cervical cancer the more dejected I was becoming. My case seemed to be out of the ordinary in every conceivable way. For a start, it was an adenocarcinoma rather than a squamous cell carcinoma. Adenocarcinomas, which account for around 20% of cervical cancers are harder to treat effectively and more likely to recur. My adenocarcinoma turned out to be mucinous – which should have been good news as it led to a very obvious symptom which should have resulted in a diagnosis. But no one recognized the symptom. Mucinous adenocarcinomas are rare, and more likely than other types of adenocarcinoma to recur. Although I had only one, tiny, cancer-positive lymph node after my 2013 surgery, my mucinous adenocarcinoma had decided to metastasize. Now I was learning that I was not a suitable candidate for immunotherapy because I had the wrong sort of HPV.

There was nothing whatsoever I could do about this. My doctor was doing everything in his power to help me keep on the right edge of the bell curve, so I let the idea of immunotherapy go and concentrated on the two tests I needed to find out more about my two hotspots. The first test was a colonoscopy to find out whether Tumour 2 was inside or outside the large bowel.

You will be delighted to read that I am not going to tell you all about my colonoscopy. The preparation is truly horrible, but completely necessary. My only advice would be to ask for the general anaesthetic, Propofol. Having undergone a colonoscopy before, in France, where all patients are out cold for the duration, I asked for similar at AMC and my request was granted. No nasty comments about my inability to speak Dutch were made before or after the procedure. Nor did the test show any tumours inside my bowel. They thought they were giving me good news on that score, but it merely indicated that whatever it was was probably outside the bowel, and potentially a lot more dangerous.

The day after the colonoscopy, I was scheduled for a biopsy of Tumour 3 in the abdominal wall. I hadn't had a biopsy before, so didn't think I would need a general anaesthetic. They would, I was told, insert a fine needle to aspirate out some of the tumour tissue for analysis, and that way we could tell if it was a metastasis or a "new" cancer – or indeed, something totally harmless. They would anaesthetize the area with local anaesthetic. Sounded reasonable to me.

On the day, the doctor explained that he would first use an ultrasound to see exactly where Tumour 3 was located. He found it without difficulty. I had a very kind nurse, Bas, with me throughout the procedure. The doctor said he would anaesthetize the abdominal wall above the tumour and give the anaesthetic a few minutes to work. After a while, I was feeling nothing when he prodded my abdomen. He warned me at that stage that with needle aspiration, they generally couldn't extract enough tissue for analysis with one aspiration.

"Do you mean you will have to insert the needle twice?", I asked, wrinkling my nose.

"Yes, or maybe three times", he replied.

As the doctor guided the needle in through my belly, I could see it going in but could feel nothing. Then suddenly, when he reached the tumour, I felt everything.

"I can feel that!", I exclaimed, trying my best not to wriggle up the bed away from the biopsy needle. "That's not anaesthetized!" Only then did the doctor explain that he couldn't anaesthetize the tumour; the local anaesthetic was working on the abdominal wall, but not on the tumour, which was some 3 or 4 centimetres deep. I was horrified. This really hurt, and he hadn't even started to aspirate with the needle yet. But we needed a tissue sample, and I didn't see any way around this. The choice was: go home now, or let him do the biopsy. So I gripped the sides of the bed and asked Bas to hold me down by the shoulders if necessary. I didn't trust myself to lie still. The doctor started aspirating. It was excruciating, but I didn't let go of the bed. I was sweating profusely, feeling nauseous and crying. But we weren't finished. He had got a good sample, but like he said, one aspiration is never enough. I had to let him go in a second time. If I refused, the first sample would be unusable on its own … and we would still not know for certain whether my new hotspot was a metastasis. So after a taking a minute to get my breath back, I nodded my assent and he went in again. I willed myself to lie still as I felt the needle enter the tumour for the second time, and then blind pain as it aspirated a sample. Then the gods took mercy on me and the doctor imparted the happy news that he had enough tissue and didn't need to go back in for a third aspiration. I cried with relief and started shivering uncontrollably with the emotional and physical shock.

After the procedure, Bas wheeled me, still crying and shivering, to a recovery ward. They wanted to watch me for an hour or so to make sure that I didn't have any internal bleeding as a result of the biopsy. As he rolled me out, I asked, "Is Peter here?" Bas replied that he wasn't. "He's probably gone for coffee",

Deny, dismiss, dehumanise

he suggested, and promised to fetch him once they had me settled in a recovery bay. In fact, Peter was exactly where I had left him, just outside the biopsy room, but I think the nurse decided that it would be best to have me nice and calm rather than crying and shivering before they let him join me. That was not the right decision.

In the recovery bay, Bas handed me over to another nurse. He explained that I spoke English, and the colleague spoke to me in English explaining to me that I would be staying with them for an hour or so. He started pulling back the curtains at the end of the bed and I asked if it was okay to leave the curtains pulled around the bed because I was crying and shivering still and wanted some privacy to recover.

"Sure", he said and pulled them closed again.

I asked if my husband could come and sit by me. The new nurse said he'd fetch him shortly. Bas and the new nurse then spoke to each other in Dutch for a minute or so, exchanging details and doing a handover. Bas said goodbye and wished me strength. It's a common thing in the Netherlands to wish people strength when they are undergoing an ordeal. I had stopped crying by then and although I was still not able to stop shivering, I smiled and thanked him for his help during the biopsy.

As soon as Bas left, the nurse he had handed me over to started speaking to me in Dutch. I assumed that he had simply forgotten to speak in English, so I said, "I don't understand. I don't speak Dutch, remember?" He said the same sentence to me again in Dutch. Again I told him I couldn't understand what he was saying to me. He was right at the end of my bed looking straight at me. He started to pull back the curtains around the left side of my bed.

"Can we leave the curtains closed for a while?" I reminded him. "I'd like to have some privacy while I'm still a shivering mess." He ignored me and started to pull back the curtains at the end of my bed and on the right-hand side. I asked again, pleading, "Can we leave the curtains closed, just for a short while, please?" He was less than a metre away from me. There was no way he didn't hear me. He continued to pull the curtains back and ignore my pleading. So I screamed. Loudly. I have never screamed in my life. This was my first ever scream, and it was a good one.

"Stop yelling at me!" he shouted, suddenly remembering to speak English. "I'm only trying to do my job!"

I was in no condition to argue with him and the reason I had screamed was that I needed someone else to come. I was afraid of this man and his sudden refusal to speak English as soon as Bas left, and his apparent inability to hear me when I spoke back in English. I had screamed for help. Help came in the form of another nurse, an Australian, judging by her accent. I asked for Bas. I asked for Peter. Bas came. I tried to tell him that his colleague refused to speak to me in English after he had left. He was confused.

"But we were all speaking to you in English", he said.

"Yes", I agreed. "But he stopped when you went away and would only speak to me in Dutch."

The offender spoke to Bas quickly in Dutch. I didn't understand.

"It's all right", Bas tried to explain. "My colleague was speaking to another patient, not you".

I indicated the three empty beds to my left and the other empty bed to my right, the last in the row. There was no one opposite me either.

"There's no one else here. He was definitely talking to me, and he wouldn't reply when I spoke to him in English. I was just asking him to keep the curtains around the bed closed until I felt a bit better."

The nurse who had answered my scream for help heard this and immediately closed the curtains around my bed.

Bas said, "I'm going to get your husband".

"Don't leave me with him!" I pleaded. I looked at the nurse who had been so disagreeable and asked him to go away because he was frightening me. He left and the female nurse stayed with me while Bas went to fetch Peter. They said he could stay with me until I was discharged.

When I was able, I filled Peter in on what had happened.

"I could have been with you", he said. "It wouldn't have happened if I'd been here. Why didn't they tell me the biopsy was finished and you were here?"

"They said you had gone for coffee", I told him.

He shook his head. "I haven't moved from my chair in the waiting room all morning."

I felt a good deal safer with Peter beside me and the Australian nurse looking after me. She was very kind.

After an hour or so, Peter and I asked her how I could make a complaint about what had happened. She said I should probably talk to the doctor in charge. She said she'd ask him to come and see me before I went home.

A short while later, the doctor who had performed the biopsy earlier came to talk to us. I introduced him to Peter and told him (I was totally calm by now) slowly and clearly exactly what had happened.

"It must have been a misunderstanding", he said. "He's a good nurse. Everyone here speaks English."

I tried to explain again that indeed he was speaking English to me while Bas was with us, but spoke only in Dutch immediately after Bas left, and had ignored me when I spoke to him in English. It was obvious from the expression on the doctor's face that he didn't believe me. He wasn't being difficult. He simply couldn't believe that anyone would behave like that with a patient. He was out of his depth and I didn't really blame him. I found it hard to believe too, every time.

"I'll talk to him", he promised rather reluctantly.

I've no idea whether he ever did speak to the nurse. Whatever transpired after I left the hospital, whatever discussions were had, whatever explanations were given, no one saw fit to ever contact me about it again.

Deny, dismiss, dehumanise

8 | May 2015 … UMC, Maastricht

Curative treatment is no longer possible, now that recurrence has been established. There will only be further deterioration and eventually Mrs Cullen will die.
Independent Medical Report on the Cullen case

The results of the biopsy showed that Tumour 3 was indeed a metastasis of the original cancer. The wisdom from Van der Velden and the tumour board was that the overwhelming likelihood was that Tumour 2 was also a metastasis. Treatment options and the prognosis were as they had been before the test results came back. Surgery was out because removing Tumour 2 would involve cutting into bowel tissue irradiated in 2013, and causing a tsunami of unpleasant complications – something I was not prepared to live with, and no surgeons were queueing up to inflict. Radiotherapy was out because both Tumour 2 and Tumour 3 were inside the previously irradiated area, and you can't irradiate the same tissue twice. Chemo was on offer, but no one was surprised when I turned down the chance to have myself injected with chemo drugs when they simply could not save my life at this stage. I had no real symptoms at the time, and I wasn't willing to disturb the delicate status quo by inflicting myself with all of the side effects of a chemo cocktail.

The decision I made on chemo was not unusual. Many people in the same position decide to maintain their quality of life and relative well-being for as long as they can. When cancer symptoms arrive, some people opt for chemo then to see if it might buy them a few more months. I was allowing myself the option of changing my mind too should I feel differently in the future, and I was assured that I would be at no disadvantage if I opted for chemo later rather than right then. Unlike with primary cancers, early chemo doesn't offer any advantages over later chemo to patients with metastasized cervical cancer.

With no treatment in the offing, I walked away from AMC for the time being, but figured I'd be back there in the future.

I had business elsewhere. As soon as I realized that my cancer had metastasized, I decided I wanted to give myself the option of euthanasia at the end of my life. I was acutely aware of my body's inability to deal with pain-killing opiates, and facing the prospect of palliative care, I wanted to put something in place that would allow me to choose how and when I died. So I resolved to find out how to make my wish for euthanasia official.

The other thing I realized when the metastases were diagnosed was that it was now Peter, and not me, who was the most important person in our story. Most couples are an economic unit, and Peter and I were no different. And like most terminally ill spouses, I was concerned about the financial effect my illness and death would have on my partner. In 2012, I had joined as the fourth member of a copywriting team attached to the IT department of Booking.com. A year later, when I was first diagnosed, there were seven writers and I had already carved out a number of niche areas within the team. Today, I am no longer well enough to be part of that team, and there are now over 30 writers, some of whom I helped to recruit and mentor and many of whom now hold senior positions.

In the two years between diagnosis in June 2013 and the recurrence of the cancer in March 2015, I had managed to get back to work part time, but I became increasingly less able to commute, and keep up with this fast-changing environment. I was being left behind. I hated that my career was ending in front of my eyes and I could do nothing to stop it. In July, my sick pay from the company would stop and I would have to try to get my salary from UWV, the organization that looks after disability pensions in the Netherlands.

But what would happen when I died also continued to worry me. However generous my employers were being, offering to supplement to my disability pension for the time being, my wages and my UWV payments would stop with my death.

We decided to talk to our lawyer again to see how we could explain the economic impact of their negligence to UMC Utrecht, and appeal to their sense of common humanity. But before we could get in touch with him, he phoned us. He had some news of his own. UMCU had finally accepted one of our nominees to act as an independent medical expert on my case. The two sides had been trying to agree on an expert since early in 2014, but each of our suggestions had fallen through – either the expert didn't want to get involved for one reason or another, or UMCU had vetoed our suggestions. We were starting to get really concerned as the expert had to be a gynaecological oncologist, and there was a limited number of suitable candidates in the Netherlands. In fact, we had begun to think of going abroad to find an expert ("you won't get an impartial doctor in the Netherlands", some of our Dutch friends advised), but the problem was that all the files were in Dutch, so an expert from the UK, France, Germany or further afield would need to have the files translated. Belgium was the obvious choice, as Flemish Dutch is one of the country's two languages, but Belgium was close enough to the Netherlands for all the gynaecologists to know each other very well.

So it was with much relief that we learned that Professor Roy Kruitwagen, head of the Gynaecology Division at Maastricht University Medical Centre, had agreed to act as an independent medical expert. He wanted to see me, so we took the train to Maastricht.

We saw him in his office on the morning of 6 May. I tried to keep in mind that Kruitwagen was an *independent* medical advisor. He was not there to take sides with me. His job was to remain impartial and to assess the medical facts and figures with an experienced and unprejudiced eye. I was afraid of him. I was afraid that he would not be able to see through the sea of medical details to the misery that had been caused by UMCU. And I was afraid of him too because he was a doctor – my faith in the medical profession had taken a beating in the previous two years.

Although all my medical records had been provided by the hospitals and should have been sent to him, he had not been brought up to date and had no idea until he met us that my cancer had metastasized. He hadn't been expecting that – and we hadn't anticipated that we'd have to fill him in on the latest shattering news. He dealt with the update that my case was now terminal very professionally and kindly, but even so, explaining my story from beginning to end was difficult for me, and even more difficult for Peter.

In order to retain some emotional control and not succumb entirely to the pain caused by answering Kruitwagen's questions, I stepped outside my story for the first time and tried to look in at it with the detached eye of an outsider. With its details laid bare and recounted in its entirety in non-emotional medical language, the story seemed even starker and painted a bleak picture of what happens when hospitals fail. At some level, I knew then that this was a story that needed to be told, and I think it was that morning in Kruitwagen's office in Maastricht that the seeds for this book were sown.

Kruitwagen had to ask questions about what effect my current state of health was having on my work life, my social life, my ability to do housework (I wonder do they ask this of male patients too?) my ability to enjoy leisure activities, my ability to urinate, defecate and have sex, and the fact that the killing of my ovaries by radiation in 2013 had pushed me into the menopause from hell. Nothing was spared. Every crevice of what's personal and intimate was scrutinized – all with a view to being assessed and totted up by Frieda de Bruin, the loss adjuster, who would come up with a monetary total that my distress added up to. "The value of Adrienne Cullen, damaged patient, amounts to ..."

None of this was Kruitwagen's fault. He was as kind as his role of independent adviser allowed him to be. After about 90 minutes, he finally ran out of questions, and our anger at retelling the story ground us to a halt.

"I'm going to tell you broadly what I'm going to say in my report", he announced. "I don't see any reason why you shouldn't know." He knew that being made to wait until his report was delivered would increase our stress. "You are the patient and you will be the owner of this report", he added. "But I need to prepare and write it in Dutch. Is that okay? I can provide a summary in English for you." We thanked him and listened to his brief run through of his main findings. In short, he found that the overwhelming likelihood was that had I been treated appropriately in 2011 for the adenocarcinoma flagged in the unseen pathology results, I would have needed only the hysterectomy (not the chemo or radiotherapy because there would have been no cancer-positive lymph node) and the certainty of my survival would have been 90% to 95%.

When his draft report came ten days later, it echoed exactly what the professor had told us in his office on 6 May: "Curative treatment is no longer possible, now that recurrence has been established. There will only be further deterioration and eventually

Mrs Cullen will die." There was a lot of medical jargon but the message came across loud and clear: Adrienne Cullen is incurably ill today because UMCU was negligent in its handling of her test results and didn't inform her for two years that she had cancer. I now felt I had a copper-bottomed case against the hospital. Now, surely they would understand.

Ostensibly, the purpose of seeking an independent medical report was to bolster our legal case against the hospital, but to me, the real value of Kruitwagen's report was that it was an independent and unemotional account of the damage, misery and impending death that had been caused when UMCU decided to move from paper to electronic records without, it seems, protecting patient data and without putting appropriate safety nets in place during the transition.

To that extent, I was pleased, but Peter wasn't. Seeing my "death sentence" written in black and white by a doctor totally unknown to us, was painful reading.

She knows she will die from the cervical carcinoma. Curative treatment is no longer possible ... the severity of the symptoms would most certainly have been less because, in the absence of lymph node metastases there would have been no indication for adjuvant chemoradiation. Moreover, the chances of curation would have been significantly better (90-95%) compared to the chances of curation upon diagnosis of lymph node metastasis (75-80%).[9]

I couldn't turn back time, so I focused on concentrating the minds of UMCU's lawyers on the fact that my life was now a write-off. Peter was focused on the fact that he was going to lose his life-partner of 33 years – a wretched waste of a valued life and a shameful disgrace that lay firmly at the door of the leadership of the University Medical Centre in Utrecht.

---

9   Professor Roy Kruitwagen's report was written in Dutch. The excerpts reproduced here
     are from a certified legal translation of the report.

9 | June and July 2015 ... UMC, Utrecht

A body of men holding themselves accountable to nobody ought not to be trusted by anybody.
Thomas Paine

We told our lawyer what had happened in Maastricht. I sent him a copy of Kruitwagen's report and we made an appointment to see him on 11 June. We had talked a little bit in the past about the compensation paid in the Netherlands to patients damaged by the actions of hospitals and doctors. The picture he had painted then had shocked me. There's a belief here that the social welfare system looks after income if the patient needs to work fewer hours or has to stop working altogether. The reality wasn't that simple. I believed that UMC Utrecht was responsible for the financial consequences of its negligence, and that passing the cost on to the taxpayer through the social welfare system was very convenient for them – and humiliating for me to have to apply for assistance from the state and prove to them how sick I was in order to qualify. And there is no way that that assistance would cover what I was currently earning, let alone compensate me for wage rises, bonuses, my freelance work and promotions as my career progressed.

The previous discussions we had had with our lawyer about compensation had all been theoretical, and had mostly taken place in February 2014 right after UMCU had accepted liability for medical negligence. At that time, although it was always a possibility, we hadn't known I was going to die, so I didn't really know what the consequences were when someone died as a result of medical negligence. But I was sure in my own mind that this was a whole new scenario, and being responsible for my early death was bound to make the hospital's loss adjuster and the hospital board see things differently.

"Now it's official", I began when we were sitting with the lawyer in his office. "I'm going to die of this disease because, and only because, UMC Utrecht left my cancer-positive test results lying unnoticed in my file for two years. If I had been treated appropriately at the time, I wouldn't be dying now."

The lawyer agreed. In a nutshell, that was the finding of Kruitwagen's report.

But my prognosis of death at the hands of UMCU wasn't going to have an effect on the compensation we could expect. Under the Dutch system, you don't get more pain and suffering compensation if you are going to die, and family members can't claim pain and suffering for your loss. Peter and I were speechless.

"Look", explained the lawyer. "Let's say a couple bring their baby to the hospital and a doctor or nurse makes a mistake that results in the baby's death. The couple aren't entitled to any specific financial compensation for the baby's death — except, of course, for the funeral expenses."

We were dumbstruck. "But why?" I asked. I was asking that a lot these days.

"The parents aren't at a financial disadvantage as a result of

Deny, dismiss, dehumanise

the baby's death because the baby, obviously, wasn't earning any income", explained the lawyer.

"But it's such a tragedy", I said "Surely there must be compensation for pain and suffering … and loss?"

Apparently not. The baby can't make a claim for pain and suffering after his death, and relatives can't claim for pain and suffering caused by the death of a loved one, even if that loved one is their baby.

"As I mentioned before", the lawyer continued, "the highest compensation ever paid in the Netherlands to a patient damaged by medical treatment was to a man who contracted HIV after a blood transfusion and later died of AIDS. That was back in the 1990s, in the days of the guilder. He received the equivalent of about €160,000. Since then, no higher amount has ever been received by any patient in a case against a hospital."

"But why haven't the courts increased the payments in nearly 20 years?" I asked.

"Almost no patient ever takes a hospital to court", the lawyer explained. "Once you take the hospital to court, you have to pay all your legal costs yourself."

I understood immediately what he meant. As soon as UMCU had accepted legal liability for the damage they caused me, they became responsible for paying our legal costs. The reason behind this is so that patients won't be at a disadvantage if they're not financially able to take a legitimate case against a hospital. (No-foal-no-fee arrangements were banned here until 2014 and although they have now been introduced on a trial basis, they are still frowned on.) When we had initially found out that UMCU would be held responsible for our legal costs once they assumed liability, Peter and I had thought what a constructive and well-thought-out system that was. Now I was beginning to see it had disadvantages too. If I were to take UMCU to court on this, they would stop paying our lawyer and we'd have to start paying tens of thousands of euros in legal fees. Because the majority of patients, ourselves included, couldn't really afford to pay a lawyer somewhere north of €300-an-hour throughout a long legal battle, cases were settled outside court. That meant there were no cases in front of judges for them to rule on, for new precedents to be set, and for the compensation guidelines to be increased periodically to match patients' needs and expectations, and to keep abreast of compensation payments in other EU countries, such as the United Kingdom, Italy, Germany and Ireland.

The bottom line was that if I died before we settled, I'd get nothing. If I survived long enough, I was unlikely to get much more than the €160,000 or so paid to the unfortunate man back in the 1990s. The lawyer promised he would do his best, and said he was going to ask for €200,000 for me. I could barely believe him. Everything I had gone through, the shock of the cancer diagnosis two years too late, the trauma of being ignored by UMCU afterwards, the surgery, the chemo, the weeks of radiotherapy, the nausea, the fatigue, the lymphoedema, the loss of dignity, the PTSD, the ongoing health complications, the bullying for not being able to speak Dutch, the reduction of my salary, the end of my career, and now the end of my life – that was deemed to be worth about €200,000 on a fair day with the wind behind us? I had seen consultants' cars in UMCU's car park worth more than that.

The lawyer saw my horrified face. He counselled me to try to come to terms with the fact that this is the way it is in the Netherlands. They didn't believe in punitive damages, and payouts for pain and suffering are among the lowest in the developed world. The hospital was not, it seemed, under any obligation to help us put our lives back to rights. Nor was the board likely to suffer in any way as a result of the damage they had caused. The paltry sums mentioned by our lawyer would barely make a blip in their annual accounts.

Our lawyer suggested we compile a list of our earnings and assets since 2010. In order to calculate what compensation, if any, Peter would be entitled to when I died. We would have to disclose all our earnings, our pensions, our investments and any other assets to UMCU's lawyers and to De Bruin. The look of horror on my face heightened. The hospital that damaged me was entitled to know every detail about our finances, solely so that they could reduce the compensation they had to pay us. Every step of this process with the hospital was causing more distress and humiliation. The violation and indignity of having to disclose our personal circumstances to heartless functionaries representing the people who were costing me my life was too much to stomach. On top of making a fatal error, then ignoring that error, now they were going to means-test us! We were disgusted. We were being "processed" by a compensation system that was a slick, well-oiled machine weighted in favour of those with power – the hospital, its lawyers and its insurers – and against the virtually powerless patients. We knew all too keenly that no amount of money in the world would ever compensate me for the loss of my future, or Peter for the loss of his wife, but offering a level of financial security was the least UMCU could do to repair the damage they had caused, and I was determined that the complacency with which this whole matter was being dealt with by the hospital would not go unchallenged. They were not going to get away with ruining our lives and then keeping their heads down while their agents threw us the usual few euros that the system was designed to dispense. Getting the hospital leaders to face the dreadful and far-reaching consequences of their actions would be my next goal.

I asked the lawyer how I could get in touch with the board. I wanted direct access to the people at the centre of this fiasco. I wanted to tell them exactly what the patients they damaged were put through in order to try to put the pieces of their lives back together. I wanted to ask them if they had any idea of the effect this "begging for compensation" was having on someone who was already terminally ill. I wanted to ask them why only the hospital's lawyers, not its doctors, dealt with patients who had been damaged by medical mistakes. I felt sure that if I could just explain it the right way to the board they'd understand.

He didn't say it, but I knew our lawyer thought I was naïve. Still, he realized I was fiercely determined to do this, so he contacted UMCU. Much to his surprise, they agreed to meet me. I was to see Arie Franx, Kit Roes and the chairman of the hospital board, Jan Kimpen, the following day, Thursday, 2 July, at 12:30pm.

****

I didn't sleep much on the night of 1 July. Everything I wanted to say crowded my mind and pushed sleep away. By eight the next morning, I wanted nothing more than to stay in bed and sleep. I washed and dressed as though it were a normal Thursday and I was going to work in Amsterdam. I hadn't told Peter about my appointment at UMCU. I wanted to do this alone. As far as Peter was concerned, UMCU could "keep their filthy money". He wanted none of it. I didn't agree. I didn't want to die and leave Peter on his own, but the least I could do was to make sure that UMCU compensated us properly. I needed to sort this while I was still able.

That Thursday was one of those summer days when the Netherlands behaves as though it were in the tropics. It was sunny and humid and seriously hot. By the time I got to UMCU at eleven, it was almost 30 degrees. I sat in the air-conditioned student area of the hospital to dry out and cool down before my lunchtime meeting. Here, it felt less like a hospital and more like a place of learning.

Kit Roes collected me at reception. I followed him, mostly

Deny, dismiss, dehumanise

in uncomfortable silence, past the shop on the left with its flowers, get-well-soon cards and shiny balloons welcoming the new-borns of Utrecht. We passed the atrium café where we had had coffee after Dr Brouwer told Peter, not me, that my cancer was probably a stage IIB. We passed the pharmacy on the left and the lifts on the right and then up a flight of stairs in a wing I hadn't noticed before. Here all was wood and carpet and plants. This was UMCU's corporate heart. There's no hospital smell here and the paintings on the wall are a better class of art. Here, there were no drip-trees, white uniforms and clogs, bolted-down plastic seating or coloured strips to follow along the shiny institution floor. This was a world of boardroom tables, bottled water, men in suits and capable-looking female secretaries. Adrienne-The-Patient slunk into the background and Professional Adrienne tried her best to gear up.

In the boardroom, I shook hands with Franx and Kimpen. No one else was sweating. They probably thought I was nervous. That annoyed me – probably because it was true. Playing host, Professor Kimpen offered me a seat on his right at the large, round table and the other professors sat opposite. Drinking my water in one go (Kimpen asked the secretary to bring more), I thanked them for meeting me and, polite men all, they thanked me for coming. The three men looked surprised when the next thing I did was turn on my iPad. I flicked through the my photo gallery at random, stopping at the ones that caught my eye: a photo taken fifteen years ago on the street in Jerusalem with a younger, healthier me on a camel called Sammy and Peter, his hair black then, holding the reins; a photo of my friend, Yeokyung, and me in a boat in Stockholm the previous summer, leaning into each other and smiling for the camera; a photo of last year's Christmas dinner at home with friends, the Christmas tree in the background with 500 lights on it – I never knowingly under-decorate a Christmas tree; a photo of the enormous pale yellow lilies in my garden the previous July; a photo the waiter of a little Italian trattoria in Amsterdam took of me with my Brazilian friends, Tati and Jaime; a photo of me near the Blue Mosque in Istanbul wearing the pink flowery scarf Mansi brought me from India, and a photo of me near the garden pond holding Georgie, our cat. There were probably fifteen or twenty photos in my selection of family, friends, home and holidays and I went around the table making sure that each man had a good look. They all nodded tactfully as I gave them a brief run down on each photo. And being smart, they probably also knew where this was leading.

I snapped the iPad closed and said: "That's my life. That's what's coming to an end. Trips with friends, the lights on the Christmas tree, the meals in Italian trattorias in Amsterdam. I'm roughly the same age as all of you, but I'm not going to be in the holiday snaps any more. There are lots of places I still want to visit – Shanghai, Tokyo, Seoul, Hong Kong, Reykjavik, Helsinki – but I'm not going to get there now. I'm going to be the missing face in everyone's photo albums. The missing person at the table. And the *only* reason is that I came to UMC Utrecht for treatment. Unfortunately, I came at a time when you were moving to electronic files and no extra safeguards were put in place during that process. I was not safe in your hospital."

Kimpen flinched. It appeared I had touched a nerve.

"I don't accept that the transition to electronic files can be said to have been responsible for what happened in your case", said Kimpen. He didn't look pleased. "There are no conceivable systems or safeguards that I can implement that would protect against someone in gynaecology and someone in pathology not managing to talk to each other."

I was fascinated. Insofar as I had ever been told anything at all about what had caused the mess-up with my test results, I had been told that the transition from paper to electronic files that had been underway in 2011 was the most likely culprit. But it seemed that the hospital's CEO didn't share that viewpoint. I was torn. I wanted to explore this further, but it looked like a sore point for Kimpen, so I bit my tongue. I had another agenda that day.

"We asked you here today to see what we could do to help", said Kimpen.

"Thank you", I replied. "I think you will be able to help me."

I told them that judging by the way they had responded to me since 2013, I could only conclude that they had no idea what happened to patients damaged by hospitals. I told them that I believed they were hiding from the real-life damage their systems had caused.

"For a start", I said, "when someone can't work any more, the salary fairy doesn't just wave a magic wand and arrange for UWV to pay them instead." I told them of the months of paperwork, humiliating meetings with HR and company doctors, the endless explanatory emails, the forms in Dutch and the unpleasant conversation I had had the previous week with UWV about attending a meeting with their doctor.

I told them that while they were entering into an exciting period in their own careers in the last decade or so before retirement, I at the same age had to watch my career drain away.

I told them that I was currently spending my days picking through our finances with my accountant because UMCU's agents wanted to know every cent of income, pension and investments we had – so they could subtract it from any compensation they had to pay Peter for my loss of earnings on my death.

I told them of my disbelief when I heard from my lawyer the amount of money their loss adjuster thinks is appropriate to compensate me for cutting my life short by 20 to 30 years. I told them that the cars they had driven to the hospital that day were probably worth more than my life was – and that my life was, according to their loss adjuster, valued at a good deal less than any one of them earned in a year.

I told them that I had gone a long way towards forgiving what had happened in the past, the human error, the negligence and even the dismissive and uncaring way they treated me after I was eventually diagnosed, but if they forced me to spend the rest of my days providing financial documents to their loss adjuster and then to die knowing that my husband was going to be paid a pittance for my loss, that I would *never* forgive.

I looked across the table at Franx and Roes and said: "When we first met last year, you said that the hospital board had not known anything about what had happened to me; they had never even heard of me – despite accepting liability for medical negligence. Well, this time, I'm not going to give you the opportunity to use ignorance as your alibi."

I shifted my focus to just Franx and said, "You said that you, personally, felt ashamed at the way I had been treated. And I believed you. Should I still believe you?" Franx nodded his head. Kimpen stiffened slightly beside me but said nothing. I looked at him and continued.

"I'm telling you now that this hospital is doing it to me again. You have washed your hands of me and handed me over to lawyers and loss adjusters to clean up the mess you made in your clinic and in your pathology lab. Your lawyers are very good at their jobs. They will ensure that Peter and I get as little financial compensation as possible – regardless of the further indignities they inflict on us in the process. It is in their interest, in your interest, to delay settlement in the hope that I will die, as anticipated, in the coming months, and so my claim will die with me. Dead patients don't have to be compensated.

"I am asking you to call a halt to what these people are doing to us under the guise of correct procedure and precedent. I'm asking you to stop 'processing' us and make your own decisions in line with your consciences about what's an appropriate way to deal with me – and to deal with all patients like me. You have a

Deny, dismiss, dehumanise

moral obligation to undo as much as possible of the damage you have caused.

"All I want to achieve is that Peter and I are not at a financial disadvantage because of what happened to me here at UMC Utrecht."

I probably would have ranted on longer, but I had started to feel seriously unwell and needed to get my breath back. Roes and Franx looked nearly as miserable as I felt, but it was Kimpen who spoke.

"This needs to be dealt with without further delay", he said. "I understand the difficulty you are in. I will see this is sorted out."

He then looked at me and said, "Do you trust me?" The answer he expected was probably, "Yes". The honest answer was closer to "No". The answer I gave him was, "I'd like to, but it depends on what you do next."

What he did next was to visit the hospital lawyers, and then he went on holidays. I never saw him or heard from him again.

10 | July 2015 … Alrijne Hospital, Leiden

The first revolution is when you change your mind about how you look at things, and see there might be another way to look at it that you have not been shown.
Gil Scott-Heron

I got home in the late afternoon, but I remember almost nothing about how I got there. I hadn't eaten anything during the day, nor did I want to. I couldn't have been thinking straight either as I was still attributing my nausea, sweating and weakened state to the stress of visiting UMCU, coupled with lack of sleep.

Once home, I flopped onto the bed and tried to fill in a bewildered and very worried Peter about what I had been doing during the day. If I had been capable of sitting upright and making sense, we might have argued about the wisdom of me going to UMCU on my own, and perhaps he would have reprimanded me for telling him I was going to work when I had a totally different agenda. But although he was keen to know what I had said to Kimpen, Roes and Franx, Peter was much more concerned about the state I was in. He knew something wasn't right and wanted me to call our GP. The last thing I wanted was more f★★★★★g

Deny, dismiss, dehumanise

doctors, so I persuaded him I'd be just fine after a good night's sleep.

Well, Peter was right and I was wrong. Overnight, I started vomiting and my temperature was rising. As soon as the surgery opened next morning, I had appointment to see the trainee GP. Her thermometer confirmed a temperature of 40.5 degrees (that's 105 for anyone happier with Fahrenheit). The next thing I knew, I was being whisked off to hospital in an ambulance.

There wasn't much beyond the rather unpleasant here-and-now going on in my head that morning, but in Peter's head, Van der Velden's words from last April were ringing ominously. He was sure that Tumour 2 had been triggered and was causing a blockage in my large bowel, which would lead to my death very soon. The trainee GP could think of nothing to reassure him otherwise.

In the back of the ambulance, I remember trying to explain to the paramedic that I didn't want to go to hospital because people would give me a hard time for not speaking Dutch. He thought the fever was making me delirious and tried his best to reassure me that everybody in the Netherlands speaks English. The more he tried to reassure me, the harder I tried to explain what had been happening to me over the past two years at AMC. He couldn't believe what I was telling him and tried, kindly, to convince me that all would be well. By the time we reached the hospital, the Alrijne in Leiden, I was crying with dread of what awaited me on the ward. As I was being taken out of the ambulance, the second paramedic, a younger man who had been driving, put his hand on my shoulder and said, "I heard what you were saying about people who don't like that you don't speak Dutch. I know it happens." Just being believed by this kind, young paramedic made me feel less alone.

On the ward, no one made any hurtful comments about my inability to speak Dutch, and this remained the case for the five days I was there. I was brought to the oncology ward – so I guess everyone else was also thinking that whatever was wrong with me was cancer-related. There were four beds in the room and the flurry of activity around me was dizzying. I was surprised. I thought they'd leave me somewhere quiet and monitor me, but there was an exhausting queue of medics looking for urine, looking for blood, asking questions and measuring temperature, oxygen levels and blood pressure. Then others came looking for veins they could use to rehydrate me and give me antibiotics.

They told me at some stage during the afternoon that I was dangerously ill. I'd had a urinary tract infection (UTI) that had developed into urosepsis. I didn't register how serious it was. Throughout the afternoon, the noise on the ward seemed to be getting louder and louder. The other patients seemed to be speaking at full volume to their visitors and the constant noise of doctors and nurses, drip alarms, chairs being dragged to bedsides and mobile phone chats was overwhelming. The July sunshine coming through the windows was blindingly bright and I begged for the thin curtains to be pulled around my bed. The nurse looking after me knew the light and noise were too much for me and apologized for having nowhere else to put me. They really had no other bed, let alone a room on my own, even though I was too sick to be where I was. They did their best. They pulled the curtains and tried to keep the noise levels to a minimum – but in a busy ward, that's not really possible. I was never left alone for more than a few minutes. There was someone beside me the whole time.

The day wore on and I wasn't getting any better. I was unable to pee, so they catheterized me, and helped me to sip the water beside my bed. I was too tired to lift the glass unaided. Peter came with clothes and toiletries but I didn't have the strength to undress. I remember a trip to the ultrasound, and possibly a CT too. During the night, I was in too much pain to sleep. I wasn't responding to the antibiotic.

Deny, dismiss, dehumanise

By Saturday morning, I had not improved. They tried a different antibiotic. During the afternoon, they moved me to the chemo room, which was not used at the weekend. Despite the smell of the chemo, which I hadn't smelt since October 2013, and which made horrid memories come rushing back, the chemo room saved my life. It was quiet and cool, and for the first time since Tuesday night, I slept. They warned me though that I could only stay there until Monday morning when the day's chemo patients would arrive.

The new antibiotic worked. By Saturday evening I was eating, by Sunday I was walking around, and by Monday I was almost ready to go home, which I did on Tuesday. Only afterwards did I realize how sick I had been. I had no idea then what caused the UTI, or what made it develop into urosepsis. The hospital didn't have any explanation either. No one was able to explain to me how I could have been totally healthy and at work on Wednesday and suffering from urosepsis on Thursday morning. The good news though was that it had nothing to do with my cancer – or so we thought at the time.

****

With the drama over and the antibiotics doing their job, my attention turned back to UMCU. I'd left the meeting on 2 July sure that the three professors had understood what I'd explained to them. I expected to hear from them any day now. I knew that Kimpen had gone on holiday, as had Franx, but the agreement was that they would put a plan in action before they left and Kit Roes would be my point of contact.

By 9 July, a week after the meeting, I had heard nothing. I emailed Roes. I got no answer. I sent it again the following day. I got an automatic reply saying he was out of the office from 10 July to 20 July. He had gone on holiday too. On 16 July, he replied to my email saying they had worked out a proposal for me before going on holidays … and had sent it to my lawyer. This wasn't the agreement. I had contacted the hospital's CEO directly because the legal channels were going nowhere. At no point had we discussed that their lawyer would get back to my lawyer – who was himself on holiday until some time in August. I responded to Roes telling him this and asking him to tell me what the proposal contained. I didn't know at the time that the UMCU lawyers and the loss adjuster had actually drawn up the proposal, not Kimpen, Roes and Franx. Roes responded saying that it would, he felt, cause complications for me if he were to proceed without the involvement of my lawyer. I disagreed. If I had wanted this sorted out by the lawyers, I wouldn't have wasted my time going to the hospital myself. And my lawyer was waiting to hear back through me what the hospital was proposing. I persisted. And eventually Roes relented and agreed to talk to me the following week, 20 July, when he would be back in his office.

The 17-minute phone conversation did not go well. The proposal that the UMCU lawyers drew up on the instruction of the hospital's CEO offered exactly the inadequate sum of money that I had already told them was derisory. For my pain and suffering and all my out-of-pocket expenses, their grand proposal was … €180,000. I felt as though I had been slapped across the face. My response to Roes was that it was "grossly insulting". It was exactly the sort of figure that I had told them had been suggested by Frieda de Bruin, and which we had found totally unacceptable. In fact, it was less than the €200,000 our lawyer had optimistically mentioned he would like to achieve.

"It's the highest amount of damages ever offered in the Netherlands", interjected Roes. "And it's tax free."

He wasn't making the situation any better.

The amount that Roes, or rather UMCU's legal department, proposed to compensate Peter for loss of earnings as a result of my

Deny, dismiss, dehumanise

death was €192,000. That, he assured me, took into consideration my salary and projected wage increases for the remaining ten or twelve years of my working life. This was even more insulting. I told him this was probably about what he earned in one year. Roes assured me that they had taken salary increases, bonuses and promotions into consideration, and again reminded me that this sum would be nett of tax.

Whatever metric they were using was weighted heavily on the side of the insurers. I was never a high earner, but my basic salary when I became ill was around €45,000. On top of that, I earned quarterly and annual bonuses. I also worked as a freelance editor, boosting my salary by a further €5,000 to €10,000 a year. My nett annual take-home pay was in the region of €38,000. Not even considering inflation, wage increases and promotions, my nett earnings up to retirement in 2027 would have totalled, at the very least, €460,000. Why was this man thinking that €192,000, or €16,000 a year, was adequate?

I struggled to stay in control. I had really believed that Kimpen and the others had heard and understood me. I knew I could never get as much compensation as I felt I deserved, but I did feel they had got the message that the "car money" sums dispensed to patients in the past were no longer acceptable – patients and their families were entitled to be compensated adequately, without having to … beg.

All I wanted was to be able to carry on with the same standard of living as we had had while I was still alive, and for that to continue after my death. The offers I had just been made showed that they had understood nothing, and that it was still the lawyers and not the doctors who call the shots when hospitals fail. I was collateral damage. It was demonstrably cheaper to compensate the odd patient damaged during a shift from paper to electronic files than to put expensive safeguards in place that would protect all.

Peter took the phone from me and told Roes calmly and in

detail what we planned to do next. He outlined the media plan we had been discussing over the past few weeks. A third-generation journalist, Peter understood the news value of my story, and as a former head of media affairs with a semi-state body in Ireland, he understood only too well how organizations in general, and hospitals in particular, hate bad publicity. We believed that it was necessary to expose UMCU for what it had done to me, how it had behaved in the aftermath, and how it was continuing to behave even now, in the full knowledge that I was terminally ill.

Roes urged us to discuss matters with our lawyer before contacting the media. I don't know whether he thought it was our lawyer's job to talk us out of going public, or whether he believed I had no entitlement to tell my story, or indeed whether he thought we could be frightened by the legal implications of going public. But I now agreed with Peter that we had nothing left to lose. I had kept silent up to now to protect the wrong people at UMCU from being hurt, and because I believed, despite the way they had treated me since 2013, that the hospital had a human heart somewhere. That belief had just been dashed as UMCU let me down for the fourth time.

11 | August to October 2015 ... UMC, Utrecht

Evil is a function of thoughtlessness: the tendency of people to obey and conform without critical thinking.
Hannah Arendt, 1963

I was at a low ebb. My lawyer's best efforts using the compensation "system" – which was all that was available to him – were having no effect whatsoever on the immovable force of Frieda de Bruin and the hospital's lawyers. And my own attempts to appeal directly to the hospital leaders had also fallen on deaf ears.

After we spoke, Roes sent an email to my lawyer summarizing my response and asking that the lawyer make it clear to me that all further communication was to be held exclusively between my lawyer and the hospital's legal department. The good professors did not want to be bothered again. Their official position with regard to their patient was now, "talk to us only through our lawyers".

I did, however, hear from Franx, head of the gynaecology division, who had given me his phone number before he went on holiday and invited me to contact him if he could help. I sent him a

WhatsApp and received a friendly reply explaining that he was at sea and would phone me in the morning. That evening however, I received another WhatsApp, with a different tone, saying that in order to manage my expectations, he was telling me in advance that he could only answer questions I might have about providing medical or psychological support for me and Peter: all other matters would have to be communicated through my lawyer. This upset me in a way that the lack of understanding shown by Roes and Kimpen didn't. When I first met him on 10 October, 2014, and then again on 2 July, 2015, I had felt that Arie Franx was listening in a way that the others weren't. His body language, his facial expressions, his admission that he felt "ashamed", his offer to stay in contact and the seriousness with which he spoke of the calamity that had befallen me in his department had made me believe that he was sincere and understood that the hospital should have been helping me. Now it looked as though he just had a better shtick than the others.

On his return from holidays, I filled my lawyer in on what had happened in his absence, and instructed him to have no further communication with De Bruin until further notice. Reactivating the old conversation between our lawyer and the loss adjuster would simply be showing UMCU that we had been put firmly in our place, and now they could carry on "processing" us along the system like the compliant patients they expected us to be.

We also asked our lawyer about other ways of holding UMC Utrecht accountable for what they had done to me. We suggested speaking to the IGZ – the people I had phoned in the summer of 2014 to tell them what had happened, and who had never returned my call. We were advised that the IGZ operated in their own way and we could not influence or take part in any investigation they might undertake. We discussed taking the incident to the *tuchtcollege*, a disciplinary board that deals with health sector personnel in the Netherlands. The problem with

Deny, dismiss, dehumanise

that was that I couldn't take a complex complaint against the leadership of the hospital. The *tuchtcollege* did not deal with, I was told, administrative errors in hospitals or calamities resulting from systems or protocol failures. I had the option of bringing a complaint against Van der Vaart, but I knew that would be scapegoating and laying complex blame, which should have rested at a corporate level, at the feet of someone who was, at most, only partly responsible for what had happened, and who was, in my opinion, all too likely to be hung out to dry by the hospital.

Part of the problem was that I was still at sea as to what exactly *had* happened to my test results in 2011. Van der Vaart had said that he believed that the transition from paper to electronic records had been at the root of the error, but the hospital's CEO had emphatically denied that this was the cause. In Kimpen's view, it was plainly and simply the responsibility of doctors ordering tests and pathologists processing tests to come up with a way of communicating with each other so that results don't get lost.

I had met Van der Vaart twice, in a private capacity outside the hospital, since the traumatic diagnosis in June 2013, and we had stayed in touch by email. The objective of this contact was to attempt to heal, in some way, the hurt that had been caused to us both, and not so that I could interrogate him about what had gone wrong. However, we did, of course, discuss what had happened. He said he did not know what safety systems and protocols, if any, were in place in UMCU in 2011, nor did he know if the hospital had put any extra precautions in place during the shift to electronic patient files. All Van der Vaart knew for sure was that under the paper-based system that was still in place in April 2011 when my sample was taken, results from pathology destined for him would be put into his cubbyhole. Other test results belonging to other patients had followed this system before and well after my test results left the pathology department in April 2011.

Huub Van der Vaart was as puzzled and, arguably, as

distressed by what had happened as I was. He had attempted to find out what had gone wrong, but didn't seem to have discovered very much detail. He had addressed groups of gynaecology fellows at UMCU twice about the incident itself and about how badly the support systems had failed me, primarily, and him too. People listened. Afterwards, kind colleagues empathized and provided support for him. Better late than never. But no one from the hospital's leadership reached out to him. No effort was made to help him find out what, precisely, had happened, which could have partly cleared his name. The hospital's view was that it had all happened too long ago, and because their system had now changed, there was no risk of it happening again. No further lessons could be learned – case closed.

I didn't agree. And nor did Peter. Perhaps it's because of our backgrounds in journalism, or perhaps it's a cultural thing, but we couldn't get our heads around the idea that a calamity had happened to a patient in a hospital, which was going to result in her death – and no internal or external investigation was carried out to find out what had happened; no one questioned any of the people who might have been involved; no one outside the hospital had been informed; other than Van der Vaart, no one at the hospital would discuss the matter with the patient or provide an explanation, and the hospital denied, without carrying out any apparent checks, that any other patients had been subjected to similar risks during the transition to electronic files.

But perhaps what bothered me most was that there was no documentation anywhere – not at UMCU itself, not at the IGZ, not at the department of health, and nowhere in the public domain – that recorded that anything at all had happened to Adrienne Cullen at UMC Utrecht in April 2011. The calamity was not on the hospital record, and so not available to learn from. The only account that anything had gone wrong at UMCU lay in the minds and memories of those involved, all of whom had been damaged in one way or another by the tragedy. Once we died, retired or moved on, the waters would close over and it would be as though nothing had ever happened.

And that is why I now agreed with Peter that going public was the best option. We contacted Esther Rosenburg at *NRC* and arranged to meet her in September.

In the meantime, Peter started to put in place another aspect of his press plan that he had outlined to Kit Roes. He started to tweet snippets of my story – photos and some of the details about what was happening to me, including that I was told I was going to die because of medical negligence at UMCU. Being a Twitter newbie, he soon realized that it wasn't working. A few people we know saw the tweets and got in touch, but that wasn't what he wanted to achieve. So he thought about it differently. He found Kimpen and some of the other UMCU luminaries on Twitter and started to follow them. He took a look to see who else followed them, and who they were following, and so he followed all of those too – doctors and nurses working in UMCU; staff, professors and executive board members in hospitals across the Netherlands; medical academics in major hospitals in the UK and the US; politicians, stakeholders in the health sector, and anyone who he thought might be interested in what was happening. That worked much better. The tweets were hitting the UMCU leadership where it hurt them most, in their egos. Within days UMCU's lawyers were on to our lawyer complaining about Peter's "social media campaign". The hospital was, according to its lawyers, "embarrassed". But what was really annoying them was that Peter was doing nothing wrong or against the law. The tweets were merely relating the story of what was happening to me – that UMCU was responsible was indisputable, they had admitted legal liability. Although the tweets were close to the bone, nothing Peter said was untrue or defamatory. He was telling my story in 140-character bites with photos on Twitter – and if the hospital was embarrassed, it was embarrassed by the recounting of its own sorry role in the damage and death of a patient.

Nor was I sitting idly by. I wanted the rest of the hospital's small executive board and the members of the larger supervisory board to also be aware of what happened to me and how badly the hospital was dealing with it. I was determined not to be shushed by the strategy of silence that UMCU espoused. My instinct was that other patients had been, or would be, suffering from UMCU's habit of tight-lipped silence. And I was determined to write to each and every member of both boards telling them the details of all that had happened since 2011. I started writing my story. I sent an open letter to every individual on the boards as well as to a number of other strategic people in the hospital.

It came as no great surprise that no one on either board ever acknowledged receipt of my letter. Whether any of them ever received it, I simply don't know. One of the other hospital seniors I selected to send the letter to was Annelien Bredenoord, Associate Professor of Biomedical Ethics at UMCU, elected Senator and chair of her political party, D66 in Utrecht. D66 is one of the country's largest political parties and has broadly liberal or centre-left policies. The "D" stands for "democracy" and the "66" marks the year it was founded. Professor Bredenoord had spoken out on several occasions about health issues and justice.

As an elected representative and someone familiar with medical ethics, I thought she'd be an ideal person to reach out to, and uniquely qualified to help. But no. She replied that she was very sorry to hear about my "disease" and what had happened, but it had nothing to do with her and wasn't something she could help with. She wished me strength, and shut the door in my face. So a medical ethics professor at UMCU didn't see the way patients were treated as having anything to do with medical ethics, nor was it of even the remotest interest to her as an elected senator of one of the country's largest political parties.

Deny, dismiss, dehumanise

Bredenoord was not the only person who had responded to my story in this way over the past few years. Her knee-jerk-sympathetic comments coupled with complete wonderment as to what it had to do with her was a response that Peter and I encountered often. We were regularly met with total incomprehension, sometimes even active disapproval, because we dared to speak out against the systems that were in place to deal with people like us in situations like ours. The difficulties we were having with UMCU's attitude and with the production-line process that was in place to dole out minimal compensation to damaged patients were as much deep-rooted theoretical difficulties as they were urgent practical difficulties. For us, it was a question of natural justice, moral responsibility, and having the common decency to put right what you have done wrong; for De Bruin, UMCU, and arguably for the whole medical-negligence legal sector, it was a matter of looking up their chart to see what figure was doled out the last time a patient was damaged. The system was a given. It could not be changed, and patients' own input into the compensation arrangement was not welcome. We were told many times: "This is the way it is. This is how the system works here". We were supposed to keep our mouths shut - and comply.

Franx and Roes got copies of my letter too, as did Van der Vaart. I imagine it was difficult for him to read what I had written. Its message wasn't aimed at him, but it would have been wrong to have others in the hospital reading it without him knowing anything about it.

The likelihood is that my letter would have gone straight into the wastebaskets of all who read it, except for one small thing. Our lawyer had put me in contact with Prue Vines, Professor of Law at the University of New South Wales in Australia. In the summer and autumn of 2015, she was a Visiting Professor spending a few months working with a team at the Free University in Amsterdam. Her specialist expertise lies in the area of how apologies affect individuals damaged by the acts of others, and influence whether or not they feel inclined to sue the wrongdoers. Our lawyer thought that Professor Vines would be interested in my case, how I was being dealt with by UMCU, and the impact that the country's compensation system was having on us both. She spent an afternoon with us at our home and, as a specialist in the area, was both appalled and fascinated to hear what had happened to me after the catastrophic error was discovered in UMCU in 2013.

I had, she declared, been "set adrift by the hospital", which absolutely should have had a serious-harm protocol – similar to Australia's "Open Disclosure" or the UK's "Duty of Candour" policies – in place to respond to my needs from the moment the calamitous error was discovered. She was also critical that I had never received a formal apology from the hospital.

It was so refreshing to speak, at last, to someone who saw the issue much as we did. We had believed right from the start that UMCU had exactly this type of responsibility to me and should have had – as any major teaching hospital in a wealthy EU country should have had – a competent serious-harm protocol. Listening to Prue Vines that day, we were reassured we were not crazy. Other hospitals in other countries in most of the developed world had had systems in place for years to support patients damaged by hospitals – in fact, there was a whole discipline internationally that dealt with the complex problems of the victims of medical adverse events. In other countries, those whose lives were ended or blighted were not expected to just suck it up and stop complaining, as the whole system here in the Netherlands seemed geared towards.

Prue Vines said that how UMCU had responded was "an enormous deviation from the principles" of an open disclosure policy. I'd had no contact from UMCU explaining or apologizing or even acknowledging the calamity. I'd had no meetings with anyone other than Van der Vaart until 18 months after the event, and even that meeting happened only because of our insistence that we meet someone representing the hospital. As far as Vines was concerned, UMCU did not adequately carry out its responsibilities to me and as a result, the damage caused by the medical negligence was compounded. UMCU had been responsible for causing "second harm".

At the end of our afternoon together, Peter asked Vines if she would write a letter to the hospital board outlining her thoughts and insights on how the two sides might move a little bit closer together. She agreed,[10] and we left it entirely up to her how she would approach such a letter and what she might say. We simply felt that she had more experience of the area than anyone else we had spoken to, her academic credentials were in exactly the right area – and her heart was in the right place too.

On 10 October, exactly two years after my last radiotherapy treatments and one year after meeting the UMCU representatives for the first time, Prue Vines' four-page letter was ready to go. With that arriving in the board members' inboxes alongside my story, it packed quite a punch. De Bruin received her copy too, as did professors Roes, Franx and Van der Vaart.

Peter and I sat and watched and waited … sending the occasional tweet to remind the hospital I was still alive.

Another recipient of the two letters was Esther Rosenberg, who we had spoken to at length in September, and who had been busy trying to gather information and find someone at UMCU who would speak to her about my case. She was working alongside another of the paper's journalists, Hugo Logtenberg, who also wrote news features on healthcare issues. The combination of the two *NRC* journalists, Peter's tweets, my letter to the boards, and the Vines letter, was starting to make UMCU feel very uncomfortable indeed.

---

10   See Appendix 1 for the text of the letter Prue Vines sent to UMCU board members.

On the legal front, the instruction we had given our lawyer in August to stop negotiating with the other side was still in place. Frieda de Bruin was now putting pressure on him to come back to the table.

"What should I say to her?" our lawyer asked me.

"Sit tight", I told him, "tell her your client is still too traumatized by their derisory offer to give you any coherent or consistent instructions." It was the truth. In all honesty, I had no idea what to do next. If putting pressure on UMCU through the media and by reaching out to the board members directly didn't work, nothing was going to move them from their arrogant silence.

I hadn't fully recovered from my bout of urosepsis in July. I was no longer well enough to continue working and had started to receive a disability pension based on a percentage of my earnings. We had been obliged to hire, at our own expense, a specialist financial advisor to look into our "global wealth" – which sounded wonderful, but consisted of a few tiny Irish and Dutch pensions, some small investments and our savings. Our accountant put us in touch with a very pleasant and helpful expert who was able to advise us what income we needed to maintain the same standard of living we had before I became too ill to work. She discovered that I had a very small partner's pension at Booking.com. That should have been good news, but under the system deployed here by loss adjusters, all social welfare payments, pensions, life assurance policies (which we didn't have), and any investments made by people to improve their financial situations would be deducted from what their clients were liable to pay surviving spouses for loss of income. My tiny partner's pension would pay out around €10,000 a year up to 2025. That would be enough to tip the balance in UMCU's favour – and mean that they would not be liable to pay any compensation whatsoever for loss of earnings after my death.

Deny, dismiss, dehumanise

My lawyer would be obliged to disclose the information about the pension to De Bruin, if he knew about it, so the €192,000 offered in July was likely to be snatched off the table in double-quick time, leaving us with a grand total of €180,000. And if I died before a settlement was signed, my own claim would die with me. All UMCU would be liable for then would be my funeral expenses. Keeping my lawyer away from the negotiations and sorting the compensation impasse in our own way was imperative.

12 | November 2015 … UMC, Utrecht

A foolish faith in authority is the worst enemy of truth.
Albert Einstein, 1901

On 1 November 2015, Professor Margriet Schneider became the new CEO of UMC Utrecht. Professor Jan Kimpen was leaving to become the new Chief Medical Officer at Philips. Before he went, he received a knighthood for his services to healthcare.[11]

My lawyer was very excited about the change of leadership, and reported that the incoming CEO had been apprised of "the Cullen case" and was anxious to see it resolved. Sure enough, a settlement offer came in late afternoon on Wednesday, 28 October. My lawyer rang me at home. He beat around the bush, talking about how concerned the new CEO was about the detrimental effect all of this must be having on my health, and how determined she was to see it settled as soon as possible. He was trying to soften me up, and held back from actually telling me what the offer was

---

11   On 27 October, 2015, Jan Kimpen was made Ridder in de Orde van de Nederlandse Leeuw, or a Knight of the Order of the Dutch Lion for his services to health. See photo on the website that accompanies this book.

Deny, dismiss, dehumanise

for as long as he could bear it. I refused to ask. He broke first.

"They have told me to tell you that they would like to offer you and Peter together, to settle both your claims, €500,000", he said. The impact of the nice round figure that my lawyer thought was a seriously generous offer was somewhat undone by his next sentence.

"Of course, the out-of-pocket expenses and advances you have already received will be subtracted from this. So it will be €500,000 minus the €45,000 you have already received."

I'm no negotiator, but instinct told me that the worst thing I could do now was to give an unthinking, emotional response. My reactions would, I was sure, be communicated back to De Bruin. Even if our lawyer didn't intend it, she would pick up my response from what he said to her, and what he didn't say. So I simply told the poor lawyer that I'd talk to Peter about it when he got home. I then asked him if there was a gagging clause, and he assured me there had been no discussion of a gagging clause. I told him we'd get back to him the next day. I think I'd rained on his parade.

Peter was, in fact, upstairs. I stayed on my own for a while in the kitchen and thought about what to do next. Despite my lawyer's enthusiasm at being the broker of the biggest pain and suffering offer ever offered in the history of the state to a damaged patient, I found it hard to drum up much excitement. Is that what it boiled down to? Was I supposed to be delighted that someone saw fit to offer us €500,000 (minus expenses)? I felt vaguely ill, and humiliated. I was sure there was no one on the UMCU boards, or no one in a senior position in the hospital, who would feel that €500,000 would put their lives back to rights in the same circumstances. So why then do they think it's enough to compensate someone whose life they will end and whose hopes they have dashed through their negligence?

But dying patients can't afford to be anything but pragmatists. So while my heart groaned "No!" my head did a quick calculation.

The nett figure after deductions, €455,000, along with our savings, was only slightly short of what our financial advisor had told us we would need to maintain our current standard of living for the rest of my life, and support Peter properly for the remaining few decades of his. I made some tea for myself and took a cup of coffee upstairs to where Peter was working. I feared that De Bruin's negotiations with my lawyer would be nothing compared to the deal I now had to sell to Peter, who was still in the I-don't-want-to-take-their-miserable-money frame of mind. My biggest fear was that I would die before a settlement was agreed, and then Peter would be invited to submit a claim for the cost of burying me. I had to get this sorted.

"That was the lawyer on the phone", I told him, my tone subdued and my face grim. "UMCU has made an offer. It's not enough."

He didn't say anything. He was doing to me what I had just done to the lawyer. I rescued him immediately. "They've offered €500,000," I said. He looked dubiously surprised. So I added, "And they just spoiled the impact by reminding us that it'll be minus the forty-five grand they've already given us."

I grinned at him and shook my head.

"And I suppose there's a gagging clause", he said.

"No, that was the first thing I asked too. He said there was no mention of a gagging clause."

I could tell that Peter was having the same internal battle that I'd had. His whole psyche was screaming at the indignity of accepting a cash offer for the loss of his wife; but a quick look at my face told him I wanted to take it.

"It's not enough", he said. "It's an insult to you."

"It's never going to be enough", I answered. We had had this conversation before in a hypothetical form. Now we were having the real version.

"The thing is, it is enough in the sense that we can stay in this house, we can keep the car, we can pay all the bills we've always paid, do all the things we always do and, with the savings, there's enough for you to be okay when my income stops."

I was resorting to moral blackmail and I had no qualms about it. "And there's no gagging clause", I reminded him.

"You know", Peter began, "the bit that really shows what these people are like is their proviso that the expenses they have already paid us will be subtracted from the offer."

"At least they didn't remind us again that it was tax free", I laughed. "Though I agree with you. That was the bit that got me too. There they are trying to persuade us that they are making a generous offer because they are so concerned about my state of health, and they've ended up making us laugh at them because of the petty reminder that the expenses already paid will be deducted from the total amount."

"If they hadn't inserted that clause, I might have been inclined to consider it", said Peter.

This was going better than I had hoped.

"Well, maybe we should get back to them and say 'no' ... but if they raise the offer to €500,000 *in addition* to what we have already received we would accept it", I suggested.

We talked around the ins and outs for a while. We sensed that the prospect of ending up all over the Dutch media horrified the incoming CEO and her board, as did the irritating tweets that were finding their way into all corners of the Dutch and international healthcare communities. We also sensed that we could push a lot harder and get a significantly higher offer. But it would take time, and I was tired. The past months had been a physical and emotional boot camp and the incessant drill had me at the end of my rope. My energy levels were nearly as low as they had been after the radiotherapy. I wanted to make the counter offer of €500,000 plus expenses, and then be done with it. Peter had had enough too. Neither of us had ever really been motivated by money. The outrage that UMCU could do what they did to me, ignore the consequences, refuse to tell me the details of what had happened, and then make a financial offer that was little short of an insult – that was what had driven us to distraction. Achieving the highest financial offer ever made in the Netherlands for pain and suffering would send a powerful message that hospitals had an obligation to their damaged patients, and it would make our lives that bit more secure and easier too.

We decided to take our time, think about it carefully and talk to our financial advisor. The offer was nothing like what we would have received in damages in our own country[12], or in most of the other countries in the EU, but was a major step in the right direction for other patients damaged by medical negligence. I contacted the lawyer in the morning and told him we wanted to think about it for a few days and take some financial advice. I asked him not to get back to De Bruin for the moment.

Another reason Margriet Schneider, wanted to resolve "the Cullen case" was that a major story about a totally separate calamity at UMCU was about to break before *NRC* was ready to publish ours.

On Monday, 2 November, Schneider's first official working day as the hospital's new CEO, I contacted our lawyer and told him that Peter and I would accept a settlement of €500,000 (plus expenses) for the negligence UMCU had committed in my treatment and for the shameful way they had dealt with me afterwards. In addition, we suggested that the hospital should set up an annual award or bursary called the Cullen–Vines Award, which would be given to the doctor or other health professional who had made the greatest contribution during the year in the areas of open disclosure and transparency after serious harm. He

---

12 In April 2018, an Irishwoman, Vicky Phelan, who had developed terminal cervical cancer after receiving a false negative Pap smear settled out of court for €2.5 million. Three months later, another Irishwoman in the same situation settled for €7.5 million.

Deny, dismiss, dehumanise

said he would pass on the good news and the request to Mrs De Bruin and get back to me.

We didn't hear anything for a while. UMCU was busy elsewhere. On the night of 4 November, during Schneider's first week at the helm, a story about UMCU broke on prime-time TV that had the whole country talking. One of the Netherlands' most hard-hitting investigative programmes, *Zembla*, had been scrutinizing the hospital for some time. The story that night claimed that ear, nose and throat (ENT) specialists at the hospital had reported their department to the IGZ a year previously because they were being subjected to a "culture of fear" that made the department unsafe for them and their patients. The IGZ went straight to the hospital leadership, who reported back that they could find nothing wrong in the ENT department. The IGZ took them at their word and closed the case without any findings.

So the staff went to *Zembla* reporter, Ton van der Ham, instead. According to the whistleblowers, doctors were being bullied, ridiculed and ostracized if they didn't carry out operations fast enough or get through a punishingly long list of procedures. Patient safety was, they insisted, being jeopardized. And the story got worse. Two patients had died, according to the story, and their deaths had not been reported to the appropriate authorities. One had died after having his carotid artery cut by mistake during surgery. And instead of reporting it to the coroner, as any hospital would be legally obliged to do in such circumstances, the department had informed the coroner that the patient had died of natural causes in the days following the surgery. So the coroner didn't visit, and an autopsy wasn't performed. The IGZ had also not been advised that a calamity had occurred, although protocol demanded that this happen in the case of an accident during surgery.

One particular senior doctor at the department, Dr Volkert Wreesmann, had left the Netherlands, to work in a UK hospital because of the alleged poisonous atmosphere in UMCU's ENT department and because the consequences for his patients disturbed him so much. Others were afraid to speak freely, but this doctor spoke openly about the situation.

"It was totally unsafe", he told the programme, describing the practices at the ENT, and explaining that the understanding at the department was that errors should not be reported.

When asked about what Dr Wreesmann had to say, a spokesperson for UMCU gave the impression that this doctor had been asked to leave UMCU because they did not find his work adequate or his attitude appropriate. But his new boss praised his clinical skills and his devotion to his patients. They allowed *Zembla* to film him performing live surgery with his new team. He was, and remains, a valued member of staff at an English hospital.

Also speaking on behalf of UMCU on *Zembla* that night was UMCU's care quality and patient safety director, Kit Roes. He was put up to defend the actions of the hospital. It didn't go well. Roes was unable to give satisfactory answers to many of the questions raised by Van der Ham. In fact, he remained silent in the face of many of the questions being put to him.

Peter and I watched the programme on the internet. Because it was in Dutch, and complicated, most of the content went over our heads, so we had to wait until the next day's papers and the help of some patient Dutch friends to translate and fill in the missing information for us. We were amazed – yet not surprised. Other patients, other families had also been damaged at UMCU, and as far as we could see, little or no regard had been given to the impact on the bereaved families. In the case of the patient whose carotid artery had been cut, what had the hospital told his family had happened to him? Did they know that their husband, father, son, brother had had the main artery to his brain cut during surgery, or did they think what the coroner thought, that the man died from natural causes unrelated to a mistake during his operation?

How had they felt when a journalist had uncovered the full details of what had happened? Was the hospital helping them now? The programme reinforced our own impression that UMCU was a kingdom unto itself, and the leadership there felt accountable to no one, certainly not to its patients.

The morning after the *Zembla* broadcast, our lawyer phoned to say that he had had a response from De Bruin.

"It's good news", he reassured us, "but it's complicated". He would visit us at home that afternoon to discuss it further.

The complication was that, although the hospital had agreed to our counter-offer, there was now a big, fat gagging clause in the settlement.[13] It was in Dutch, so our lawyer translated it for us. It went something like this:

By signing this agreement, parties declare not to further make public this case nor the course of the medical treatment. They will not, in any case, contact written press, radio, television and/or internet or internet forums. They also agree not to inform third parties about the agreed arrangement and about the settlement agreement, and/or about how these were created, either in person or via third parties.

Concerning existing contacts with the media, Cullen/Cluskey will declare to these media, via their lawyer, that they have reached an amicable settlement with the hospital.

The bottom line was that in order to receive any compensation, UMCU wanted us to sign our names to an agreement that would stop us from speaking to the press, or to anyone else, about what had happened to me.

"No", Peter and I said in unison.

"I'm not going to sign any agreement that says I can't talk about what has happened in my own life", I told the lawyer. "They have no right to ask this of me. It's in the back of my mind

---

13   This was Clause 4 in a Draft settlement agreement between UMCU and us, with the hospital's head of legal affairs. See Appendix 2.

to write a book about all this in the future, if I live long enough to get it finished. A gagging clause would mean I couldn't do this. No way."

"Anyway", added Peter. "You know and they know that we have already told everything we know to NRC. Do they expect us to contact the paper and tell them not to use the story? Even if we were willing to do that – and we are not – they'd most likely refuse. We have no control over what *NRC* wants to do with the information we gave them. It's already in the public domain."

The lawyer told us that he had discussed the *NRC* story with De Bruin and he felt that they would probably accept that the story would go ahead.

"What they want to control though is having any more bad publicity for the hospital", he explained. "They are particularly worried about the tweets."

What we didn't realize until long after this conversation with our lawyer on 5 November 2015 was that the Minister for Health, Edith Schippers, had explicitly asked hospitals not to add *geheimhoudingsclausules*, or confidentiality clauses, to settlement agreements with patients they had damaged. It was an issue that had come up in the past, and although she had not gone so far as to introduce legislation to ban them, the minister had strongly urged hospitals not to compromise their professionalism by doing this, explaining that pledges of secrecy worked against any attempt to monitor the quality and safety of care given to patients. We didn't know about this because we are not Dutch, and so had a limited knowledge of what had happened in the past in the Netherlands, but everyone else involved in negotiating our settlement agreement with UMCU would have been very well aware that the minister had specifically spoken out against them and asked hospitals not to demand that patients sign them.

We spent a long time with our lawyer that afternoon. When he left, it was with the agreement that he would talk to Mrs De

Bruin again and tell her that we would not sign her gagging clause.

It was Monday, 9 November, before we heard from the lawyer again. It was my 55th birthday. He had spoken to De Bruin several times. She, and UMCU, were digging their heels in.

"She is adamant that something of a gagging clause – we didn't use those words, of course – remain in the settlement agreement", the lawyer reported.

So much for the new CEO's concern about the effect that all of this must be having on my health. She suggested that our own lawyer write a clause that Peter and I could agree to. She gave permission for him to write it in English, so that we would understand it. Here's draft two of UMCU's gagging clause:

By signing this contract both parties agree that they will not divulge any of the facts of this case, any information about the medical treatment, or any information about this settlement agreement and the negotiations preceding it by proactively or independently seeking out any Dutch media, such as the press, radio and television. Nor will they proactively or independently use any social media, such as Twitter, Facebook and LinkedIn, to disclose the facts and/or information mentioned above.

"No!" said Peter and I again in unison. "We will not agree to anything that tells us we can't divulge the facts of the case." Peter was adamant.

I agreed wholeheartedly. I would not be silenced by people who, by their own acknowledged negligence, had presided over an unsafe situation that is going to cost me my life, and who now wanted me to tell nobody about it! I was beginning to agree again with Peter that it was preferable to receive no compensation than to join UMCU in their shameful silence and help them to bury their ignominious secrets.

The lawyer got back to us by email late the same night. I was having a great birthday. De Bruin didn't like the wording our lawyer had come up with. Well, we hadn't either, but it seems they were discussing it anyway. She emailed a third draft.[14] It was in Dutch, but translates, more or less, as:

By signing this agreement both parties agree that they will not proactively approach the media, including the newspapers, radio, television or approach internet forums or any social media. Where there are already contacts with media, Cullen/Cluskey will confine themselves to the facts and refrain from making negative statements about the UMC Utrecht, ▇▇▇▇▇▇▇▇▇▇▇▇▇, specific therapists, work processes, the treatment of their claim and this settlement. If Cullen/Cluskey decides to publish independently, for example in the form of a book, the same condition applies (facts only and no negative statements).

This was even worse than what we had rejected earlier in the day. What on earth did "facts only and no negative statements" mean? And now my book had entered the debate. How had they found out about that? This would be a legal nightmare that we had no intention of inflicting on ourselves. Who was to adjudicate what was a "fact" and what was a "negative statement"? It's a fact that UMCU was legally liable for my cancer results being incorrectly handled leading them to being unseen for two years while my tumour grew – but it's also a very negative statement. That Peter and I believe that UMCU behaved deplorably throughout the aftermath of the calamity is a negative statement … and it's a fact.

It was too late at night to talk to the lawyer, but we were beside ourselves. The stress of the past two-and-a-half years had been immense. When the offer of a settlement came on 28 October, I had allowed myself to relax and let my guard down. Then, only after we had come to an agreement on the settlement amount, were we informed that payment was contingent on signing a gagging clause that would forbid us from speaking openly about what had

---

14   See Appendix 3 for the email containing this draft of the gagging clause. The name of the hospital's insurers has been blanked out because we are likely to be sued if we mention them.

happened. Twelve days had now passed since the settlement offer and three separate iterations of a gagging clause had been put in front of us, each one worse than its predecessor. I had no resources left to deal with this, and nor had Peter. What sort of healthcare was this? Dealing with fatally damaged patients the way UMCU did in my case should not have been allowed. First, they had caused damage to me when I had attended their hospital; then they had ignored the fact that anything untoward had happened to me there; and now they were using their lawyers to pressure me into keeping silent about it. I felt like I had stepped into a John Grisham novel. The hospital appeared to see nothing wrong with exerting all their corporate legal might against a patient who was terminally ill because of them – while simultaneously passing messages through our lawyer that the CEO was terribly concerned about the effect the settlement deal was having on my health. I couldn't understand this behaviour, and I couldn't believe that Schneider could possibly realize what her lawyers, her loss adjuster and her insurers were doing.

So we decided to write her an email. Peter and I stayed awake all night writing a letter to the new CEO. We filled her in on the background, and told her that we had been refusing to sign a series of gagging clauses produced by the lawyers, and that the stress of this was unendurable. And inexcusable.

We finished it at around five in the morning. We sent it to our lawyer first for his opinion, and then we tried to sleep. Before nine o'clock, the lawyer was on the phone. Under no circumstances were we to send the letter to Schneider. We couldn't understand why not.

"She needs to know what's happening to us", I pleaded.

I was assured that Schneider did know, that she had been apprised by De Bruin and the hospital lawyers. I had my doubts then, and I'm still not convinced that Schneider knew what was being done in the name of her hospital. If she did know, shame on her. We did as we were told for a change and didn't send the email. In retrospect, we probably should have, but now our lawyer was promising that he could make this go away, that he would deal with the matter of the gagging clause and have it removed.

By lunchtime, he was back to us. The gagging clause stays. De Bruin is still adamant that there would be some type of gagging clause in the settlement. She suggested again that our side write a gagging clause that we could live with, and she'd see if it met the needs of her side. Clever move that. It leaves very little in the way of a paper trail if UMCU is accused afterwards of demanding a gagging clause. All but two of the gagging clauses were written by us or our own lawyer at the instigation of the other side. The excuse was so that they could be in a language we could understand. But one way or another, the bottom line was still, "there will be *no* settlement (read 'compensation') without a gagging clause".

To give him something to bargain with, Peter and I assured our lawyer that we had no intention of saying anything slanderous or writing anything libellous, ever, about UMCU. We were highly critical of the hospital's behaviour, but we weren't so stupid as to break the law voicing that criticism. We sent him a draft of a clause that, if they absolutely insisted on including in the agreement, we would be happy with:

We, Adrienne Cullen and Peter Cluskey, undertake never to say in any media in any country anything libellous, slanderous or defamatory about UMC Utrecht, the doctors who treated me or any other parties such as the insurers, or to use any invective or to say anything that we know to be untrue about anyone at UMC Utrecht, about the treatment I received, about the insurers, the process ....

This is what we had said from the beginning. We would sign this undertaking, and nothing more. If UMCU wanted something different, the deal was off. We would then sign nothing – and if the hospital decided there would be no compensation, then so be it. We gave the lawyer leeway to put it into legal parlance.

We didn't threaten any further publicity. We didn't have the heart left for it, but I guess UMCU's negotiators finally realized that they had pushed us too far. If they retracted the offer, we would have nothing left to lose. A dangerous position to force anyone into. It seems clear in retrospect that all we had to do was hold our nerve, but we are not hardened corporate lawyers or shrewd business executives, and this was not a commercial deal. This was our lives and our dignity – what was left of them – and any nerve we had left was in tatters. We also had a time clause ticking away. De Bruin, the hospital lawyers and the UMCU boards knew that I knew that the agreement had to be signed while I was still alive.

Predictably enough, De Bruin and the UMCU lawyers still weren't keen on our new iteration of the gagging clause. They spoke to our lawyer further about the hospital's position, and urged him to have yet another go at writing yet another gagging clause to silence his own clients. He came up with draft four:

Prior to this contract, Cullen/Cluskey have had contacts about this case with the media and the press and expressed themselves through social media about what has happened. Regarding future media and press contacts, UMCU/███████████ stipulates that Cullen/Cluskey are free to disclose the facts of the case and the impact this has had on their lives. In these contacts – and this includes utterances from Cullen/Cluskey published through social media or otherwise – Cullen/Cluskey will be mindful of the intention of the parties in entering this settlement agreement, i.e. to cease bringing charges or making reproaches and accusations to each other and to once and for all end their dispute. Practically, this means that Cullen/Cluskey will not use any invective or say or write anything that can cause harm to the reputation of the UMCU/███████████ and its employees.

We asked the lawyer to explain the implications of the latest clause to us.

"It allows you to say and write what happened and how you feel or felt about it", he explained. "It also allows you to speak to the press or the radio and write a book."

That was good to know.

"Are there any hidden traps?" I asked

"No", reassured the lawyer. "What this clause aims to prevent, is that you would, for instance, say that UMCU is a useless hospital and that it should be burned to the ground or such comments that might damage the reputation of the hospital. If you stick to the facts and what this did to you, you cannot damage the reputation of the hospital, because that damage has already been done and acknowledged by the hospital themselves."

It was late afternoon at this stage, and Peter and I were reeling from lack of sleep. But this sounded really good. Our lawyer assured us that it *was* good. To all intents and purposes, the gagging clause had been removed.

"And the Cullen-Vines award?" asked Peter.

"Mrs De Bruin says that the hospital will give the idea sympathetic consideration", replied the lawyer.

"But will they write it into the contract?" persisted Peter.

Apparently not. We'd have to trust them on that. This was our only contribution to the settlement agreement, and it wasn't going to be included.

The following day, 11 November, a draft agreement was drawn up awarding me €350,000 for my pain and suffering claim and €195,000 for Peter's claim. A "gagging clause" similar to that agreed the previous day was inserted. It differed slightly from what we had discussed. It seems that the hospital's insurers wanted to insert a sentence instructing us not to mention them by name, ever. So the new sentence inserted at the end read:

Regarding ▮▮▮▮▮▮▮▮▮▮▮*, the underwriter of UMCU, Cullen/Cluskey will make no mention of* ▮▮▮▮▮▮▮▮▮▮ *in further discussions with media and/or press in all forms from the date of settlement.*

I'm told these insurers stopped dealing with Dutch hospitals shortly after "the Cullen case". Settlements for patients damaged by hospitals in the Netherlands had threatened to get a lot higher.

13 | November and December 2015 ... UMC, Utrecht

Every society honours its living conformists and its dead troublemakers.
Marshall McLuhan

The photographer sent by *NRC* was a delight. Peter and I, more used to reporting the story than being the story, were stiff and awkward subjects. I was expecting a 15-minute visit to snap a few head-and-shoulder shots – but the photographer had a totally different plan. First I was photographed on my own in the living room. Then it was Peter's turn, and then the two of us together holding hands like self-conscious children. Then we rearranged the furniture for a different perspective and went through it all again. And then more furniture got moved, and a few pictures taken off the walls, and we tried for a third and a fourth angle. When we moved into the garden (it was November!) Georgie, our 15-year-old tabby cat, wanted a piece of the action, and the photographer obliged. Seems that the cat was cooler in front the camera than either of her parents. The photographer clicked away until she had charmed and disarmed all three of us. By the time she left, we felt we had met a new friend, and even

Deny, dismiss, dehumanise

the ever-conservative Georgie had forgiven her for moving every stick of furniture on the ground floor and taking most of the pictures off the walls so she could have a clear, white background.

One of the reasons we had decided to go to the newspaper was that I still knew so little about how things had gone wrong in UMCU in 2011. We believed that an investigative report carried out by the *NRC* journalists would get to the bottom of what had happened – and I would then know the details of my own story.

But UMCU was still refusing to speak to the newspaper. In October, I had heard that Arie Franx was going to meet the journalists. I heard that a list of questions had been prepared by the paper and sent to the hospital. The meeting was postponed. Then, on 20 October, it was cancelled definitively. Without being allowed to talk to anyone from the hospital, *NRC* had difficulty digging deeper into the case.

Days before the story broke, UMCU changed its mind. On 16 November, we heard that the hospital was going to issue a statement. At last, I thought. Now I might find out something more about what had happened to me. But I didn't want a situation where the hospital would tell everything they knew … to the media. So I contacted my lawyer and reminded him that the correct protocol would be to discuss the matter openly – with the patient *before* telling the newspaper. The lawyer passed my request on to the loss adjuster, the loss adjuster passed it on to the UMCU lawyers. The head of legal affairs replied to my lawyer telling him that they would not be sharing with *NRC* any information that we didn't already know about and asking him to pass that reassurance on to me. Which he duly did. All that took two days.

On 19 November, the day before publication, UMCU issued a press release, which was later published on their website.[15] I was mentioned in the press release. In translation, Margriet Schneider,

---

15   See the full text of the press release translated in Appendix 4.

whom I had never met, said:

What happened to Mrs Cullen is terrible. It's indefensible that everything took so long, and Mrs Cullen did not receive any support from the hospital. Our first priority is to care for our patients and to support them, especially if something unexpected goes wrong. The example of Mrs Cullen shows that we failed.

We have to do this differently in future. We will take this case into account. It is extremely brave of Mrs Cullen that she talks about her experiences so candidly. She can be assured that we will pick up the gauntlet.

No one had thought I was "brave" when I was writing letters to the supervisory board, complaining to Australian law professors, demanding fair compensation and asking repeatedly to be told what had happened to my results in 2011. No, UMCU had made it quite clear that I was a pest.

The statement continued: "We reported this incident to the IGZ two years too late. That should not have happened." In other words, they were saying that they had finally reported the incident to the IGZ, and acknowledging that they should have done so when the calamity was discovered – when we had first asked them to.

The statement also said that the incident had been investigated in 2014. Now this was news. We had been asking since 2013 to be involved in any investigation that was being conducted. We had been told at the meeting on 10 October 2014 that there had not been an investigation. Most recently, in mid-September, our lawyer had requested the hospital to inform us officially about what had gone wrong in my case. We never received a reply. I didn't believe that an investigation had taken place. Everyone agreed that we were entitled to know the details of what had happened to me, but efforts to achieve this had met with a blank wall every time. We could not understand why the hospital, a publicly owned organization, funded by taxpayers' money, patients' money, was behaving as though it were not accountable to its patient or to the public who paid for it. UMCU genuinely seemed to think that if they told us my test results had gone into my electronic file and so my doctor didn't see them, that this was an acceptable and sufficient explanation. It might have satisfied the hospital's curiosity, but not ours.

But this statement, despite its shortcomings, was quite a breakthrough. It acknowledged publicly, for the first time ever, that what had happened to me was a terrible calamity and that the way I had been treated in the aftermath was indefensible because I had received no support from the hospital at a time when my needs should have been their priority. By issuing this press release, UMCU had done something, so we were told, that no other hospital had ever done – to publicly acknowledge that it had made errors, not reported them, and acted in a way that was not in their patient's best interest in the aftermath of a medical calamity. As far as the public was concerned, UMCU had just held its hands up and apologized. And in a way they had. But in a civilized society, hospitals don't apologize to patients in a press release. They make contact with the patient and apologize to her directly. We asked our lawyer to explain to the hospital that a public proclamation was not the same thing as an apology, and we would really like the hospital to say these things to us properly and directly – rather than being cc-ed in their media communication through two layers of lawyers. That request, like all our requests to date, was ignored.

On 23 October, Arie Franx had emailed me. Franx and I had not been in contact since July when he had sent me a WhatsApp saying that he could talk to me only about medical treatment, anything else had to be channelled through my lawyer. So it was with a great deal of trepidation and distrust that I opened his email. He was inviting me to come to the hospital and talk to him. I thought about it for a few days. I really didn't trust him any more.

On both occasions I had met him, he had seemed approachable and genuinely concerned. After the meeting in July, he had sent an email asking about my health and telling me to contact him if I needed him. But then he had all but turned me away when I actually did contact him a couple of weeks later. Twice now he had turned his back. I was wary of setting myself up for another disappointment and more pain.

But of course I wrote back.

"I have heard references to some investigation being made into the events surrounding the negligence after we met you in October 2014", I wrote, "but I know none of the details of what you discovered, or indeed the nature of this enquiry. Because of the ad hoc, inconsistent, sparse and hearsay nature of the communication we have had on this subject so far, I would like to ask that if I meet you to discuss the matter definitively and openly, that we have the meeting recorded by a stenographer."

Suggesting a stenographer had put the cat among the pigeons. I also suggested an alternative venue – I had no desire to return to the UMCU campus again – and suggested the offices of our lawyer in Amsterdam. It didn't occur to me at the time, but the distrust was working both ways – Arie Franx was as wary of me as I was of him. Our email exchange was tetchy and guarded. He didn't want any lawyers present. That was fine by me. I didn't either. I had only suggested the lawyer's office because Amsterdam was equidistant from Utrecht and our home, and it wasn't the hospital. Franx balked at the idea of a stenographer, and at my alternative suggestion that we record the meeting, just for our own record afterwards. He offered to have notes taken and a report prepared. I didn't want someone else's summaries and paraphrasing. My own note-taking would not have been up to such a meeting, and anyway, I wanted to concentrate on the conversation, which was likely to be fairly complex in places, and not be distracted by taking notes. I thought an impartial, professional, English-speaking note-taker would have been the ideal solution. It wasn't meant to be a trap.

I pushed for an early meeting, but all that was on offer for weeks to come were meetings at seven o'clock at night. I was in no condition to be travelling to meetings in the dark over an hour's drive away. These days, I was often exhausted by lunchtime and regularly had to go to bed in the middle of the afternoon. Often I stayed there. I needed to be sharp for this meeting. I declined the night-time suggestions.

Another matter that seemed to be bothering Franx emerged in our email exchange. We still hadn't reached a settlement with UMCU at that stage, and he didn't want to get embroiled in the middle of it. With echoes of our WhatsApp conversation in July, he stressed that he would not be able to talk to me about financial compensation, and remarked that he understood it was close to being settled. On 3 November 2015 when I read this, Peter and I certainly didn't feel that a settlement was imminent. That was the day after we were presented with the first gagging clause and we were being told there would be no settlement until we signed one. I was finding it hard to keep my fury out of my correspondence with Franx. It was really a bit rich to have the hospital lawyers trying to prevent me from speaking about what had happened, while the hospital had yet to tell me what actually had happened.

Throughout November, the correspondence between Franx and me continued. Huub van der Vaart was going to join us. This was the best possible combination, as without him, there would be large gaps in the story. But then the NRC story broke, and some departmental bureaucrat I had never met was going to come instead of Van der Vaart. I wasn't having that. Although Van der Vaart was partly responsible for the calamity, I trusted his integrity. In fact, he was the only person at the hospital who I felt had always been truthful, who had expressed heartfelt sorrow, and who appeared to care what happened to me. I wanted him there.

✴✴✴✴✴✴✴✴✴✴✴✴

On Friday, 20 November, our story ended up all over the front pages of *NRC Next* and *NRC Handelsblad* – odd socks, tabby cat and all. Before we were awake, the phone was ringing off the hook. We didn't answer it. Our lawyer spoke to some other reporters and ended up on a radio programme, but I was too ill to handle a media circus, so we stopped all further communication with the press.

The day after the story broke, I ended up in the emergency GP clinic at Antoniushove Hospital near my home twice in one night. My own GP had diagnosed another UTI earlier in the week and started me on antibiotics. By Saturday night, it was clear they weren't working. The antibiotics were changed by the clinic, but by 2am I was in so much pain that I had to ask Peter to drive me to the hospital again. I hated waking him. We were both under a great deal of pressure, and he was exhausted. I knew that every time he drove me to hospital he was thinking: "Is this it? Is this the cancer kicking in and causing this pain? Is this the end? Will I be bringing her home again?" The stress of night-time hospital visits and emergency trips to the GP fuelled our fury at UMCU.

"Where are the good people from UMCU now?" Peter asked as we drove to the hospital for the second time that night. "Why are we driving around in the cold and the dark in the middle of the night while the people who caused this are sleeping comfortably in their beds? Why are we doing this alone?"

I had no answers. The questions weren't helping. But he was one hundred per cent right. Why were we rattling around trying to deal with medical emergencies on our own?

The GP I had seen earlier in the evening at the hospital's out-of-hours clinic had wanted to know my medical history. They always do. It's a totally reasonable request. So I told her the history. It's not an easy story to tell at the best of times, and it's a good deal harder when you're in pain, with a fever and exhausted.

Deny, dismiss, dehumanise

It brings the trauma up to the surface and I usually end up crying. That doctor had gone home by 2:15am when we arrived for the second time. I had to give my history to another kind, bleary-eyed doctor. It wasn't any easier to tell the second time.

"Was there nothing about my history in the notes from when I was here earlier?" I asked him.

Apparently not. No doctor ever writes down that I have incurable cancer because of medical negligence at another hospital. And that it has left me with complex PTSD. They all agree that it is vital that all staff treating me need to know this important background as it affects my treatment, but no one ever puts it in my file. So each time, I have to tell the story over again. I ask Peter to wait in the waiting room. Having one of us in tears is enough.

The doctor catheterized me, gave me two urine bags and a painkilling injection. I was to see my own GP on Monday.

By Monday, 23 November, I was sufficiently recovered to resume my correspondence with Franx. I sent a list of questions. I was aware that some questions might never be answered, but these were the questions that had echoed around in my head since April 2013. In the main, they were the obvious questions.

Van der Vaart wrote to me. He would, after all, like to come to the meeting. Good. I climbed down on the stenographer/recording issue. Both men seemed to feel that they couldn't speak freely if they were conscious that the meeting was being recorded, that they would have to watch their words. Although I tried to reassure them that I wasn't setting a trap or planning to run to the media, I merely wanted to be able to remind myself of exactly what was being said, they weren't having it. I think they were afraid that they'd be hearing themselves on *Zembla* in a few weeks' time if they agreed to being recorded. I wasn't used to people being afraid of me. When and how had I become so scary?

I was bringing a friend, Petra, with me. Peter and I had agreed that Petra would be a better person to accompany me. He was still raw with fury and anyone from UMCU was likely to get the full verbal force of his wrath. For both our sakes, I replaced Peter with Petra. I was totally comfortable with her. She knew the whole story and had given support beyond anything I had ever experienced in a hospital.

I was told that an appointment would be possible at three o'clock on 16 December – and that a venue would be found near my home. So, daylight hours and no travelling. The message was getting through. So much precious effort had gone into setting up a meeting to finally find out how my treatment at UMCU over four years previously had led to me being left with terminal cancer.

14 | December 2015 … UMC, Utrecht

*I think the currency of leadership is transparency. You've got to be truthful.
I don't think you should be vulnerable every day, but there are moments
where you've got to share your soul and conscience with people and show
them who you are, and not be afraid of it.*
Howard Schultz, Executive Chairman of Starbucks

Franx, Van der Vaart, Petra and I met in a private room in
the Van der Valk Hotel a short walk from my home. By the
time it ended at around five-thirty, I was drained. I walked
the short distance home arm-in-arm with Petra for support.

There had been no great revelations. We didn't go
through the list of questions ticking them off one at a time. It
wasn't that sort of meeting in the end. On the negative side, I
discovered that between them, the two professors didn't know
a great deal more than I already knew, and there remained large
gaps about the role of the pathology department in events. It
was frustrating to realize that questions about the pathology
department could only be answered by someone from there.
Gynaecologists and obstetricians, however senior they might
be, had no insight into the workings and procedures of the

pathology lab. Some input from the hospital board would have solved that.

Because the run up to the meeting had involved so many promises from me that I was not planning a media ambush or trying to record their words for use against them afterwards, I find I can't, in all decency, tell everything that happened. But there are things I must tell, and they are the most important things.

The two men tried to paint a picture of what happened in April 2011 when my cancer-indicative result left the lab. Huub van der Vaart explained that with the hospital's old, paper files, results were hand-delivered to the gynaecology department. One of the secretaries would place the results into the cubbyhole of whichever doctor had ordered them. Doctors would then check the contents of their cubbyholes, sign at the bottom of each result that they had seen it, and it would then be transferred into the file of the appropriate patient. Notes would be made to contact the patient about the result. And then it would be added, by someone else, to the electronic version of the patient file, which was being compiled at the time.

This was the way that all the tests I had had at UMCU between January 2011 and March 2011 had been handled. As far as Van der Vaart was concerned, this was also the way they would be handled in April 2011. If anything different had been arranged, he was unaware of it, as was Arie Franx.

Of course Van der Vaart and Franx, and indeed everyone in the gynaecology department and the entire hospital, had known that UMCU was changing over to electronic files – but the final changeover date for the gynaecology department was 11 June, not any time in April. And indeed doctors continued to get paper test results in their cubbyholes throughout April, May and June 2011.

Both professors remembered something of what the changeover period had been like. They were aware of outside staff coming into the department to do what was needed to organize the transition. When asked if they knew who was responsible for scanning the paper files into the electronic system, or by whom they were supervised and in what way, neither man knew. They were just aware that the switch was happening and that people had been drafted in from outside to do various aspects of it. In 2011, Franx was not in charge of running the department, and Van der Vaart wasn't made a professor until the following year.

My famously "missing" test result that showed I had a probable adenocarcinoma of the cervix never got as far as Van der Vaart's cubbyhole, it seems. It was added to my electronic file on a date unknown without any doctor's signature at the bottom. The new system does not record who scanned the results into my electronic file.

As far as they could tell, the two professors concluded that when the paper results had been delivered to gynaecology, someone unfamiliar with the procedure – or perhaps indifferent to it – had taken a shortcut and scanned it straight into the electronic file instead of putting it into the doctor's cubbyhole first. What they then did with the original paperwork is unknown. All that exists is the unsigned scan in the electronic file.

Van der Vaart has had many results back from the laboratory throughout his career as a doctor, and from time to time, he would receive worrying results for some of his patients. On all previous occasions, when one of his patients had an unexpected cancer-positive result, he was contacted directly by the pathologist who was sending the test results back to him. It had never occurred to him that it was possible that a cancer result would not be proactively communicated to him.

He was not alone in assuming this. I have spoken to several senior doctors in the years since my distressing diagnosis. Doctors in other Dutch hospitals, doctors in UK hospitals and doctors working in Irish hospitals. All of them believe that it simply can't happen that a lab result can "go walkabout". Some of the doctors described systems in their hospitals that safeguarded patients' results by preventing a pathologist from signing off on a result until he or she had received a confirmation of receipt from the ordering doctor. This seemed eminently sensible, but such a system didn't exist in UMCU, and still doesn't. (So you would wonder what they mean when they say they have learned lessons.)

But you don't necessarily need a fancy, computerized system to have an effective protocol. Almost all of the doctors I spoke to expected to receive a phonecall from their colleagues in the lab if something completely unexpected was going on with one of their patients. They base their careers and their peace of mind on this trust in their colleagues. It appears that there was no specific protocol or policy on this in the pathology department at UMCU. It was left to the judgement of individual pathologists whether they saw fit to contact a doctor about a test result. In my case, the pathologist did not see fit to contact Van der Vaart.

There was another safety net that could have, indeed should have, kicked in with my test results. The cancer-positive result that Van der Vaart sent to the lab on 13 April 2011 was cryosurgery of the cells on the tip of the cervix. According to professors Franx and Van der Vaart, if pathologists see a disconnect between the nature of the procedure being performed (cryosurgery) and the finding of a particular test (cancer), as was the case with me, they should have realized that neither the ordering doctor nor the patient would be expecting bad news. This is normally enough to prompt a pathologist to make doubly sure that the doctor sees those results. But that didn't happen either.

All major teaching hospitals have tumour boards for their major divisions and UMCU is no exception. Of course, not all cancer diagnoses end up being sent to the tumour board for scrutiny, but unexpected results do. Mine was an unexpected result, but it wasn't sent to the gynaecology tumour board. No one knows why.

Deny, dismiss, dehumanise

In short, the safety nets that should have been in place in pathology and gynaecology to protect me either didn't exist at all or weren't being deployed that day. And no extra, hospital-wide safety nets were put in place as the hospital went through the process of scrapping hundreds of thousands of paper patient files and replacing them with electronic files. We also don't know if the outside staff contracted to help with the switch to electronic files had any training in how to deal with patient data.

What none of us in the hotel room knew that day, but which would be reported by investigative journalist, Hélène van Beek on the TV programme, *Hotline!*, in January 2016, was that seven Dutch hospitals, overwhelmed by the logistical task of converting a veritable mountain of patients' tests, scans, images, biopsies and assorted medical notes into electronic format, had enlisted the help of private companies. Between 2011 and 2014, according to *Hotline!*, one of those private companies, Belgium-based iGuana, had taken patient files out of the Dutch hospitals, out of the country and into Belgium. Here, they had been transferred to the jail in Leuven where prisoners were paid by the kilo to do such tasks as remove staples, unfold pages, remove images and prepare the confidential patient information to be scanned. UMC Utrecht was among the hospitals who commissioned iGuana to help it with its paper-to-electronic transition.

But we didn't discuss that on 16 December 2015 because we didn't know about it. Whether the paper version of my cancer result took an illegal trip to a Belgian prison cell where it was processed for a few cents per kilo is unknown. But it's as likely an explanation as any.

Having exhausted the few available scraps of the story of what might have happened in 2011, I turned the focus of the meeting to 2013, after the calamity was discovered. When Van der Vaart was shown the unseen test result on 3 April 2013, he had contacted me, and reported it to his line manager at the time,

Bart Fauser. (He was the man who looked up from his work just long enough to advise Van der Vaart to go and report the matter to the lawyers.) Fauser stopped being Van der Vaart's line manager in the summer of 2013, when Franx took over. Franx admitted that he was the person who should have stepped in to help Peter and me after the calamity. I hadn't realized, through all the dealings we had had, that Franx was the head of the entire gynaecology division. The buck, he was telling me, stopped with him. I hadn't really been expecting this. I thought Fauser had still been in charge throughout 2013. I'm not sure exactly what I said when I realized this, but I do remember asking him repeatedly, "Where were you? Where were you?" I wanted to know where he had been when Peter and I were hurtling around the hospital dizzy with grief and disbelief. I wanted to know where he had been when De Bruin informed the hospital that my cancer was now incurable. I wanted to know where he had been when the hospital lawyers were baring their corporate teeth and trying to prevent me from telling my story. I wanted to know where he had been when I was asking for information for over two-and-a-half years about what had happened to my test results. Spitting Mad Adrienne was in full howl.

He tried to explain. When something went wrong, the hospital usually left it up to the treating physician to break the bad news to the patient and see they got whatever treatment they needed. That was the extent of what happened in UMCU after serious harm. He had not been aware that hospitals in other places and in other countries had multidisciplinary, serious-harm protocols. Franx said he believed that other Dutch hospitals did the same thing as UMCU. The first time it had dawned on him that *of course* hospitals have to step in to help patients after harm had been caused was when he had read the letter sent by Prue Vines to the UMCU board in October 2015. That, accompanied by my letter explaining the consequences of being "set adrift" by my hospital, had opened his eyes. I looked at him in disbelief, mouth open and ready to continue my tirade.

And then something happened. He said, "I didn't know then that there was something we should have been doing to help you and Peter. I am sorry. I had never come across open disclosure as described in Prue Vines's letter. It seems obvious now, but at the time I didn't know. I really didn't know."

I sat motionless. I stared at him. It was plain that he was telling the truth. He had just shown me who he was. He wasn't being professor anyone any more. He was Arie Franx and he had just told me the truth, regardless of how it made him look. Spitting Mad Adrienne shut her mouth and declared a permanent ceasefire.

"If it's not too late, can I start to help now?", he asked. "If you would like it, if it would help, we could keep in touch. I want to help." And in that instant, I forgave him. Of course it wasn't too late to help. I was going to need all the help I could get, and all the allies I could muster.

As my anger abated, so did my energy. There was a perfect December sunset outside the window and I just wanted to stare at its mix of electric blue and ridiculous pink and savour the last warm yellow glow of a rare fine day just before Christmas. The human consequences of the misplacement of a scrap of paper in 2011 had rippled further out than I had realized. I had always known that Huub Van der Vaart had been hurt by the calamity and his life and career permanently changed, but now I was seeing another, different type of victim and another sort of pain. I didn't know what to do. I also realized that all my protesting, complaining, writing letters and emails, talking to Australian law professors, contacting the press and digging in my heels like a madwoman had actually succeeded in a way that I hadn't recognized. It had all got through to Arie Franx – and changed him.

The rest of the meeting is a bit hazy. We talked about the alleged "investigation" that the UMCU press release had said had taken place in 2014. What had happened was that the gynaecology department had carried out an anonymized SAFER (Scenario Analysis of Failure Modes, Effects and Risks) report – the object of which is to ensure that errors are not repeated. The report, which was not carried out until early 2015, nearly two years after the discovery of the negligence, did not investigate what had happened in my case, rather it examined the protocols in place in 2015 to see if any recurrence of my case was possible. The report did not unearth any more information than the department already knew because it was designed to be a predictive analysis of existing protocols, not an investigation into what had gone wrong in 2011. It later transpired that it was this report that was handed on to the IGZ as evidence that UMCU had investigated "my calamity". The IGZ felt that, as an investigation, it was adequate. Not for the first time, I found myself unimpressed with what the IGZ found acceptable.

We discussed too what I referred to as a "proper investigation" and which Franx called a "root-cause analysis" or SIRE report. That, it seemed, was beyond the pay grade of division heads. Only the hospital board could sanction a root-cause analysis – which is why the toothless and ineffective SAFER report was carried out in 2015. The gynaecology division had wanted to investigate, but SAFER was the only mechanism available to them. I asked how we could get the board to agree to carry out a root-cause analysis. Franx said he would ask them again. It was pretty obvious to me that he didn't think he had any chance of getting them to agree – but, to me, it was important that they be asked, on my behalf.

I asked who had decided in 2013 that they did not need to inform the IGZ that a calamity had occurred in my case. When we had asked for the calamity to be reported, our lawyer had been told that it was not necessary to do so because two years had passed since the incident and different procedures were now in place. The inspectorate, we were told at the time, would not be interested. I wanted to know who had made that call. The decision, it appears was made by the hospital lawyers. They, not the department where the calamity occurred, got to decide when to contact the IGZ.

It all sounded like a strange and alien setup to me. Hospital lawyers deciding when to admit liability for errors *without informing the board*. Hospital lawyers also deciding what needs to be reported to the IGZ *without informing the board*, and hospital lawyers deciding when it's appropriate to gag patients and delay compensation deals.

The instant Huub van der Vaart informed the lawyers about what had happened with my test results, I became a plaintiff first and a patient second. When Peter and I realized in mid-June 2013 that we were at the centre of a calamity that could cost us my life, we told Van der Vaart that we wanted to make a complaint. Peter asked him, by email, "Will you please contact the appropriate hospital authorities as quickly as possible and tell them what has happened, so that when we make contact they will at least have some idea who Adrienne is and what has transpired? This would be a big help."

Always determined to help us, Van der Vaart did so immediately. He contacted a member of the hospital's legal team. Her advice was that we could make a written complaint to the *klachtencommissie* (complaints committee) who would judge whether the complaint was justified or not, or we could write to the board and make a financial claim. She wasn't being impudent or "smart". These are the only things a patient could do after an adverse event. There was no one else in the hospital to deal with those traumatized by being harmed by the hospital. The lawyers deal with us, or the *klachtencommissie*, which is led by a high-court judge. We were waiting for the cavalry to arrive to help us pick up the pieces, and their only suggestion was that we fill in a form. Meanwhile, the UMCU lawyers prepared themselves for litigation, to run the error into the sand, keep it out of the public eye, dole out as little compensation as they can get away with and counsel patients that if they talk about what happened, they will get no settlement at all. As a patient, I find this mind-boggling in a modern western democracy. If I were a doctor, I would find that it totally undermined my duty of care to my patient, emasculated my professional integrity, and demoralized me as a human being.

That day, at the meeting, I told Franx and Van der Vaart that the way UMCU had mishandled every single thing, from their lack of safeguards in 2011, to their indifference after the calamity was discovered in 2013, to the way we had been "played" by the gagging-clause lawyers in November 2015 had been devastating. The public proclamation in the form of a press release that the hospital seemed to think was an apology had really put the tin hat on it. I asked that a message be passed to the board that the decent thing to do was to apologize to us properly.

Over two hours had passed since the meeting began. Petra, realizing that I was a spent force, came to the rescue. She had been making notes occasionally throughout the afternoon. She suggested we write down who was to do what, and what had been agreed. There were just five things on her list:

1. *Professor Franx would ensure that Adrienne receive a written apology from the board of UMC Utrecht.*
2. *Professor Franx would find out whether Adrienne can have access to the SAFER report carried out in 2015, and would ask the board for permission to carry out a root-cause analysis.*
3. *Professor Franx agreed to look into ways of providing a support person if Adrienne needed to call an emergency doctor outside the surgery hours, or if she needed to be admitted to the local hospital.*
4. *Professor Franx suggested keeping in touch by phone from time to time and Adrienne agreed. Professor Van der Vaart said he would be available too.*

Deny, dismiss, dehumanise

5. *Adrienne offered to use her own experiences to help UMC Utrecht to implement/improve their procedures for patients affected by adverse effects or calamities caused by hospital treatment.*

15 | New Year 2016 ... Bronovo Hospital, The Hague

And silence, like a poultice, comes
To heal the blows of sound.
Oliver Wendell Holmes, 1836

Christmas 2015 came and went. Peter and I were relieved that the wall-to-wall worries had been stilled, for the moment at least. But we were weary. Never has half-a-million euros been lodged into a bank account with so little joy. All the same though, I was hopeful it would do what I wanted and rectify the financial damage enough to allow us to live as we had done before the negligence. We spent the Christmas holiday quietly at home with just some close friends popping in from time to time to have a drink, a bite to eat, and to laugh at the number of lights on the Christmas tree.

My energy levels were at an all-time low. I put it down to the fact that it was the middle of winter. By 31 December, I figured there was something else going on, but there was no way I was going to start looking for an out-of-hours GP. New Year's Eve in the Netherlands is crazier than Carnival in Rio. Everyone is on the

Deny, dismiss, dehumanise

streets outside their homes with sacks of fireworks as neighbour vies with neighbour to produce the loudest, brightest and most lavish display. Public post boxes are sealed shut for days to prevent pranksters from "posting" live fireworks to see how loud a bang they can make inside the post box, and how much smoke they can generate as the contents burn. Technically, festivities shouldn't start until midnight, but usually people start gearing up as soon as it gets dark. Emergency rooms start filling with hand, eye and facial injuries from tea-time on. Mostly, I enjoyed the amateur and professional displays all over the neighbourhood, and liked the camaraderie and the unmistakable smell of *olliebollen*, doughnut-style balls of dough, being deep-fried and dredged with icing sugar. But this year, the fireworks seemed just too loud and too bright. Georgie had already retreated into her New-Year's-Eve refuge at the back of the wardrobe. I too felt safer hiding at home, thank you, and whatever was wrong with me would keep until Monday.

In the early evening, Arie Franx phoned. He managed to winkle out of me that I was feeling ill, in a way that was more than just tiredness. I told him I wouldn't drag Peter around to whichever GP service in Leiden or The Hague had the misfortune to be operating that evening. Franx had the sense not to argue with me. But he phoned back about half-an-hour later. He had contacted a gynaecologist colleague at Bronovo hospital in The Hague, a 20-minute drive away. He had given her a brief rundown of my situation and my background. She wanted to help and was on duty that evening. If I could get myself over there, she would look after me and make sure I was back home before the worst of the festive ballistics started exploding overhead. I couldn't argue with that. His position was totally reasonable, and mine wasn't. And I was more than a bit stunned that he had arranged this. It was the first time that anyone in the medical profession had ever gone out of their way to help me by doing something outside the strict confines of their job or the rules of the system. I had asked for exactly this sort of help, and I had just got it. I wasn't used to that.

We arrived in the almost deserted Bronovo car park just before 7pm. The occasional firecracker sounded like sporadic incoming fire in the distance and, closer, a *gillende keukenmeid*, or screaming kitchen maid, set off in a quiet corner of the car park made us jump. We felt like unarmed troops abandoned in no man's land.

I asked at reception for Dr Janke Molenaar. She came and collected me. She was great! While we were waiting for the urine sample she took from me to come back from the lab, she started to fill in my details on a patient file. Franx had filled her in enough on what had happened to me to give her a starting point. For about 45 minutes, we talked and she extracted my story with as little pain as she could manage. It was much easier telling it to her because I didn't have to deal with the incredulous faces that usually accompanied an account of my medical history. I confirmed what Franx had told her on the phone earlier, and explained about my PTSD and the terror I now felt when I was in hospital. I explained that I found it very hard to trust, and as a result, had a lot of difficulty explaining my medical background to nurses and doctors I didn't know. She assured me that that was perfectly understandable.

"And now everything anyone needs to know is in your medical file here", she said. "You'll never have to tell your story again in this hospital."

I smiled and felt reassured. I had found an ally in no man's land.

Shortly after, the result came back from the lab. Sure enough, I had another UTI – my third in six months. She prescribed an antibiotic, told me to phone her on Tuesday, and Peter and I went home.

On New year's Day 2016, I was feeling much better. Over the weekend, I continued to feel more comfortable, but on Monday, I started to feel unwell again. I figured I'd been pushing myself too hard, so I took it easy.

Late Tuesday morning, Molenaar texted. She had seen the antibiogram. I needed a different antibiotic. The one I had been taking wasn't going to cure my infection. She had already faxed the new prescription to my pharmacy. I went and got it immediately and took the first sachet. Unfortunately, the infection was more advanced than I had realized. The antibiotic got chucked up, and so did everything else I tried to drink. I knew now that I had urosepsis again. I sent an SMS to Janke Molenaar.

Late afternoon, Peter and I were on our way back to Bronovo, this time with an overnight bag full of hastily chosen clothes and toiletries that Peter had helped me to pack. Trying to figure out on my own what I needed to bring was too difficult. I still had enough sense though to grab a basin and a roll of kitchen paper on the way out the door. I was throwing up constantly and really didn't want to mess up the car. On the trip over, I kept taking deep breaths as I was starting to feel lightheaded and breathless. I knew it would totally spook Peter if I passed out in the car. I willed myself to stay alert and nipped my lips and scratched my arms gently to help me focus.

Molenaar had said to come to the delivery suites on the fifth floor, where she was on duty that night. So we went straight there. If you say, "Bronovo Hospital", to anyone in the Netherlands, Dutch or expat, they will immediately respond, "Ah yes, that's where the royal family go to have their babies". And indeed they do. All three princesses, Amalia, Alexia, and Ariane, daughters of the current monarch, King Willem-Alexander, and his wife, Queen Maxima, were born there. And even in my septic state, I could see that Bronovo's fifth floor was indeed fit for a queen.

The baby being born there that evening might not have been

royal, but her family, gathered jovially outside the main doors to the ward, were as happy as though she were. The new father kept popping in and out through the doors. Their new baby was a girl, and they were going to call her Delilah. There was a round of applause and cheering and the relatives burst spontaneously into the chorus from the Tom Jones hit. "My, my, my Delilah", they sang. And then, "Why, why, why, Delilah?" I hoped they didn't know the rest of the words of this cheery-sounding song that told a bitter story. It felt weird coming to a hospital and ending up in the labour ward. Here, it was all about birth and new life and hope. I felt like the grim reaper at a kids' party.

Molenaar came and rescued me. The peaceful room she brought me to was on the ward called after the next queen of the Netherlands, Princess Amalia. The usual clatter of hospital wards was absent. Rooms were private and the equal of any swish hotel. The automatic glass doors slid soundlessly open and closed as friendly nurses came and went. There were no drip alarms, no harsh lights, no feeling of being in an institution. If you had to be sick, this was the place to be.

I wasn't allowed to rest though. They needed to get me on a drip. I needed IV antibiotics, I needed something to bring my fever down and I needed fluids. They couldn't find a vein. My dehydration wasn't helping. They'd send the best nurse on the ward for finding veins, they promised. She came quickly, tried twice and failed. They called the doctor. She couldn't do it either. They called the anaesthetists. They were too busy to come up, but told the nurses to bring me down to post-op. I wasn't strong enough to walk, so they wheeled me down to the third floor. The anaesthetists were rushed. Two of them tried, and failed to find a working vein. They weren't very nice about it. Anaesthetists prided themselves on finding veins where others couldn't.

"Have you ever used intravenous drugs?" one asked as he was sticking a needle into a vein that wasn't there.

Deny, dismiss, dehumanise

"No", I answered, glowering. I hadn't the energy to retaliate appropriately.

Another, who didn't speak to me directly, answered his mobile phone while looking for my elusive veins. It was in a frayed leather case and looked filthy. After a few more minutes poking and slapping every inch of my hand and arms and another abortive attempt with a needle, he gave up.

"Bring her to intensive care", he instructed the others and walked away. Lovely bedside manner.

The people at intensive care were much nicer, but not any luckier finding a vein — and they were the experts. They tried with an ultrasound machine. No luck. They sent for the guy who finds veins in newborns. No go either. They tried the smaller, blue cannulas instead of the pink ones, and then one like a butterfly with green wings and a long tail. Two hours had passed since I had first come into the hospital. They were running out of options, and I was conscious of how much time had passed without an IV. I knew how serious urosepsis was. They had drummed that into me in the Alrijne Hospital last July. I knew it could kill me. That was beginning to look like a good solution. I was tired of feeling sick.

"I have a DNR", I told them.

"Why?", asked one of the team.

"I have an incurable cancer", I explained. "It's in my notes. They told me the average survival was 11 to 18 months. If I'm not going to get better, then it's best to just let me die. Don't resuscitate me if I lose consciousness. I can get you the paperwork."

I was assured it wouldn't come to that. They'd get a line in somehow.

"Have you ever had a central line?" asked one of the kind ones.

I hadn't, but I knew that it hurt. I shook my head.

"Let me see", said a new voice, a man in a suit. He had just come in. He looked all over my arms and hands, now covered in bruises and pressure plasters from the previous failed attempts to strike red gold. He seemed particularly interested in the inside of my left arm. "Will you let me give it one more try?" he asked. It was nice to be asked. I'd lost count of how many attempts had been made so far – three in the ward, three in post-op and a further three or four in intensive care.

"If this doesn't work, we'll do a central line", he reassured me. "It'll be okay."

I love people who can find my veins and make them stay still long enough to get a line in. He took his time, but ten minutes later, the cannula was in. The IV antibiotics could be started and they could give me something to bring down my temperature and rehydrate me.

I was glad to get back to "my" room on the fifth floor. But Molenaar and the nurses pointed out, not unreasonably, that I was in the labour ward and I didn't really belong there. They couldn't predict how many women would go into labour over the next 12 hours, or whether they would need my room. They really should move me downstairs. There was something about the way they were talking about downstairs that convinced me I wasn't going to like it. I begged them to leave me where I was, just for the night. Like with my last urosepsis, I just wanted somewhere quiet, dark and private to rest and recover. I was exhausted after my trip down to post-op and intensive care. They didn't want to distress me any further. They took a chance, and I promised to go immediately if a woman came in in labour and needed the room. Luckily, no more princesses, princes or Delilahs needed the room that night and I was allowed to rest as best I could in the quiet, safe, dark space.

Next morning, I was starting to feel a bit stronger. I was able to sip water and not chuck it up. My temperature was heading towards normal. Still no mothers and babies were clamouring for my room, so I was allowed to stay there for the morning. A specialist in internal medicine came to see me. He sent me for an ultrasound. Back in my room afterwards, he told me that something was pressing against my left ureter, blocking it and causing my kidney to swell. Given my history, he told me gently, he thought it was likely to be a tumour.

"Is there anything we can do?", I asked. I was told a CT scan had been scheduled for 2pm. That would, hopefully, give them a better picture. We would discuss the options later.

"Don't have lunch", he warned. "You need to fast for two hours or so before the CT."

That was no problem. The thought of food still horrified me. It was now time to pack and go downstairs.

The sweet and kind transport lady who had brought me to the ultrasound earlier came to bring me down to the fourth floor, to Wilhelmina Ward, called after another royal. Wilhelmina was Queen of the Netherlands from 1890 until 1948, the longest-reigning Dutch monarch. A rather severe black-and-white image of her hangs at the entrance to the ward. The difference between Bronovo's fourth and fifth floors could not have been starker. Gone were the quiet, private rooms, the peace, the soothing ambiance, the flooring that was silent underfoot, and the friendly nurses. Down here, it was like I had stepped back into the days of Queen Wilhelmina's reign. The noise levels were nerve-shreddingly high, drip alarms were sounding from the rooms, everything clanged and echoed. The décor was institution classic, there were people everywhere and it smelt unmistakably of hospital. The nurses weren't so friendly either, but they did look rushed off their feet.

Through a warren of corridors with no natural light, I was wheeled into a small, odd-shaped room, sort of like a boomerang with one arm shorter than the other. The nurse who had guided the transport lady showed me the bell and left. The curtain was pulled around the bed to the left of me from where an unhappy keening sound was coming. To the right of me, along the short arm of the boomerang, there were two more beds. Their occupants, one woman and one man were facing straight at the newcomer. The way the beds were angled meant that I was right in their line of vision. The occupant of the bed closest to me, the man, looked resignedly glum. The woman, in the bed by the window, had her head wrapped in an enormous Crimean War-style bandage and looked very ill. She wasn't moving or speaking and was being attended to by five female relatives. Two were puffing up her pillows, holding and stroking her hands and arms and talking to her all the time. A third, wearing an abaya and veil, sat at the foot of the bed and was giving what sounded like a running commentary of events over her mobile phone in a language I didn't recognize. She seemed to be passing on instructions to the two women tending to the patient. The fourth woman, also veiled but younger, was moving around the room and placing saucers of orange segments and chopped apple along the windowsills and on the room's small table. The fifth woman, older than the others and dressed in a black abaya, but not veiled, was going back and forth between the bandaged-head patient and whoever was moaning behind the curtain next to me. It was a full-on chaos of sound and motion. I tore my gaze away from the noisy, busy women for a moment and stole a glance at the male patient. He was watching me watching the sideshow. Our eyes met and we exchanged a moment of camaraderie.

The noise, the chatter, the passing around of fruit and the constant commentary into the mobile phone continued. I watched and listened for about half an hour, trying to figure out what was going on. The moaning occupant of the bed behind the curtain came out and walked over to the bandaged-head lady and joined in the stroking of her arms and general lamentations. I wasn't sure whether that patient was alive or not. She wasn't responding to anything the others said or did. She was very pale. The keening patient started to head back to her own bed behind the curtain, but stopped on the way at the foot of mine. She started talking to me, but I don't know what language it was. I knew it wasn't Dutch. I gave her a half smile and said, "Sorry, I don't understand". She tried harder to explain whatever it was to me, becoming more agitated and stopping from time to time to gesture to herself and to the patient with the bandaged head. She was telling me her story, but unfortunately, I couldn't understand. Eventually, the young woman in charge of the fruit came over. She apologized to me in Dutch, and led the upset woman back to her bed. The keening recommenced.

A nurse came in. I think she was asking them to keep it down a bit, and telling them there should only be two visitors per patient. The thing was, the two female patients seemed connected, so five visitors between them wasn't all that far outside the rules. The noise levels lulled for a bit, but only while she was in the room. Ten minutes later, another nurse came in to try again to quell the mounting crescendo. She had much the same success as her colleague. When she left, I made a decision. I figured that my chances of survival had just taken a major step backwards when I was wheeled into this room. No nurse had come near me in the hour I had been there, and it was obvious that the ward was well out of control. Being here mightn't actually kill me, but I figured there was a good chance of it. And anyway, if my days were numbered, I wasn't going to spend any of them here. I didn't fancy an argument, so I picked up my rucksack and put it on over my pyjamas, draped my fleece across my left arm and used my right hand to wheel my drip tree out of the room. I thought my escape was foiled at first base when I bumped into a nurse in the doorway. She was on her way to have another go at restoring order. But she swept past me, clapping her hands for attention over the noise of the busy visitors and moaning patient. I kept moving, using instinct to find my way back along the dark, labyrinthine corridors, back past the photo of Wilhelmina, and out of the ward to the lift. At each step, I expected someone to run after me and drag me back. But no one batted an eyelid at a patient carrying her rucksack and outdoor coat wheeling a drip tree out the door. The lift came mercifully quickly. There was another woman already inside. She was carrying some paperwork. Probably a hospital administrator. She noticed when I pushed the button for the fifth floor, and was surprised when I stepped out.

"Do you know that's the delivery suite?" she asked when I stepped out with my drip tree. I smiled and nodded.

I went to the reception desk and asked for Dr Molenaar. The nurse on duty looked surprised. Dr Molenaar wasn't available. I asked for the nurse who had been looking after me that morning. The receptionist nurse disappeared into a room behind reception and picked up the phone. I didn't understand what she was saying to whoever was on the other end, but I don't think she was happy with me. Luckily, the nurse who had looked after me earlier happened to walk past.

"What are you doing here?" she asked.

I described in detail what I had seen in Wilhelmina Ward, ending with, "And I am absolutely not going back down there again".

"But you can't stay here", she said. "We don't have a room for you and you need a different sort of nursing."

I saw her problem, but I knew I didn't need what was on offer downstairs.

"I can't allow myself to be sent back there", I told her. "No patient should be in such a place. It's overcrowded and chaotic. My chances of survival are less if I go back there. That room I was in is not fit for purpose – four patients crammed into a tiny room and visitors all over the place. The noise level was ridiculous. The staff are totally overstretched. I can't recover there. I need rest."

I was getting upset, but I was adamant. I was not going back to that room. If necessary, I would discharge myself after my CT scan. The nurse brought me into a labour suite across from the reception desk and told me to sit down. She would look for Dr Molenaar.

A few minutes later, I heard Peter at the reception desk. He knew I was scheduled for a CT, but I hadn't got around to telling him I had been moved off the fifth floor, so when he had arrived at the hospital, he had come straight to the ward where I had spent the night. I could hear the situation was becoming confused as a new receptionist nurse was telling him I had been transferred to Wilhelmina, while the nurse I had just spoken to was saying I had come back up and was in the labour suite. I could see this becoming very confusing so I got up to rescue Peter. I was surprised at how shaky my legs had become.

"I'm in here", I said to Peter, opening the door to the room. "It's a long story."

The nice transport lady was back again to bring me for my CT. She was looking confused too. Why was the foreign lady she had brought to Wilhelmina an hour ago now back on Amalia Ward?

The long-suffering nurse who had been looking after me said I could come back to the fifth floor after the CT scan, but I couldn't stay. The bed manager would talk to me and look for a solution.

While waiting for the CT, I filled Peter in on what had happened earlier. He was horrified.

"I don't care what the bed manager says", I told him. "I'm not going back to that room. I won't recover in there. It's total bedlam. There's barely enough room for the patients, let alone a room full of visitors on mobile phones going back and forth between patients. It was well out of control."

Back on the fifth floor after the CT, the bed manager came to talk to us. She was telling me all about how the hospital was really busy because it was January, and lots of people got sick in

January. She was trying to persuade me to go back to that room in Wilhelmina! It wasn't going to happen. I told her in graphic detail what had happened during the hour I spent there. I told her there was no way any patient should be asked to put up with that.

"But what am I supposed to do?" she asked. "I'd love to be able to find a room for you, but there just aren't any."

Before I could reply, the door opened and the internist walked in. He saw me and started saying something about getting another ultrasound and thinking that whatever was blocking my ureter might be a kidney stone and not a tumour. Then he stopped, realizing he had walked in on something.

"Oh, I'm sorry", he said, glancing from Peter and me to the bed manager. "Have I interrupted a meeting?"

"Never mind", I said. "If you have some news that means I have a kidney stone, not a tumour, I want to hear it."

"We need you to go back for another ultrasound."

"When?"

"Now," he said.

I glanced at the bed manager. "Go", she said. "We'll talk later."

By now the transport lady and I were firm friends and she laughed as she arrived yet again on Amalia to bring me to radiology.

This time, the ultrasound hurt. The doctor doing it was digging as deep as he could to try to get a better view. The internist was there too and another doctor, probably a consultant radiologist, peering over each other to see the swirling grey images on the ultrasound screen.

"What are you seeing?" I asked.

"Your left kidney is dilated", replied the doctor doing the ultrasound. "The left ureter is blocked, but we can't get a clear view because there is fibrosis there and surgical clips are in the way."

I had told the internist earlier that previous scans done at AMC had shown that I had an asymptomatic kidney stone in my left kidney.

"There's no stone there now", said the man with the ultrasound.

"It's likely that the stone has dropped and is blocking your ureter", said the internist. "Have you passed a kidney stone recently?"

"I don't know", I answered. "I had bad pain with a UTI in November, but it went away with antibiotics."

All three doctors assured me that if I had passed a kidney stone, I'd know about it.

I was beginning to see a thin shred of hope glimmering in the distance. If I had a kidney stone, this wasn't another tumour.

"We can't be sure", warned the internist. "What we are seeing near the left ureter also looks like a tumour."

"Could I possibly have a kidney stone *and* a tumour in the same place?", I asked, wondering how unlikely life could get.

The doctors shrugged, not committing themselves one way or the other. The internist and the consultant radiologist left. The poking into my lower abdomen and the left side of my lower back continued for several more minutes. I had never realized ultrasounds could hurt. The doctor kept apologizing for the discomfort. He was frustrated that he couldn't get a clearer picture and a definitive answer.

Afterwards, I waited outside again with Peter and the transport lady came to bring me back upstairs. She wheeled me out of the lift at the fourth floor. My heart skipped a beat. We were heading towards Wilhelmina. I didn't know what to do.

We were stopped in the corridor by Molenaar and the internist. She had filled him in on my eventful day. While she was my "guardian angel" at Bronovo, she wasn't my treating physician, the internist was. He had been bewildered to learn from her that in between my various visits to radiology I had walked out of Wilhelmina Ward, had "occupied" a delivery suite in her labour ward and had threatened to discharge myself. Molenaar had met the bed manager.

"You can't go home", the internist told me. "You are on IV antibiotics. You need a urologist to treat your ureter and kidney. You need to stay here. And in bed, preferably."

I was close to tears. Molenaar stepped in. It was going to be okay. The bed manager had found me a bed. I could have a room on my own. It was in Wilhelmina Ward, but it wasn't the room I had been in before. I wasn't sure whether to believe them. The bed manager had made it crystal clear that there wasn't a bed in the entire hospital other than the one I had walked away from earlier. The idea that I could have a room on my own was too good to be true.

The internist said he'd talk to me later, and Janke Molenaar accompanied Peter and me to my new room. The bed manager found us en route and came too.

"Is it alright?", asked the bed manager, ushering us into the room like a proud hotelier.

"All right?", I echoed. "It's brilliant! Thank you very much."

It was a simple room with a bed, a table and a chair. It was perfect. Whoever had the idea that sick people can recover if you put them into a room where they're cheek-by-jowl with other sick strangers was surely a sadist. In the fullness of your health, it would be traumatic to share such small personal space and amenities with strangers. When you're sick, it's little short of hell. Prisoners aren't expected to share so little space with so many others, so why are patients expected to? Pretty much all major studies from Europe and North America for decades have indicated that not only is the patient experience improved with the privacy and dignity of a single room, but patient safety is improved, the number of medication errors is lower, recovery times are faster, the cross-infection risk is lower, healthcare professionals can have more in-depth consultations with their patients because confidentiality is not an issue, and, here's the surprising one, operating costs are reduced in single-occupancy rooms. [16]

I didn't really need the research to convince me. I knew for sure that with my own space, my recovery had taken a giant leap forward.

---

16   See the articles and reports on the website accompanying this book for information on multiple-occupancy versus single-occupancy rooms in hospitals.

16 | January 2016 ... Bronovo Hospital, The Hague

A surgeon accused of killing a patient by removing the wrong kidney admitted that he may have held the X-rays back to front ...
John Roberts, 60, a consultant urologist in charge of the operation, told police the X-rays were not marked in the usual way and he may have mistaken the healthy kidney for the diseased one.
As a result, he and Mahesh Goel, 39, who performed the operation, removed the healthy kidney from Graham Reeves, 70, a Korean War veteran, leaving him with no chance of survival.
Richard Alleyne, *The Telegraph*, 14 June, 2002[17]

The day's events had exhausted me, but the new antibiotics had started to do their job. I was now able to drink without throwing up. The internist had visited me again, congratulated me on my "new room" and said that he had contacted a urologist for me. Although they still couldn't tell from the imaging exactly what was going on in the left ureter, they knew that they needed to intervene to save my left kidney. They also knew why I kept getting UTIs, and why they were quickly

---

17 Wrong-site surgery occurs far more often than we think. See the articles on such cases from all over the world on the website that accompanies this book.

Deny, dismiss, dehumanise

developing into urosepsis. The blocked ureter was stopping the antibiotics from working. We would need to find a way of keeping the ureter open, or possibly taking me into surgery and draining my kidney through my back. A urologist would come to see me in the morning and work out a plan.

I slept like a log in my quiet room. Next morning, I was still feeling a bit shell-shocked, but my batteries had recharged and I was relaxed – or at least as close to relaxed as I can ever be in a hospital.

Mid-morning, the urologist arrived as promised. She seemed nice and friendly and started to explain to me what the plan was.

"We see from the CT scan that your right ureter is blocked, causing your kidney to become dilated ...", she began.

I interrupted. "Don't you mean my *left* ureter", I asked politely.

She didn't miss a beat.

"No, I'm talking about your *right* ureter and kidney", she said.

I was confused. Was there a problem with my right kidney now too? This would be a disaster. "Oh! Is my right ureter blocked now as well?"

"Yes, your right ureter," she answered. "I'm talking about your right ureter and kidney. I'll show you", she said, starting to draw a diagram of a right human kidney, ureter and bladder viewed from the front. She drew in the blockage and explained that the blockage stopped the kidney from draining normally. I wasn't really listening. I was thinking. I watched her draw for a minute or so while I tried to get this straight in my head.

I stopped her again. "Are you absolutely certain that it is my right ureter that is blocked and not my left?" I asked. "Because yesterday, they were all talking about my *left* ureter."

"No, no, it's your right ureter that's blocked. There's nothing wrong with your left kidney", she said, trying hard to be patient with me. She had probably heard that I was the woman whose cancer diagnosis had been lost by UMCU, and who was very distrustful of doctors as a result. She was visibly doing her best to be tolerant of my persistent disbelief. The relaxed feeling from my good night's sleep vanished. I went into "protect" mode. All my critical faculties were screaming at me that I was right and she was mistaken. But I knew better than to take her on head-on in her own area of expertise. I was a lay person, and part of me really didn't want to believe my own logical reasoning. But if this woman wanted to give me a general anaesthetic and take me into surgery to insert a stent into a perfectly functional ureter or possibly drain a perfectly healthy kidney through my back, I couldn't keep silent. I had to speak up now.

"This isn't making sense", I began, cautiously, keeping the pitch of my voice low and my tone as calm as I could manage. It was a struggle. My mouth had gone dry. "I am almost sure it is my left ureter and kidney. Yesterday, the guy with the ultrasound was digging into me on the left side. It hurt", I added, pointing to my lower-left abdomen. "No one has ever mentioned my right ureter. The kidney stone was always in my *left* kidney. The pain is on the *left* side."

She looked at me with as much patience as she could muster.

"Look", she said, "I'll go and get the computer and I'll show you. We can look at the scan together."

She left then, leaving me wondering which was worse, a urologist who didn't know left from right or having to accept that I had somehow got the whole story wrong and was misremembering everything that had happened the previous day. Neither option thrilled me, but I decided that if she turned out to be mistaken after I had suggested four separate times in the six minutes or so she had been in the room, that the problem was on the left, I was not going to allow her to operate on me. I did not want to be unconscious and in theatre with her in charge.

She was gone a long time. I passed the time writing down the conversation we had just exchanged. The longer she was gone, the more sure I was that I wasn't mistaken. But I was also seriously afraid and I could feel my heart racing. Over half-an-hour later, she came back. She had brought the internist's registrar with her – a nice woman whom I had met the previous day and liked.

"You're absolutely right", began the urologist. "It's the left ureter that's blocked, just like you said."

She said other stuff too, but I didn't hear any of it. My brain was shouting, "Yes! I'm *not* crazy!" My soul was shouting, "Oh God, no! Not again!" I couldn't believe that this was happening. It's like a bad joke – the patient goes into hospital with a bad eye, lung, leg, arm, ear, brain whatever, and the surgeon operates on the wrong side. I thought that only happened in hospital sitcoms. I put my hands over my face. I didn't want to be here. I asked myself, why did it have to be my responsibility to make sure the specialist operates on the correct ureter? This is not my job! Is there no one I can trust?

The urologist had stopped talking and was looking at me. "Please just go", I asked her.

She stayed where she was, looking confused.

I tried again. "Go away, please. I told you many times that it was my *left* kidney and you wouldn't believe me. The very first time I said to you, 'it is my left kidney', you should have questioned yourself, but you didn't. You just kept on being sure you were right. I don't trust your judgement. I don't trust you to treat me."

I was struggling to keep control. I wanted to howl in despair. How can hospitals do this sort of stuff? How often are calamities averted only because patients intervene? What happens to patients who don't, or can't, speak up? What sort of person trusts their own judgement so much that they cannot allow the possibility that the patient knows which kidney was scanned and which kidney hurts?

Both doctors left, and I was alone. I was very shaken. I had often felt unsafe in hospitals, but I had usually blamed myself for being too fearful. I wasn't going to blame myself any more. If one patient, me, has experiences that *have* caused her serious harm and experiences that *could* cause her serious harm in two out of three hospitals in a four-year period, you can be sure it is happening to others too.

My horrors were interrupted by a visitor. A friend, Christine, had come to see me. She had brought a present. Some chocolates and an adult colouring book called, *Colour Yourself Calm*. I started to laugh at the irony, and then explained to Christine what had just happened. She was horrified, but her main concern was that I could handle this. She knew my story, and knew I needed another medical mishap like I needed a hole in my head.

"They all know what happened to me at UMCU", I told her. "They agreed that nobody should be asked to treat me unless they had been informed about the calamity and my PTSD. If this is the care they take when treating a patient known to be vulnerable, what are they doing to the other patients?"

I was getting upset. It was hard not to. Christine suggested I phone Peter. Peter was supposed to be having the morning off. He had been in the hospital with me for over eight hours the previous day and had been up half the night when I was admitted. I had told him that Christine would be with me during the morning, so he could take a break. He was due in during the afternoon. It was still only 11:30. I didn't want to spoil his peace and quiet, but I also didn't want to keep him in the dark. If our roles were reversed, I would want to know, and would feel annoyed at not being told. I decided to compromise and try to get myself as calm as possible before phoning him. If I called him now, I would lose it on the phone and upset him more than was necessary.

"Have some chocolate", suggested Christine, with a smile offering me the box of tulip-shaped chocolates she had brought.

I laughed. Normally, I'd agree that chocolate is good for shock and boosts the morale, but my mouth was still as dry as sand. Christine stayed with me, probably much longer than she intended. I phoned Peter around 12:30, and told him what had happened. He asked a lot of questions, but didn't say too much over the phone. He said he'd see me in a short while.

Lunch came. I declined.

"You should try to eat something", Christine encouraged. She was probably right. But my mouth was still as dry as sandpaper. All I wanted was sips of water.

Around 13:00, I had another visitor. It was Ankie Smeets, the hospital's complaints officer. Peter had phoned her and told her what had happened to me with the urologist. I asked Christine to stay with me for another while. We spoke to Smeets for about 20 minutes. Peter had filled her in on my medical background, and referred her to my medical file and the information Molenaar had entered into it on New Year's Eve. Smeets could see why I was upset. It is her job to mediate and smooth ruffled feathers, so she wasn't going to try to persuade me that what had happened was unimportant and had had no serious consequences. The reason it didn't have any consequences was only because I had stood my ground against a specialist convinced that her version of events was correct and mine was wrong. She asked me what I wanted her to do.

Here we go again, I thought. Another hospital that has zero idea how to behave when something goes wrong. I asked for three things: "First, I need a new urologist", I said. "I need someone who knows which kidney is damaged and whom I can trust not to get things wrong if I need to put in a stent, or if I need my kidney drained. I need to talk to this new urologist as soon as possible.

"Second, I want to make sure that there is a record of what happened so that the department can look at it, see how things got confused, and put some protocol in place where urologists always know whether they're looking at a left kidney or a right kidney – and more importantly, that they listen to what their patients are saying.

"And finally, I'd like to know what's happening. This incident occurred almost two-and-a-half hours ago and not a single member of staff has come by to see if I am okay or to tell me what's going to happen next. Is that some sort of punishment meted out to patients who complain?" I asked her.

She assured me it wasn't. She said she'd find someone to talk to me. I asked her to find Janke Molenaar. I knew my kind internist from yesterday was not in Bronovo that day. In his absence, I trusted only Janke Molenaar.

Christine stayed on. She knew Peter was on his way. Unlike the hospital staff, Christine had the compassion to realize that I shouldn't be left on my own. Just before 2pm, a nurse came in. She mentioned nothing about what had happened earlier or the visit from Ankie Smeets.

"I've called transport to take you down for your CT", she said.

"What CT?" I asked.

"Your CT", she answered. "You have to have a CT."

"No one told me I was scheduled for a CT scan."

"Well I'm telling you", she answered.

"Well, I don't mean to be rude, but can you tell me what I need to know about the scan?"

"All you need to know is that transport will come and bring you down shortly", she replied, turning to go out the door.

"Hang on a sec", I called after her. "Generally, if a patient is to have a CT scan, she can discuss it with the doctor who ordered it. Who ordered the CT scan?"

"The doctor", replied the nurse.

"Which doctor?" I asked.

There was no reply.

"Can I talk to the doctor who ordered the CT scan?", I asked.

"The doctor is too busy to come", she replied.

"I'm not going for any CT scan unless I know who ordered it and can ask some questions about it first."

"I can answer your questions", offered the nurse.

"Okay", I said. "Can you tell me what they are hoping to find in this CT scan that they couldn't see in yesterday's CT scan? What's different about what they are doing today? Has something changed?"

"I don't know", admitted the nurse.

"Another question", I said. "Aren't I supposed to fast before a CT scan?"

"Yes, you should have nothing to eat or drink for two hours before the scan."

"I'm having a scan in half-an-hour", I told her. "And this is the first I've heard of it. I have been drinking water all morning. I've just been brought chocolates and the lunch trolley was here a while ago offering me lunch."

"Oh, you weren't supposed to have lunch", she said. "Did you eat lunch?"

"Luckily, no."

"So there's no problem then", said the nurse.

"I still need to talk to the doctor before I go for the scan", I told her.

"The doctor is busy", she said again.

"No doctor, no CT scan", I told her.

Today was turning out to be every bit as wearying as yesterday. All I wanted was to relax and rest, but the adrenalin was pumping constantly as I tried to deal with what was happening to me. I wasn't even convinced that I was supposed to be going for another CT. I had had one less than 24 hours ago, along with two ultrasounds. What was different today? What were they hoping to see?

The internist's registrar, the transport lady and Peter all turned up at the same time minutes later. I told Peter I was going for another CT right now. He was as surprised as I had been.

"Why didn't you mention it on the phone? I would have got here sooner."

"I just found out a few minutes ago", I replied.

And then, turning to the registrar, I said, "Why am I going for a CT scan? What do you hope to see today that wasn't possible to see yesterday? What is different now? And why was I not told this morning that I was scheduled for a CT scan? I had no instruction not to eat or drink."

The answers were that they felt a blank CT scan would give a clearer indication of whether a stone was present in the ureter than the scan I had yesterday. A "blank" CT was one where no contrast dye would be given to me – it gives a different sort of image. Yes, I should have been told earlier that I was scheduled for a CT scan, but the registrar was called to an emergency elsewhere, and anyway, she didn't realize that the urologist hadn't told me.

Christine finally felt free to leave and Peter and the transport lady brought me down to radiology. She was the same transport lady as the previous day. Her good nature was infectious and her compassion for the patients she wheeled about the hospital was evident. She didn't speak much English, but we communicated just fine. I caught her eye and she laughed.

"Let's go!" she said.

Molenaar came mid-afternoon to see how I was. Smeets had spoken to her about the urologist and the wrong kidney. She was her usual, kind, supportive self, but I think she was beginning to be sorry she had ever heard of Adrienne Cullen, and would probably not answer the phone the next time Arie Franx rang.

My new urologist turned up too, a little later in the day. Oh my god, it's the Milky Bar Kid! I thought to myself. In my mid-fifties now, I had started getting used to everyone looking

Deny, dismiss, dehumanise

younger. But this guy was the image of the slight, freckled boy on the white-chocolate bar wrappers. And he looked terrified. Someone had probably told him I had swallowed my last urologist whole.

He started to explain what the blank CT had told them – nothing new, as it happened – and what they proposed to do now. As he talked, stumbling a bit over his words and getting wrapped up in the details, I realized that I needed to show him that Peter and I weren't ogres. We were just more terrified than average. So I started asking questions and nodding encouragingly as he explained the answers. I then asked his opinion, and that did the trick. He relaxed, and communication became a lot easier and clearer. Tomorrow, he would take me to theatre and insert a Double-J (JJ) stent through my urethra, through my bladder, through my left ureter and into my kidney. I had hydronephrosis in my kidney, and the JJ stent would keep the ureter open, allow it to drain normally and enable the antibiotics to reach the kidney. There was a slight possibility that the kidney stone that he was convinced was lodged in the ureter, would prevent the JJ stent from being inserted. If that happened, I would have to go to an intervention radiologist to have my kidney drained manually through my back. This would have to be a separate procedure though as they did not have the facilities to carry this out in the ordinary theatre while I was still under general anaesthetic.

"But I'm confident we'll be able to get the JJ in", he reassured.

I'd have to fast from midnight as he wasn't sure what time the surgery would happen. I didn't mind. All I wanted was to know what was happening and why. I liked this doctor. He was clear, direct, and didn't seem affronted if I asked questions about why something was needed or how something worked. I sensed he found my questions reasonable – and more or less what he'd ask himself if he were in my shoes. After meeting the Milky Bar Kid, aka, Zander van Houten, I felt a lot more confident about going for surgery.

Next morning by seven o'clock, I was showered and dressed in a blue surgical gown. Clean sheets were put on my bed and I was ready to go. I sat and waited for a theatre slot to become available. While I was waiting, I picked up Christine's present and tried to colour myself calm. It sort of worked. Or it passed the time anyway. Around 11:30, my door opened and a man in surgical scrubs walked in. I didn't catch his full name, but his first name was Marius. He was one of the anaesthetists. He had heard about my traumatic experience with the first urologist the previous day, and had read about my medical background. In the circumstances, he decided it would be better for me if he came to my room to talk to me about the surgery. He was exceptionally kind. He had brought a black, felt-tip pen with him.

"We do this now to make sure there can never be any chance of wrong-side surgery", he said drawing a bold, black arrow on the left side of my lower abdomen, over where the ureter would be. I thought at the time that he was humouring me, but now realize that this is common practice in hospitals worldwide. It works very well if and when the surgeon sees it. But anyway, after talking to Van Houten the previous evening, I felt confident that he knew very well which ureter was blocked. Marius promised that he would be with me in surgery too, as the anaesthetist. He understood that I found it difficult to keep having to trust new faces.

After nearly a week of not eating much at all, I was starting to feel hungry. But more importantly, I was really thirsty. The urinary infection was making my body crave fluids. My mouth was bone dry. Marius said I could moisten my mouth with tiny quantities of water and showed me how much I could safely swallow. The quantity was less than a teaspoon, but it kept my mouth feeling comfortable. I promised to have no more than one tiny sip every half hour. I was glad he had come to see me. I desperately wanted to have confidence in the people treating me, and now between Marius and Van Houten, I felt that a trip to the operating theatre wouldn't be too daunting.

Around 16:00, I was wheeled down to pre-op. Like many hospitals, pre-op and post-op are largely the same physical space. The last time I had been here was on New Year's Eve when the anaesthetists on duty had tried in vain to find a vein. But today, they were taking better care of me. I was wheeled into a small room and the person who welcomed me knew I spoke English. He chatted away telling me what he was doing and trying to make me laugh. It makes such a difference when people know from the start that I don't speak Dutch. Normally, in hospital, I say, "I'm sorry, I don't understand", dozens of times a day as each new nurse comes on shift, each new doctor approaches me, and often to the same people over and over again as they forget that I can't understand them. Someone had made a real effort here today, and it made a world of difference to me.

The stent was inserted as planned with no need for the intervention radiologist, although it still wasn't absolutely clear whether there was a stone in the ureter. I stayed in my room at Bronovo for another five days. I then had to return to Emma Ward every day for another week or so to receive IV antibiotics. I was on the mend. My urologist had sorted out the immediate problem with the stent, which could stay in place for three or four months. Once the kidney had returned to normal size and the ureter was less infected and inflamed, I would need more imaging to see if they could figure out what was going on in my ureter – and answer the Big Question, is it a kidney stone, a tumour or both?

17 | January 2016 ... UMC, Utrecht

A stiff apology is a second insult ... The injured party does not want to be compensated because he has been wronged; he wants to be healed because he has been hurt.

G. K. Chesterton

I didn't hear any more from Bronovo about the incident with the urologist and the wrong kidney. Nor did I ever find out how it had happened, or what – if anything – had been done to prevent reoccurrence. As for an apology, the urologist did say she was sorry after she breezed back into my room that morning, but it was a knee-jerk apology, and it came only after I put my head in my hands and asked her to leave.

I was beginning to realize that hospitals didn't put any value on apologizing to patients when things went wrong. It was well into January and I was still waiting for my apology from UMCU. We had asked for an apology in November and our lawyer had been told that UMCU would like to apologize, and would do so "soon". Then, a month later, when Petra and I met professors Franx and Van der Vaart on 16 December, I explained that I was still waiting. Franx told me that he had been told that the board

Deny, dismiss, dehumanise

had agreed to apologize and would write to me "soon". I couldn't understand how, after agreeing to apologize in November, they would persist in not doing so right into January. I was seriously contemplating visiting the hospital and refusing to leave the CEO's office until I had received an apology – or that was the plan until I ended up with urosepsis again, making a protest trip to Utrecht impossible. So instead, I emailed Schneider to point out that when people say they would like to apologize, they generally do so immediately rather than waiting for months. The idea that an apology to The Cullen Patient was at the bottom of someone's to-do list was just a further humiliation.

The apology had become really important to me. I didn't, of course, believe that UMCU was genuinely upset about what had happened – except insofar as their failures had ended up all over the front page of *NRC* – but the fact that it had never occurred to them that an apology was appropriate, really disturbed me. I kept hearing the voice of my lawyer telling me that hospitals didn't ever apologize to patients they harm, and each time, my inner dissident demanded, "Why on earth not?"

In everything I had heard and read about serious-harm protocols, and all the systems in place in various countries to deal with the aftermath of hospital calamities, medical errors and negligence, the whole question of apologizing to patients was central. And I knew exactly why. Huub Van der Vaart had apologized in June 2013, and I knew that he meant every word he said to Peter and me. Arie Franx had apologized with absolute sincerity in December 2015. These two sincere apologies had made a huge difference to me, had changed my relationships with the two men and turned us from opponents into allies. Forgiveness follows naturally when you receive a genuine apology because it is impossible not to empathize with someone who is feeling bitter remorse. Without those two apologies, I would not have been able to forgive; and without the assuagement brought by forgiving, I would not have been able to heal.

But Van der Vaart and Franx were not, by any means, the only people responsible for what happened to me. UMCU as an institution was much more responsible for the damage caused than the human error of any man. I was determined to set a precedent. It didn't really matter that it was extracted under duress, and so was not going to be entirely heartfelt. What mattered was that this apology would be a first – and I hoped it would be the first of many, and that future patients will come to expect that hospitals that hurt them, will help them to heal. Anything else is an affront to the relationship of trust that should exist between patients and hospitals.

It still surprises me that UMCU's leadership still did not seem to understand that an apology is therapeutic – if it's sincere, it heals the transgressors as much as the victim. Prue Vines had explained some of this in her letter to UMCU's board in October 2015. Apologies are not made to make the wrongdoer look bad or to assign blame, they are made to forge a human connection between the person who has been hurt and those who have hurt her. None of the other steps in a serious-harm protocol can take place properly unless and until there has been an apology.

The apology from UMCU eventually turned up on 14 January. It was in English – which was a kind gesture, and much appreciated – and signed with CEO, Margriet Schneider's, automatic signature. It was obvious though that some effort had gone into it, and the writer had endeavoured to say the right things. It did refer to "the unforgivable mistake made by us", which was important, as it underlined that the hospital itself had been at fault. And it used the words "honestly sorry".

It went on to say that she hoped it would bring solace to us to know that UMCU had learned something from the "enormous tragedy". It didn't explain what exactly the hospital had learned, and I still don't know. It would be nice to know what they learned. The apology also mentioned that she hoped the meeting I had had with Franx and Van der Vaart had given me some of the answers I was searching for, as though the questions I was asking were metaphysical or spiritual in some way. I felt this was disingenuous, as what that meeting had revealed was that most of the questions I had will remain unanswered until a root-cause analysis is carried out.

I don't accept that a hospital that causes a calamity – or in the case of UMCU, several calamities – is the best judge of whether or not an investigation needs to be carried out into what caused it. Most organizations resist investigations of their own mistakes, and UMCU was no different. An outside, impartial, body should investigate the circumstances surrounding every calamity, serious harm or unexplained death in any hospital. This is the standard in most EU countries, and the fact that it doesn't happen here is not to the advantage of patients.

The apology rather undid some of the good in its first paragraphs by referring to a "missed diagnosis" – which is absolutely not what happened to me. There's a big difference between a missed diagnosis and a clear diagnosis that remained unseen for two years.[18] But hey, I wasn't expecting miracles. We had succeeded in persuading the CEO, and maybe even the lawyers, to stop and think for a while about the consequences of their actions, their public accountability and their behaviour towards their patients. Maybe when the next calamity hits UMCU, the damaged patients and their families won't be further injured by a hospital leadership that is guided more by its lawyers than by compassion.

---

18 A "missed diagnosis" describes a situation where a doctor fails to identify or diagnose a medical condition at the time they're presented with it. What happened in my case was that no one knew for two years that there was a cancer-probable diagnosis in my file, or how it got there.

18 | January to March 2016 ... AMC, Amsterdam

*It is not because I cannot explain that you won't understand, it is because
you won't understand that I cannot explain.*
Elie Wiesel, April 22, 1993

When my Bronovo CTs and ultrasounds found their
way to Van der Velden at AMC, he saw something
he wasn't expecting – something that was at odds
with his view of what was going on with me. We travelled to
Amsterdam to see him.

"I'm confused", he told us. "And I don't like being confused."
Peter and I smiled. We weren't used to seeing Van der Velden
confused either. He had always been refreshingly methodical
and meticulous and crystal clear in everything he said and did.
As a practising gynaecological oncologist for over 30 years, there
wasn't much he hadn't seen.

In his consulting room, he called up on screen the CT scan
taken a year ago at AMC and pointed to Tumour 2, the tumour
believed to be on the outside wall of the sigmoid colon. He then
uploaded the CT taken the previous month at Bronovo and
pointed to the same tumour.

Deny, dismiss, dehumanise

"It's in a different place", he said. And it was clear from the two scans that Tumour 2 was more than a centimetre away from where it had been 12 months before.

"Oh! I didn't know tumours could move", I said.

"They can't", replied Van der Velden.

Now we were confused too.

"So what's going on?", asked Peter.

"I'm not entirely sure", admitted Van der Velden. He said that it was certain from the Bronovo scan that there was a gap between Tumour 2 and the colon wall. This gap had not been visible the previous year. We looked back at the 2015 scan again, and sure enough, Tumour 2 was snug against my colon wall.

"If it's not on the colon, then what is it attached to?" I asked. "What else is there? Could it be attached to my ureter?"

"The only thing we can think of is that it is an ovary", replied Van der Velden. "Ovaries can move, which would explain why it's against the colon wall in one scan and in a different position in another scan. And it might explain why you are getting UTIs and urosepsis so often. The tumour, or ovary, is indeed pressing against your left ureter."

"So I *do* have a kidney stone blocking my ureter on the inside and a tumour pressing against it on the outside", I said.

"Well, whether or not you have a kidney stone is up to Dr Van Houten, but if there's a tumour pressing against the ureter from the outside, then it would prevent a kidney stone from descending."

"This sounds like good news?" I asked tentatively.

"We can't be sure yet what's going on, but if this tumour is in your left ovary, then it can be surgically removed", he explained. "But I do have to warn you that cervical cancer metastasizing in an ovary is very rare. There's about a one-in-a-hundred chance of that happening.

"And the other tumour?", asked Peter. "If you can now

remove this ovary-tumour, can you also remove Tumour 3 in Adrienne's abdominal wall?"

The answer was "yes". If Tumour 2 turned out to be an ovary, it could be removed, and Tumour 3 had always been operable. The only reason it hadn't been removed before was because it made no sense to perform invasive abdominal surgery for one metastasis while the other metastasis was believed likely to kill me first.

"So then I would have no tumours at all?" I asked, hardly daring to say it. "If I haven't grown any others in the meantime …"

"It is possible that we can remove both tumours, and it is theoretically possible that you will get no further metastases, yes", said Van der Velden. "But we have to be cautious, and take one step at a time."

I heard the hope, I heard the caution. I was well used to getting bad news, but *good* news … I had no idea how to deal with this psychologically. I had spent over a year internalizing the message that my cancer was terminal, my tumours inoperable, and I was going to die in the near future. I had fully absorbed it, practically, mentally, emotionally and spiritually. Even in my dreams, I knew I was a dead woman walking. But now, this news might mean I wasn't going to die after all. My already upside-down world gave another dizzying flip. I hung on tight. Don't get carried away, I warned myself. If I were lucky enough to have two operable metastases, the greater likelihood is that surgery will buy me more time, not cure me. But I'd settle for that.

"I'll order a PET-CT scan for you." Van der Velden's words brought me back to the here and now.

The PET will show if I have any metastases other than Tumour 2 and Tumour 3, and the CT will provide definition for what the PET lights up. Then we'd decide what to do next.

****

The waiting times in Dutch hospitals tend to be mercifully short, especially for cancer patients. So just a few days later, I received a missed a call from the PET-CT department. The voicemail message asked me to phone them. I got through to the hospital's main switch. As always, I asked politely if it was okay to speak in English. I was answered in Dutch. "Wat zeg je? *(What are you saying?)* I then said, in my best effort to communicate, *"Sorry, Ik spreek geen Nederlands. Kunnen we Engels spreken?"* (Sorry, I don't speak Dutch. Can we speak English?). There was an irritated sigh at the other end and the line went dead. This was the third time that the phone had been hung up on me by an AMC staff member when I asked to speak English.

It was almost a year since we had met hospital CEO, Professor Marcel Levi, to discuss with him the series of unpleasant encounters I had had as a result of not speaking Dutch. Apart from an initial promise to, "plan the most suitable way to explain to our staff that patients who do not speak Dutch, for any reason, [should not be] quizzed or even reprimanded about this", we had heard no more. I emailed him, telling him what had just happened and giving the details of the number I had rung and the exact time. A week later, I got a reply.[19] He said that after my complaint in March 2015, they had formulated a consensual policy to offer all non-Dutch-speaking patients, other than those who spoke English, a translator for phone and face-to-face appointments. They felt that because most nurses and doctors speak English, this would not usually be required for English-speaking patients. For administrative staff, if they were unable to communicate in English, they should transfer the patient to a colleague who was.

At the same plenary staff meeting where the translator policy was agreed, Levi wrote, "we also discussed whether we would

---

19   The email I sent to Marcel Levi and his reply to me can be found in Appendix 5.

find it appropriate to ask a patient why he/she did not speak Dutch. While many of us believed this question was just intended [to be] friendly and possibly out of curiosity and many of us also thought Dutch is such an erratic language that it is not strange at all if someone with another mother tongue would choose not to speak it ... we agreed that it might be better to abstain from this question as it apparently evokes a negative feeling from the patient (as you explained). Also this policy was implemented in our regular training program. All these policies will be published on our internal website as official AMC policies."

In the case of my phonecall on 1 February, Levi had tracked down the person who had answered the phone. I had got it wrong (again). He explained. "I spoke to the operator who answered your call", he wrote. "Her story is that she did understand that you wanted to speak in English ... but was not able to answer you in proper English and wanted to transfer you to a colleague who could do so. However, when completing the transfer, the line was interrupted. I am not sure what happened but she convinced me that she did not actively hang up on you."

The thing is, unlike Levi, I was sure what had happened. I know the difference between someone trying, and failing, to communicate with me and someone giving an irritated sigh. I also know the difference between being accidentally disconnected while the operator is transferring me and being hung up on. But Levi had decided − despite the numerous unpleasant incidents related to language intolerance that Peter and I had described to him − to believe that I was yet again mistaken and misunderstanding the best efforts of AMC staff to help me.

In order to demonstrate further to me that I was totally mistaken, Levi told me that he had asked a group of Masters students he was mentoring to phone the hospital on a number of occasions in November 2015 and January 2016 and to speak English to the operators, receptionists in the outpatients clinics and in radiology and to ask them questions. He was happy to tell me that none of the Masters students reported any "irregular behaviour". While I appreciated his enterprise in running this project, I don't think that Dutch-speaking medical students pretending they couldn't speak Dutch to their fellow countrymen is likely to result in a very realistic scenario. I had asked Levi to consider recording phone calls – and related to him how successful this had been in the case of the taxi company employee who had been so unpleasant in 2013 – but he had replied that patient confidentiality regulations meant that phone calls to hospitals could not be recorded. I'm not sure whether patients would object to this. I, for one, would be delighted if all calls were recorded – and all areas of the hospital equipped with CC-TV video and audio if the patients consented. Patients, and staff, would be a lot safer.

Towards the end of his email, Levi reprimanded me for the way I described incidents such as being hung up on, shouted at and staff suddenly forgetting how to understand or speak English once their colleagues had left the room. He said: "I must take exception to your use of words like 'offensive behaviour', 'mistreatment', 'abuse' or 'bullying'. That is certainly not what our staff is doing, for which I can vouch personally, and the use of these words certainly [does] not relate or contribute to the friendly and helpful atmosphere we want to create for our patients." I was seriously confused. I had described to this man how a physiotherapist had put her hands on her hips and shouted at me, "Why don't you speak Dutch? You live in the Netherlands!" when I was a post-operative patient in the ward in 2013. I had also described several of the other incidents to him, but the only thing he was "taking exception to" was how I was describing them. If such incidents are not "offensive behaviour", "mistreatment", "abuse" or "bullying", what is?

I started to realize that, as far as the AMC leadership was concerned, I was the problem. The incidents I was complaining about had simply never happened, and my saying that they had was what needed to be stopped.

When we had met in 2015, Marcel Levi had asked why, if staff were behaving in the way I described on as regular a basis as I seemed to think, he wasn't hearing complaints from other non-Dutch-speakers. I tried to explain to him that it was something I too had discussed with colleagues and other friends who didn't speak Dutch or who spoke only a little. While several who had been to AMC had told me that there had been comments about the fact that they lived in the Netherlands but didn't speak Dutch, they had decided not to make an issue of it. A very small percentage of hospital patients complains about anything at all that happens in hospitals. Patients are, by definition, sick; complaining is difficult and upsetting and they don't like alienating those looking after them. For foreigners, there are other forces at play too. When people are living in a foreign country, we often feel ashamed that we are not able to speak the language of our host country, or speak it well enough to cope while we are in hospital. As a result, foreign patients often feel guilty when someone points out that they have been living here for X number of years but can't speak Dutch. As a result, many of us feel it is, at least partly, *our fault*, and that our own shortcomings have caused the staff member to say what they said – and so we don't report it. It is, with a few exceptions, usually fairly low-level unpleasantness. Many of us also feel that reporting it would lead to more trouble for us, something I was beginning to see was absolutely the case. What we experience as non-Dutch-speaking foreigners in the Netherlands is a classic response to bullying – we are ashamed to be victims, and the less we draw attention to it, the fewer people we have to admit our shame to. That's a reasonable enough strategy, and often it works. In a lot of cases, we foreigners go home to our own countries if we can when we're seriously sick, and most of us who stay don't need ongoing treatment, so we don't have to come back to the hospital and experience the disagreeable comments repeatedly. That makes it easier to walk away and forget. My situation was different. I spent a lot of time in hospitals, particularly AMC. I was suffering from the cumulative effect of low-level unkindness as well as a handful of instances of pretty nasty bullying – and I was determined not to fall into the trap of blaming myself for the way a bigoted minority chose to treat non-Dutch-speaking patients.

★★★★★★★★★

The PET revealed no hotspots other than Tumour 2 and Tumour 3, which were still shining as bright as fairy lights in my pelvis. Surgery was scheduled for first thing on Monday, 7 March. Because there was an element of uncertainty about what he would find, Van der Velden wanted a bowel surgeon and a urological surgeon on standby. Imaging is never totally accurate, and it was still possible that Tumour 2 was adhered in some way to my colon, or attached to my ureter, from where removing it could compromise the ureter and the kidney. Van der Velden also wanted to have a general surgeon available too. Tumour 3 didn't appear to be attached to any organ, but removing it and the surrounding tissue was going to leave a "hole". Some reconstruction work would be needed. If Van der Velden couldn't do it himself, he'd need the input of another surgeon.

It was with a great deal of trepidation that I turned up at AMC the evening before the operation. Van der Velden had interrupted his Sunday evening to make sure I was settled and to discuss any outstanding issues. With his help, and the help of a friend, we had contacted the head nurse on the ward and explained my medical background and the unfortunate incidents there had been in the hospital during my previous admission because I couldn't speak Dutch. I was assured that everyone on the ward understood my circumstances, and efforts would be made to have just one nurse on each shift caring for me. Visiting times would be relaxed so that I could receive as much support as possible from family and friends. The gynaecology ward, H5 Zuid, was determined that my stay would be without incident and would be as stress-free as possible. They are, in the main, good and kind people. I set up a roster with some close friends who were willing to come and sit by me for a morning or afternoon to make my hospital stay less stressful, and give Peter an occasional break from the daily commute up and down to Amsterdam.

On the morning of the surgery, a nurse accompanied me downstairs to the pre-op area. She stayed as long as she was allowed to. Van der Velden came into the operating theatre before they put me under. It was reassuring to see him. I asked him to tell me what had happened in surgery as soon as I woke up.

"Patients often don't remember what's said immediately after surgery", he warned.

"I'll remember", I assured him.

And I did. What seemed like seconds after I was put under, I was aware of voices speaking to me in English. I was either throwing up or coughing out the intubation tube. Whatever it was, it seemed to be the right thing, as the voices continued to speak to me encouragingly. My eyes were still closed, but I heard Van der Velden's voice.

"What happened?" I asked him. "How did it go?"

"Everything was fine", he answered. "I got everything out. It was an ovary."

"Wow!" I exclaimed hoarsely, and promptly slipped back to the fuzz that follows a general anaesthetic.

Next time I came to, I was in post-op recovery. Gerard was looking after me. I remembered him from 2013. He was very kind. Van der Velden arrived shortly after with Peter in tow. They both looked very pleased.

Deny, dismiss, dehumanise

"It *was* an ovary", I told Peter.

"I know", said Peter, taking my hand.

Van der Velden said he'd come back later, smiled and walked away. I could tell he was really pleased. It must give doctors a tremendous buzz when things go well.

Over the days that followed, I basked in the knowledge that I was tumour-free. It mightn't last forever, but right now, I had no cancerous growths. All I had to do now was recover.

I was discharged as planned on Friday, 11 March, but found myself being readmitted the following Wednesday, 16 March. I had developed an infection in my abdominal wall. The pain there made it hard to empty my bladder, so another UTI had also kicked in.

I was horrified at finding myself back in H5 Zuid. Julia, one of the kindest and most understanding of nurses, helped to ease the shock by making me as comfortable as possible, and someone managed to find a vein for the IV drip. I was sent for another CT – my fourth or fifth since the start of the year. A student nurse, Naomi, came with me. The ward was still aware that I was afraid to go to other departments and take the risk that I would encounter more people with something hurtful to say about my lack of Dutch. I was glad of Naomi's company, and the other staff members were all kind and professional – even when I held up proceedings for half an hour because the cannula that had been put in earlier had stopped working and they had to send for an anaesthetist in order to give me the contrast dye.

The IV antibiotics kicked in and I began to feel a little better overnight. The CT scan was not giving enough information, so I was sent for an ultrasound. This time, another student, Eva, came along. It is a privilege to get to know these young nurses starting out on their careers. They are full of hope and compassion, and driven by a desire to use their skills to make a difference to the lives of others. But sometimes, when I talk to them, I fear for them.

Health systems can be as tough on nurses and doctors as they are on patients. It takes a strong constitution and a brave heart to hold onto the vision that brought them to the job in the first place. I knew H5 Zuid was a good place to train, but I had seen other wards and other hospitals where trainee nurses and doctors did not fare well.

My main worry now was that Van der Velden was going away on 18 March. We had always known this, and planned the surgery for 7 March so that I would be recovered before his departure. But we hadn't counted on infections. I was told that, Dr Gertje van Leen, would look after me in his absence. He reassured me that she would take good care of me, but I was afraid all the same when I said goodbye to him on Thursday evening.

On Friday morning, I was more comfortable and the pain had gone from a howling seven back down to a whimpering five. The antibiotics were doing their job. My cannula was blocked again, so I couldn't be given my Friday evening antibiotics until a new cannula was inserted. Netta and a student nurse, Sara, wheeled me down in my bed to the anaesthetists in post-op just before 18:00. I was still not anywhere near strong enough to go downstairs under my own steam. On the way down in the lift, Netta explained that they had to rush a urine sample (mine) to the laboratory before it closed, so they would not be able to stay with me in post-op. They had also not had their break yet. My heart missed a beat and fear clenched my stomach.

"That's okay", I said. "Everything will be fine."

The doctor who came to find a vein was kind and professional and we chatted away while she took her time making sure she had located a working vein. She pierced it and it co-operated first time. The cannula was in. Not one hundred per cent satisfied though, she said she wanted to ask her boss to take a look. A man arrived in the large bay where my bed was parked with an ultrasound machine. We could see the vein on the screen. He was kind too.

Deny, dismiss, dehumanise

He explained to me that it wasn't possible to see the cannula on the ultrasound because it was made of plastic. Anyway, he too was satisfied that the cannula was in place and went away. The first anaesthetists said to me, "I'll call your ward and tell them they can come and get you." I thanked her, and she left.

I had been aware that my phone had buzzed a few times while the vein hunt had been going on. It was the WhatsApp chat from my team at work deciding where to go for Friday drinks. Peter had been texting me too. I was replying to him when I heard someone call out to me. I looked up from my phone and saw two nurses walking past the bay I was parked in. They were wheeling another patient in a bed. One nurse, dressed in the white uniform of the wards, was pushing the bed and the other, dressed in the blue scrubs of the post-op unit was walking backwards and pulling the bed along with her. It was this nurse who was calling out to me. The only word I understood was *Mevrouw*, the Dutch form of address for women. It's used like the French, *Madame*.

"I'm sorry", I replied. "I don't understand."

"Ah! Hah! She doesn't understand!" came the ringing reply from the nurse, with the emphasis on the last syllable of the word "understand". It was accompanied by a side-to-side movement of her head and was at full volume. She finished with a loud laugh. Because she was walking backwards, I could see her face and I heard what she said, loud and clear. They were only a few metres away from me.

I was shocked. Even after all that had happened to me before, I couldn't believe that someone was ridiculing me at full volume for not understanding her, and then laughing. They continued steering the bed towards the doors. I called after her, "It's not *that* funny!" but my reply sounded shaky and lame. They didn't respond and continued walking out the doors to the lifts. They were bringing the patient back to her ward. I was very shaken and my heart was thudding in my chest. I struggled to stay calm and not get upset.

The nurse who had ridiculed and laughed came back through the doors a couple of minutes later. She walked over to my bed. I saw her coming, but didn't make eye contact. I didn't know what to expect.

"Hey", she said, nudging up against the end of my bed with her thigh, "What ward are you from?"

Without looking up, I mumbled, "H5 Zuid", and indicated the sheet of paper at the end of the bed that gave details of who I was and where I belonged.

"Ah, H5 Zuid", she acknowledged. "I will call them for you."

I mumbled thanks. She walked over to the white phone and I heard her speaking briefly to someone.

A few minutes later, Netta and Sara turned up to bring me back upstairs. When I saw them, I felt I had just been rescued. The emotion I had been keeping from erupting came to the surface and I started to cry. I tried to tell them what had happened.

"Who was it?" they asked. "Was it a doctor or a nurse?"

"I can't tell", I replied. "Everyone here wears scrubs, so it's hard to know. But she was pushing a bed, so I guess that means she's a nurse. Doctors don't push beds."

Just then, the laughing nurse came into view nearby.

"That's her!" I said. "That's the woman who mocked me for not understanding Dutch."

The woman walked away and Netta and Sara followed. Netta and Sara came back almost instantly with a man, also dressed in scrubs, but with a white coat over them.

"I'm Dr Karsen", he said. "I'm the registrar in charge of the ward this evening. What happened?"

I told him what had happened: that I had been looking at my phone, that one of the nurses had asked me something in Dutch as she passed by pulling a bed with another nurse, that I had replied that I didn't understand and then there had been this ridiculing out loud, "Ah! Hah! She doesn't understand!" And then the nurse had laughed out loud and walked away through the doors and out of the ward.

It was plain to see that Karsen was astonished.

"I find it impossible to believe that that could have happened", he began. "I know Sonja to be a compassionate nurse, and I can't imagine her doing that. I can't imagine her laughing at a patient."

"I'm not making this up", I told him. "She was looking straight at me. I heard exactly what she said. It was as clear as a bell, and as real as the conversation you and I are having right now."

"You're clearly not delusional", remarked Karsen. "And I understand why you would find such a thing, if it happened, very upsetting."

He wasn't intending to be cruel. I had seen this type of response before. As an experienced doctor in his early forties, Karsen "knew" with his rational mind that the patient in front of him was telling the truth and was not "delusional". But he could not – or did not want to – believe that a colleague, who he felt he knew well, could possibly have ridiculed a patient out loud for not understanding Dutch and then laughed at her. It was beyond his capacity to believe that such a thing could happen, let alone believe that it had just happened on his ward. I knew I was going to have an uphill struggle to get him to believe me, but I tried to explain again exactly what had occurred, with as much detail as I could remember. I was desperate for him to believe me.

After two or three minutes trying to persuade Karsen that I was telling the truth, another man joined the small group around my bed and the laughing nurse, Sonja, returned too.

"That's not me", she said emphatically. "I didn't say that. I didn't laugh at you."

It probably wasn't wise, but I started to argue with her. I knew what was going to happen. Everyone was going to believe her and not me. She is the healthy professional doing her job, I am just a patient — and patients are generally not seen to be reliable witnesses. We're sick, maybe we're on medication, maybe we're in pain — all of which call our judgement into question. I knew I was not on any medication other than IV antibiotics and paracetamol. I also knew that I had never in my life imagined that something was happening to me when it wasn't, or that someone had said something that they hadn't. I was as clear-headed as anybody working on that ward and I heard distinctly what Sonja had said when I apologized for not understanding her question. I had also seen her face and her head movements as she replied slowly and clearly in a sing-song voice, "Ah! Hah! She doesn't understand." And I saw her put her head back and laugh.

"I heard you clearly", I argued back to Sonja. "You made a smart comment in a sing-song voice about me not understanding and then laughed out loud. Why else would I have called after you, 'It's not *that* funny!'?"

Sonja was shaking her head.

"There was another nurse with you wheeling the bed", I continued. "Why don't we ask her what she saw and what she heard?"

"I will phone her right now and ask her if she heard me ridiculing you or laughing at you", countered Sonja.

"I think it would be a better idea if someone not involved spoke to her first", I replied quickly. I was afraid that Sonja would contact this independent witness from another ward and persuade her to vouch for her version of events. I sensed that loyalty to the colleagues one had to work with day-in, day-out ran deeper than loyalty to patients, who are outsiders, who come and go, and who no one really knows. And anyway, I was not the patient of the "witness nurse". She had no reason to back me up.

The other man who had turned up, but who hadn't introduced himself or hadn't spoken, exchanged a glance and a nod with Sonja. The message was to go away, but I'm not sure whether it

Deny, dismiss, dehumanise

was an instruction to go and call the witness nurse or to go away because her presence was making the situation worse. She left and I continued to try, and to fail, to make Karsen believe me. I could see he was conflicted. He couldn't really know who was telling the truth. On the face of it, it seemed that what I was describing so emphatically and clearly must have happened, but his mind, just *couldn't* allow the idea that it had happened.

Throughout the conversation, Sara had been holding my hand and the anaesthetist who had found the vein earlier had come back and was trying to help. Netta was trying to get me to take deep breaths, but there was absolutely nothing wrong with my breathing and I wasn't having a panic attack. I think they just wanted me to stop talking. They didn't like what I had to say. Karsen was still getting himself tied up in knots trying to persuade me that he understood how upset I was while denying that anything upsetting had happened. The others took their cue from him: whatever had happened to this patient, it wasn't what she said. I could think of nothing more I could say or do. In retrospect, I was sorry that I didn't ask Sonja to give her version of what had happened. All she had said was that it hadn't happened. I hadn't noticed this at the time, because I knew exactly what *had* happened, so the absence of another version of events didn't seem like an omission. It was only later that it dawned on me that she had given no explanation of what she thought had taken place.

Netta wanted to bring me back to the ward. I was getting nowhere, so I agreed. Back in my room on H5 Zuid, Sara and Netta hooked up the antibiotics now that I had a working cannula and asked if there was anything I needed. I assured them there was nothing, but asked them to close the doors of my room. I just needed to be on my own for a while. They left, closing the doors behind them. They still hadn't had their break.

I concentrated on trying to calm down properly. I meditated a bit. It was going to take a while, but I had at least stopped crying.

Then the door opened and a woman walked in. I knew it was Dr Gertje van Leen, who was looking after me while Van der Velden was away. I had never met her, but I recognized her from her photo on the gynaecological oncologists' website. I had been hoping to be the model patient in Van der Velden's absence, but as soon as Van Leen asked me how I was, the whole story of the nasty episode in post-op came tumbling out. She listened carefully and then won my undying gratitude by believing me. She had never met me before, but I knew that she believed I was telling her the truth. That alone made such a difference. Being bullied is devastating, but not being believed afterwards compounds the hurt. When I realized I didn't have to try to convince her I was telling the truth, I relaxed. I told her something of the other experiences that I had had over the previous three years at AMC. She listened. She believed me about those events too. She didn't try to persuade me that I was exaggerating, or misunderstanding, or being too sensitive, or misinterpreting friendly banter. She simply believed that what I was telling her was true and that it had happened just as I said. She didn't seem all that surprised either.

"So it's not about language, it's about power", she summarized, when I had finished. She was absolutely right. She had hit the nail on the head.

She stayed for a while and we talked a bit. After she left, Sara came in to see how I was. She checked the drip to make sure the antibiotics were going through the line, asked if I was comfortable, gave me some paracetamol and then made to leave again. But she stopped at the door and came back.

"You are absolutely right to fight back", she said, surprising me totally. "I know there are people who have things to say about people who don't speak Dutch. You are very brave. Keep doing what you're doing." Then she turned and left.

I hadn't replied to her. I was too surprised. I'll reply now. Bless you Sara. Your words gave me courage when I needed it, and

Deny, dismiss, dehumanise

gave me faith in the goodness and compassion of the majority of people working in AMC. It is partly down to you that this book got written. I don't know how else to "fight back".

19 | May 2016… Bronovo Hospital, The Hague

What I propose, therefore, is very simple: it is nothing more than to think what we are doing
Hannah Arendt

I wasn't long out of my room in AMC's H5 Zuid when urosepsis struck again. As with the two bouts in 2015 and again in January, it came on suddenly. I had been warned that urosepsis was potentially fatal. I had been warned to look out for the symptoms and to contact the hospital right way if I had a fever and suspected I had urosepsis again.

So when I woke up on the morning of 12 May, vomiting, with cloudy urine and a temperature of 38.6, I rang Bronovo. Peter and I were there by 9:00, and I was sent to the lab to give a urine sample. Back at urology outpatients, I was told to go home and someone would ring me later to tell me if I had an infection. I told the receptionist that I was already certain that I had urosepsis, and wasn't happy to go home without speaking to a doctor. I was told that it was very busy that morning. I insisted. I was told I could wait in the waiting room and Dr Hoevenaar would try to fit me in at the end of his morning surgery.

Deny, dismiss, dehumanise

The JJ-stent that had been inserted in January was still in place. I already had an appointment to have it changed in two weeks' time, on 25 May. It had been in situ longer than normal, but because I had had major surgery in March, followed by two post-operative infections, there hadn't been an opportunity yet to replace it safely. Unfortunately, my body had decided that it wasn't able to manage another two weeks, and had succumbed to another bout of urosepsis.

After about half an hour, my own doctor, Van Houten, joined Hoevenaar for the outpatients' clinic. He saw me immediately, and confirmed within an instant that I had urosepsis and needed to be kept in hospital.

"I'm going to have to admit you", he told us. He saw my face. He remembered what had happened the last time I was in Bronovo.

"Can I not just come back into Emma ward every day for antibiotics?" I pleaded. The prospect of again being sent to that crazy ward I had walked out of after an hour in January horrified me. I was feeling really sick and knew I wouldn't be able for that.

"I think the responsible thing is to admit you", persisted Van Houten.

"Another hospital then", I tried. "Antoniushove, maybe? Westeinde?"

Van Houten promised to see what he could do, and in the meantime, I was sent back to the lab to have bloods taken and then for a CT. He would see me afterwards.

I collected the various lots of paperwork from reception and went to the lab. I was finding it hard to stand and walk, even sitting in the chairs at outpatients had been desperately uncomfortable. I hadn't yet fully recovered from the surgery and post-operative infections two months earlier in AMC, and now the vomiting and dehydration and going from floor to floor in the hospital had me feeling weak. While the nurses were taking the blood they needed, I did something I never do. I started to pass out. I had almost fainted once before and knew the warning signs. First, I started to yawn uncontrollably, then I started to throw up. The nurses raised my legs and opened the window, and I stayed conscious.

I didn't want to miss my CT slot, so after ten minutes' rest, I went to Radiology on the ground floor. I missed my friend, the transport lady. I could have done with her help that day.

By the time we got back to urology outpatients, they had all gone to lunch and the clinic was closed. To ensure my place in the afternoon queue, I dragged a chair across to the reception desk and prepared for the 20-minute wait for Van Houten's return. When he walked past with Hoevenaar five minutes before the start of afternoon surgery, he found me asleep in the chair at reception.

Van Houten had already received the urine results, which verified that I had an infection, and the CT results, which showed that my left kidney was dilated again. I had urosepsis and hydronephrosis. I needed IV antibiotics immediately and might need a replacement of the JJ stent the following morning. He said that although he could get a bed for me, and probably my own room, in Antoniushove, he didn't want to send me there.

"You might need to have your kidney drained manually", he explained. "That has to be done by an intervention radiologist, and there's none in Antoniushove. It would be irresponsible to send you there now only to have you brought back here again tomorrow because they couldn't treat you. There's also a chance that you might need to have another JJ-stent inserted in theatre tomorrow, rather than waiting until 25 May."

Sick as I was, I knew this made sense. But I really didn't want to face the chaos of the ward that I had been in in January. Van Houten said that I would be admitted to a different ward, Henriette. I had to give them the benefit of the doubt. I realized that Van Houten didn't have much choice. He had a patient with sepsis and she needed to be admitted, now. I agreed. I didn't have a choice either.

In Henriette, I was deposited in room 314 just before 14:00. Peter was still with me. The room was an exact replica of the small, four-bed room I had been admitted to in January, and was just as chaotic. All three other beds were occupied by men. They looked despondent. A nurse called Ilse told me in a loud voice to ring the bell if I needed anything and promptly left. That was all she said. No details were taken from me. No vital measurements such as temperature, blood oxygen and BP were taken. Nobody asked me if I was in pain. Nobody discussed with me what treatment I would receive. In fact, apart from being given the bell in a very loud voice, nobody spoke to me at all.

Because I had been admitted to hospitals before with urosepsis, I expected that the nurses would be trying to get an IV line into me as soon as possible to give me paracetamol to get the fever down, and to start me on fluids and IV antibiotics. I was also expecting that someone would ask me if I was able to urinate. I had been aware for the past couple of hours that I was not peeing. I knew this was not right. I was expecting the nurses to tell me I'd need a catheter.

None of the things I would have expected to happen to a repeat urosepsis patient with a blocked ureter, a swollen kidney, a four-month old JJ-stent, a high temperature, a full bladder, level-7 pain and PTSD was happening. Over 45 minutes passed, but after my brief conversation with Ilse, nobody had come near me. Nobody seemed aware that I was on the ward. I knew I was in trouble, so I started looking for help.

I had noticed a pleasant nurse coming into the room from time to time, dealing with the other patients. She wasn't coming over to me though. I knew I wasn't her patient, but I figured she was my best chance. I called out to her as she passed my bed and asked if my antibiotics were coming soon. She knew nothing about antibiotics. I asked her to find out what was happening and told her that Ilse was looking after me, I thought.

The nice nurse returned shortly after and said that I had to have IV antibiotics. The doctor had sent the prescription to the pharmacy. I told her I knew this, that the doctor had explained what was going on and that I had had the symptoms of urosepsis since 06:00 that morning, some nine hours previously. She said they hadn't been ordered from the pharmacy yet by the ward, and that she'd chase them herself. She was now the only nurse looking after the four patients in room 314.

The nice nurse obligingly did what I asked, but I knew it wasn't right that I'm the one asking for my medication to be ordered up from the pharmacy, that *I'm* going to have to explain that I need an IV put in by an anaesthetist, that I need my temperature and BP to be measured and that I need a bladder scan. I shouldn't be the person in charge of my own treatment when I'm admitted to a hospital ward. I couldn't understand why there had been no admissions procedure why no one had spoken with me to get information and discuss treatment. I wasn't sure which nurse was supposed to be looking after me and there didn't seem to be any senior nurse in charge making sure things were done. There also didn't seem to be any doctors on the ward. Nobody appeared to be aware that I had a serious infection, and, most worrying to me, no one was aware of my medical history or the fact that I was a cancer patient who was terminally ill because – and only because – of an error made at UMC Utrecht. I was terrified. And so was Peter. Like me, he had seen urosepsis in action before, and like me, he knew how serious it could be and how fast I could go downhill.

In the corridor, Peter overheard the nice nurse on the phone looking for my antibiotics. He went out and told her a little about my medical history – terminal cancer diagnosis, the medical error, my frequent bouts of urosepsis, the PTSD and the difficulty I had being in hospital. She nodded, but didn't seem to register

Deny, dismiss, dehumanise

what he was saying. In her defence, she was rushed off her feet — and I wasn't her patient.

I rang the bell. I wanted to explain everything to someone in charge of me. It wasn't fair to be hassling the nice nurse. Ilse came into the room and turned off the bell. Even though she knew from earlier that I didn't understand Dutch, she started asking me something in Dutch before I had a chance to say why I had called. I figured out from the fingers she was wrapping around her own wrist that she was asking whether I had a wristband. I told her I hadn't. She insisted on seeing my left wrist, which was under the sheet. I showed her that that wrist was also bare. She made an annoyed noise, threw her eyes up to the ceiling and left the room. I never saw her again.

Two of the other patients in the room, both elderly men, were receiving physiotherapy. First one, then the other. Both physiotherapists were speaking "at" the patients in loud voices. The men replied in normal voices. They were obviously not hard of hearing. There was little engagement between the patients and the physiotherapists, and no warmth.

The nice nurse came and told me the antibiotics had just been ordered. It was now a little after 15:00, and I had been on the ward over an hour. I explained that I had bad veins and that each time I needed a cannula, I had to go to the anaesthetists or to intensive care. To her credit, she believed me and rang the pre-op ward and wheeled me there herself. She noticed as we were leaving Henriette that I had no wristband. I told her I thought Ilse was making one for me. She said nothing and went into a small cubicle in the corridor and made me a wristband herself before continuing to the anaesthetists.

Unfortunately, Marius and the other anaesthetists who had looked after me so well in January were not in evidence that day. Instead, there was the same fraught and irritable atmosphere that there had been on the first evening I had been there, when they were unable to find a vein. The nice nurse explained the problem to one of the anaesthetists who, without speaking to me or looking at me, took hold of my left arm. He then began to point to what he thought was an obvious vein, and berated the nurse for not making any attempt herself to insert the cannula. I was only able to follow bits of his reprimand, but when I saw the nice nurse looking embarrassed from her unreasonable dressing down, I jumped in.

"It's not her fault", I said. "I told her that it was always very hard to find my veins and that I always needed anaesthetists. I'm very dehydrated at the moment from vomiting, so I assumed it would be difficult again today to find a working vein."

The angry anaesthetist looked at me in astonishment. My impression was that he was surprised that patients could talk at all. He still didn't say anything to me, but he pulled over one of the trolleys with cannulas and tourniquets and chose a pink cannula. Normally, I'd have advised any doctor that the smaller, blue, cannula was much more likely to be effective in my veins. But I figured my attempts to communicate with this guy had already got me into his bad books. So I bit my tongue – and let him find out the hard way, at my expense.

With about as much gentleness as a country vet wrestling an unco-operative cow, he stuck the needle into where he saw this perfect vein. It hurt like hell. I have had several dozen cannulas in my arms and hands over the years. I know some degree of pain is unavoidable, but this was off-the-scale pain. It wasn't right.

"That hurts like hell!" I told him. "There's something wrong. It shouldn't be that painful!"

He tried injecting some fluid into it, and it wouldn't go in. He tried tweaking it this way and that, but whatever he did, he couldn't get any blood out or fluid in. His efforts were punctuated with exclamations of, "Eh? Eh?" and he looked totally bewildered as to why the cannula wasn't working.

Deny, dismiss, dehumanise

"It's not in properly", I told him. "Please take it out!"

It's probably not a great idea to tell a grouchy anaesthetist his job, but whatever had happened with the cannula in my arm, it was extremely painful. He continued to tweak it, causing more pain each time he touched it. I tried again, a little louder this time, hoping to attract the attention of some colleagues working nearby.

"Please just take it out", I begged. "It's obviously not in properly. I have had dozens of these and I know that there's something wrong."

It had the desired effect. Two colleagues started to come over to us.

"Alright! Alright! I'm taking it out! I'm taking it out!" he snapped.

"Please stay here", I said to the two colleagues.

They watched him take it out. The unkind anaesthetist turned to the nurse who had brought me from the wards and started to snap at her again. He was telling her to go back to the ward. Again, I intervened. I wanted this nurse to stay with me. She was the only kind person I had encountered since my admission an hour-and-a-half earlier.

"Please let her stay with me", I pleaded. "I asked her to stay with me throughout. I trust her."

But the man wanted her gone.

"She has work to do", he said. "She can't waste time standing around waiting for you. Someone else will bring you back afterwards."

One of the watching colleagues intervened.

"My name is Caroline", she said. "Will you let me try to find a vein? I will stay with you while you're here and make sure you get back to the ward afterwards."

"Will you stay with me throughout and not go off and leave me?" I asked.

She promised she would. The unkind anaesthetist got up and

walked away without any more comment to anyone. I'm used to being bruised from needle-sticks, but the huge bruise that was left on my arm was the largest and blackest bruise I have ever seen. It remained on my left arm for months.

Caroline was as good as her word. It took her a long time to find a vein, but eventually she had the smaller, blue cannula inserted in the underside of my right wrist and I was ready to go back to Henriette.

I didn't know at the time, but in the 45 minutes or so I was away, Peter had again explained my circumstances to another of the nurses on Henriette. He told her that there was a full medical history in my file from my previous admission in January. He told her too about the medical negligence at another hospital and the terror of hospitals I had as a result and my bouts of urosepsis. She listened politely, but didn't reply, and didn't seem to understand what point he was making. I wasn't her patient either.

When I arrived back on the ward, I urgently needed to pee. I called the kind nurse over, and she directed me towards two doors in the corner of the room. I hadn't noticed them before because they were so close to the bed just inside the door. I had to squeeze past one of the other patients who was sitting on a chair beside his bed. I apologized for disturbing him and he smiled.

The first door I opened was the wrong one. It was the shower. The second door revealed a tiny toilet. It stank. The toilet seat was wet and the floor around it was wet and soiled. This tiny toilet was to be shared by four patients. It was far too filthy for me to sit on and use. I started to clean it with thin, hospital toilet paper. I remembered that when I'd stayed in this hospital in January, no one had cleaned the bathroom the entire week I had been there. Peter had brought sponges and cleaners from home and we had done it ourselves. But this was different. I couldn't be expected to clean a shared toilet.

Whether it was the smell and general dirtiness of the toilet or

Deny, dismiss, dehumanise

the state of my own bladder, I found I still couldn't pee much. This was pretty typical of urosepsis, and needed to be dealt with. I was certain I needed to be catheterized. I washed my hands thoroughly and went back to bed. The short journey to the toilet had left me weak and shaky. The pain was getting worse. I flopped into bed.

Where were the antibiotics? Where was the paracetamol to bring down my temperature? It was now after 16:00. I had been in the ward two hours and had been in the hospital since 9:00 that morning. I was burning up. Still no one had taken my temperature or my blood pressure. No one seemed to know I was septic, and that I urgently needed antibiotics, fluids and paracetamol. I wasn't able to look after myself any more. But none of the nurses seemed to know what I needed.

I called the nice nurse again and told her that I couldn't pee and needed to be catheterized. She nodded.

"I have had no antibiotics yet", I told her. "And I really need something to bring down my temperature. Have you paracetamol for me?"

She told me that the paracetamol would have to be given IV too because I was still nauseous. She would go again and look for the antibiotics.

Peter was at the end of my bed trying to be patient. We were horrified that nearly two-and-a-half hours after admission and seven hours after arriving at the hospital, I had still not received any medication whatsoever and no one seemed to be responsible for looking after me. The noise in the room was now a risen to a crescendo – dragged chairs, chattering and laughing visitors and general hospital clatter. Peter went to talk to the nurses a third time.

At the nurses' station, he explained yet again, as urgently as he could, that I was very distressed and needed treatment now. He told the nurse that I had a history of urosepsis, that I was terminally ill, that my entire medical history had been explained in detail when I had been a patient in Bronovo in January, and that it was available to her in my file. He told her that we had been assured then that we would never again be put in a situation in Bronovo where we had to explain my distressing story to yet more staff. He stressed that everyone who has ever been involved in my treatment has agreed that it is essential for them to know these aspects of my medical history. Everything she needed to know was in the hospital system, in my file, but no one was looking at it.

The nurse listened to him in silence. When he finished, she said nothing at all, and made it very clear through her silence, facial expressions and stance throughout that she had no interest. At that point, in an attempt to get through to her he said "There are two doctors in the hospital that know all about Adrienne's history, Dr Zander van Houten in urology and Dr Janke Molenaar in gynaecology. They will verify that what I'm telling you is true. Can you contact them?" Still no response. He was getting nowhere and was conscious that he had left me alone for too long. He said he was going back to me and walked away.

Back in Room 314, I had a put pillow over my head to block out the noise. While my inability to deal with noise was absolutely a symptom of my sepsis, it was, objectively, really very noisy in the room. There were now four patients and six visitors. The cumulative effect in that tiny room was a cacophony. The light from the window opposite me was blazing in and my eyes were throbbing painfully.

When he came back, Peter took the pillow off my head as he was afraid I would overheat or suffocate. I just wanted silence and darkness. He pulled the curtains around my bed, but that couldn't blot out the noise. I couldn't cope any more. I put the pillow back over my head and tried to escape.

A few minutes later, a nurse I hadn't seen before suddenly pulled aside the curtains at the opposite side of my bed from Peter. She was the nurse with whom Peter had been speaking at the nurses' station. Her body language and facial expression

Deny, dismiss, dehumanise

were very annoyed. Ignoring me, she said loudly to Peter across my bed, "Can I talk to you outside?" and indicated towards the door. Quite rightly, Peter had no intention of going anywhere with someone who was visibly angry. I said to her, "Please stop shouting. Please get me out of here. I simply can't deal with this any more." She ignored me and continued to insist that Peter go outside with her. I was terrified that she was going to make him leave the ward. Then I would be totally on my own and I knew I was no longer able to look after myself. I don't know her name. She never said who she was.

At about 16:20, the nice nurse turned up with the antibiotics and paracetamol. She explained she could only give them through the drip one at a time. She would give me the paracetamol first because the antibiotics took much longer to be delivered. I told her again that I couldn't pee. It still didn't seem to register. She promised I'd get the antibiotics as soon as the paracetamol was finished. She had picked up that there had been a disagreement with the angry nurse. I told her it didn't involve her. She had been kind to me from the beginning, and I wasn't even her patient.

"Whose patient are you?", she asked.

"I don't know", I replied. "Ilse's, I think."

The angry nurse who had wanted to remove Peter from my bedside came back and said gruffly that she was looking for a solution. I asked her what solutions there were. She replied in a very irritated way that she didn't know what the solution was until she found it. She said she'd look for earplugs for me because at this stage even she could hear that the noise levels were intense. I felt as though I were in a busy, noisy and dangerous public place. The PTSD makes it terrifying for me to be in this type of chaos in a hospital. I never got those earplugs, but I probably wouldn't have used them anyway as they would have added to my disorientation and would have meant that there was no way of communicating with me.

Shortly after 16:30, a different nurse and a woman in ordinary clothes arrived at my bed and spoke to me. I had to explain (for the fourth or fifth time that afternoon) that I didn't understand. They were surprised. No one had mentioned that I didn't speak Dutch. No one ever mentions this to their colleagues. The woman's name was Manuela Lucas. She was in charge of the ward. She said she wanted to have a conversation with me. I said we couldn't have a conversation there because there was no privacy. The three other patients and their five visitors all had a full view and full audio of what was happening at my bed. I was conscious of being a sideshow playing out with a lot of spectators who should not have been hearing about my medical details or seeing how ill I was.

Mrs Lucas gave a signal to the nurse and they wheeled me out of the room. The instant silence was pure bliss. I was brought down a long corridor, past the black-and-white picture of a woman whom I assumed must be Queen Henriette. I'm not sure these black-and-white images of severe figures from the dour past gladden the hearts of passing patients. Lucas opened the door to Room 340 and I was wheeled in. The cool silence within was a blessed relief. I had been at the end of my tether. I had tears of gratitude as I thanked her for her kindness.

"It's okay, you can stay here", she said, patting my hand.

For some time, I lay, and Peter sat, in the cool, quiet room drinking in the silence and the calm. It was just after 17:00, and the paracetamol drip had finished. The nurse who had been with Lucas came in at around 17:20 to finally give me the antibiotics – three hours and twenty minutes after I had been admitted and eight-and-a-half hours after we had arrived at the hospital. I told her too that I had been unable to empty my bladder all day. She told me that I'd be able to manage better later. She also told me that I would be able to stay in Room 340. I drifted off to sleep, and so did Peter, exhausted from the sheer stress of the day.

Shortly after 18:00, Van Houten arrived. He had been in

Deny, dismiss, dehumanise

surgery at another hospital all afternoon. We told him something of what had happened since I left outpatients four hours earlier. I told him about my concerns about not emptying my bladder. He instructed me to try again to pee and went off to find a nurse. He came back on his own with a bladder scan. Despite having my own, clean, toilet, I was still unable to pee and the scan revealed that I was retaining over 500mls of urine – about the maximum quantity the average female bladder should hold. Van Houten looked again for a nurse, before deciding to catheterize me himself. This could have, and should have, been done four hours earlier when I was first admitted.

Van Houten told me that he would be away the following day and that Theo Hoevenaar would look after me. He might want to replace the JJ-stent, and because of that, I would have to fast from midnight. No problem. Food was way down my list of priorities. All I wanted to do was rest and sleep in the cool silence of my room.

20 | May 2016 ... Bronovo Hospital, The Hague

The single biggest problem in communication is the illusion that it has taken place.
George Bernard Shaw

Peter and I had had the afternoon from hell, but we didn't realize that we would have to go through it all again the following day. Nothing that had happened during the eventful afternoon of 12 May was entered into my nursing notes. The next shifts came on duty knowing nothing about my urosepsis, my PTSD, my terror of hospitals, my medical history, the delay treating me when I was admitted – and not knowing that I had been promised I could stay in Room 340.

At 8:00 the next morning, Friday 13 May, Hoevenaar did his rounds. He saw that I was responding well to the antibiotics and decided not to replace the JJ-stent. It could wait until the scheduled surgery on 25 May. He told me that I would have to stay in hospital until Monday or Tuesday, would need to remain catheterized until the following day, and would have to stay on IV antibiotics, possibly until the JJ-stent was changed. During this conversation, he was accompanied by a nurse from the night shift.

Deny, dismiss, dehumanise

What Hoevenaar said was not passed on to the nursing day shift. They got the message that I would not be going to surgery, but didn't know what was wrong with me, what my treatment plan was, or whether I was to be discharged.

Over the next hour or so, several nurses came in, one at a time, to question me. Each time, I explained I couldn't speak Dutch. Each time, they were very surprised. Each asked what the doctor had said, why I was in this room, and what my treatment plan was.

At around 9:00, a fourth nurse, this time from another ward, arrived with the belongings of his patient, who was going to be brought to Room 340 when she was out of surgery. He stuck a printout of her name on one of the cupboard doors, locked her belongings inside, and placed her slippers under the bed furthest away from me. I was, it seemed, going to have a roommate.

Some time after, a fifth nurse came in, again surprised to find I couldn't understand her.

"Do you know what your treatment plan is?" she asked.

I explained yet again what Hoevenaar had said.

"Well, you know more than we do then", replied the nurse, a bit miffed at not having been informed.

"You can't stay in this room though, because it's closed", she added.

I pointed out that the belongings of another patient had just been placed in a cupboard with her name on it and that her slippers were under the bed.

"That's complicated …" the nurse began. "That's something different … it's to do with another ward. This room is closed. We'll be moving you to another room."

"But this room isn't closed if another patient is in here", I persisted pointing to the bed with the pair of slippers underneath. "And Manuela Lucas told me yesterday, twice, that I could stay here."

"She meant you could stay here just for yesterday", replied the nurse authoritatively. "We'll move you to a room with just one or two others in it."

I was shaking my head. That wasn't what Lucas had said, and I was sure it wasn't what she had meant.

"A room with just ladies in it then", the nurse cajoled.

I became upset and told her that Manuela Lucas had said I could stay here. I asked to speak to Lucas. I was troubled that again nobody seemed to know anything about me – least of all what was wrong with me. I was right back to the madness of the previous afternoon.

"We'll have to talk to the nurse", the nurse replied confusingly and walked out of the room.

Ten minutes later, yet another nurse came in, the sixth that morning. As had the others, he began speaking to me in Dutch, and again I apologized and explained I couldn't speak Dutch.

"Oh, I'm sorry", he replied. "Nobody told me. My English is not so good, but I'll try", he smiled at me. "My name is Willem. Can you tell me why you're here, what your treatment plan is, and why you have been put into this room? We don't know anything about you."

I was close to losing it. But I could see that this kind man was doing his best.

"Did nobody tell you what happened yesterday?", I asked. "It must all be in the nursing notes from yesterday afternoon. My husband gave them all the information about my medical history." I said. "Mrs Lucas knows." His face remained blank and he shook his head.

"You know nothing about the urosepsis, the PTSD, the medical negligence, my fear of hospitals and my terminal cancer?" I asked, despair creeping into my voice.

"No, we know nothing", replied Willem kindly. "But you can tell me now. I need to know why you were put into this room.

Deny, dismiss, dehumanise

You shouldn't be here."

I started to cry. The prospect of telling the whole sorry story to yet another person was exhausting. I couldn't believe I would have to fight to keep the peace and privacy that Lucas had offered yesterday. And even more worrying, this man plainly had no idea why I was on his ward.

I tried again. "Janke Molenaar wrote my full medical history into my file last December, on New Year's Eve. She said I would never again have to tell my story in this hospital."

"I can see nothing in your medical file", continued Willem. "But tell me. I want to help."

Having no other option, I told my story again. I stumbled through what had happened in UMCU, what had happened in other hospitals that had made it worse (including the wrong kidney episode in Bronovo in January), my terror of being in hospital and the disbelief I felt that after explaining all this at great cost the previous day, still nobody knew anything about me. It was terrifying me that the nurses on this shift had had no communication from the previous day, or even about what the doctor had said that morning. At the best of times, I don't feel safe, but it was seriously frightening me that Peter and I had to keep explaining to a constant flow of new nurses who never passed on a word of what we said. For any patient, this would be stressful, for a patient with PTSD, it was a nightmare.

Willem listened patiently. Somehow, he made sense of what I was saying through my tears and frustration. He promised that he would enter everything into the system and that I would never again have to tell it to a new shift of nurses. He agreed that everyone looking after me absolutely needed to know my distressing medical history, and promised that no one would treat me who didn't know my background and my terror of being in hospital. He promised that only one person on each shift would be in charge of looking after me, and that while I would be removed from Room 340 because it was "closed", I would go to a one-bed room so my husband and friends could be with me for as much of the day and night as we wanted without disturbing other patients. I really wanted to believe him, but I didn't dare.

Shortly after Willem left, Peter phoned. I filled him in on the morning's events. He turned up at the hospital shortly afterwards and could see that I was weary. I was also hungry. He offered to go to the cafeteria downstairs to get me a coffee and something to eat. Because I was in a "closed" room, food was not finding its way to me. I had received no meal the previous evening and had missed the breakfast trolley that morning.

Fortunately, while Peter was gone, I fell asleep and had no idea that he was gone well over an hour. This is what he did.

First, he went to the nurses' station to find out why there had been such a breakdown in communication. Willem admitted that he couldn't explain why still no one knew the medical history. Peter had told three nurses the previous day, or why nobody knew what Hoevenaar had decided when he made his rounds with a nurse at eight that morning.

Peter then tried to find Ankie Smeets, Bronovo's now all too familiar complaints officer. There was just a recorded message on her phone, so he went to the 4th floor. Her office was empty and a woman in an office nearby said that Smeets was not in the hospital that morning. She also told him that Smeets has no deputy. Peter asked if she could tell him the name of the person in charge of nursing. He was told that there was nobody in charge of nursing, that each ward had a manager. He asked to speak to the manager of Henriette ward. The helpful woman made several phone calls. The manager of Henriette, Manuela Lucas, was not in the hospital that day. Peter asked to speak to the chief executive or someone from the chief executive's office. Again, there was no one available to speak to him.

Peter asked, "Are you saying to the husband of a seriously

sick patient who is having ongoing problems on Henriette that there is nobody in the entire hospital that I can talk to about it or who can help us?"

He suggested that he'd sit down in this lady's office until somebody was found who was willing to address the situation, or else she could call the police and get them to remove him, if they felt that was appropriate after hearing what he had to say.

She offered Peter a cup of tea, and started making phone calls. She found a manager of one of the other wards who was willing to cover for the absent manager of Henriette. This manager, Lisette Beugelsdijk, arrived after five or ten minutes. Peter asked her how it could have happened that none of the medical information he had given to the nurses on Henriette the previous day was known to any of the nursing staff that morning and how none of the nurses knew what his wife's treatment plan was despite the fact that the doctor had done his rounds at eight that morning, in the company of a nurse. Peter told her that the last words he had exchanged with Manuela Lucas the previous evening when he met her by chance in the corridor were to thank her for understanding the situation and for putting his wife in a quiet room. She had replied to him, "Your wife can stay there". Yet by the following morning, no one knew any of the medical history that had been told in such distress the previous day. There was no record of it, and there was no record of Lucas, the manager of the ward, instructing that I was to be left in Room 340.

Peter also told Lisette Beugelsdijk that Henriette was out of control. He described what had happened the previous afternoon, when I had waited for nearly three-and-a-half hours for antibiotics to treat my sepsis. She suggested calling Hoevenaar. Peter replied that what was happening was purely a nursing issue and had nothing whatsoever to do with Hoevenaar, who would be unable to help. She said she would make enquiries and get back to Peter as soon as she could. Peter thanked her for her time and returned to room 340, remembering to pick me up a coffee and sandwich along the way.

The coffee began to do its job and I gradually realized Peter had been gone for ages while I had slept. As he was telling me what happened, Willem came in, followed by Lisette Beugelsdijk. Theo Hoevenaar showed up too, although we had not asked for him. Both Peter and I reassured him that what he had said that morning had been crystal clear and that the issues we had were one hundred per cent to do with nursing on the ward and total lack of communication. Having confirmed his instructions with me, Hoevenaar left and let the managers sort out the nursing problem.

Beugelsdijk reinforced and wrote down what Willem and I had agreed earlier and things settled down for 48 hours. As promised, I was moved to a single room. Beugelsdijk drew up a list of the nurses on each shift for the coming weekend who would be looking after me. Where possible, it would be the same nurse each day. I was promised that everyone on the ward would be made aware of my history and that no one who didn't know my history would treat me. She also said she would try to find out why nobody seemed to be able to see the medical history Janke Molenaar had put in my file. Willem said he would write a summary of it and put it into the system for the nurses. Peter and I were even promised an evening meal. (It never turned up though because I had moved to another room by dinner time. But food was not our priority.) This arrangement was largely stuck to throughout the weekend, thanks to the efforts of Willem and another nurse, Paul.

Hoevenaar arrived alone to do his rounds the next morning. He's not the chatty type. He likes to affect a gruff exterior and a saturnine temperament. But that's fine with me. I didn't feel much like chatting either. So I was a little surprised when he raised the matter of the previous day's fiasco. I filled him in on what had happened. He shook his head despondently.

"Do me a favour?" he asked.

Deny, dismiss, dehumanise

"What?" I replied, surprised.

"Make a complaint. We can't change anything because nobody ever complains."

Inside, I groaned. Was I destined to spend the rest of my life making complaints to hospitals, I wondered.

"I don't know", I replied. "I've spent the past three years in battles with hospitals. This is not even my country."

He nodded his understanding, but I felt he was thinking, "Here's another one who won't complain, typical."

"I'll think about it", I promised. "I totally get what you're saying."

"Just five or six sentences", he encouraged. "That's all that's needed."

I nodded. I knew I'd probably do what he asked. He was right. Maybe it would help. I didn't think I'd manage to stick to five or six sentences though.

I saw him again the following morning. It was a holiday weekend, and he was the urologist on duty across all three hospitals in The Hague. We didn't say anything more to each other about making a complaint. He was back to his moody, brusque self. And what I had planned made him even crankier. I was feeling considerably better – and I wanted out of the hospital. I remembered that in January, I had been on the same IV antibiotic as I was on now, and I had been able to come to the day-patient ward, Emma, every day for an hour for antibiotics. I had persuaded Paul, the nurse looking after me that morning, to ask if I could continue my treatment as an outpatient. Hoevenaar wasn't happy. He grumped at me for a bit – and then went away and made arrangements to discharge me. I would have to return to Henriette the following afternoon, Whit Monday, for my next dose because Emma would not be back in business until Tuesday.

I was free. Paul was on the afternoon shift again the next day, and when I arrived, he hooked me up to the antibiotic drip, flushed the line afterwards, and I was ready to go home within the hour. Before I left, Paul reassured me that he and Willem had written all the necessary information about me into the system, so that when I went to Emma next day, they would know who I was and what antibiotic I needed, would understand my history and be aware of my tremendous fear of hospitals.

When we arrived on Emma the following day, no one knew anything about me. I was quizzed by a tetchy receptionist who could see absolutely zero reference to me in her list for the day.

"You were last here on 12 May?" she asked, peering quizzically at her screen.

"Not really", I replied, trying to stay Zen. "I was an in-patient from the 12th to the 15th and I came back to Henriette yesterday for IV antibiotics."

I invited her to phone Henriette, who would corroborate my story and explain what I needed. She declined. I offered to go to Henriette, just across the hallway, and get someone to phone her. She ignored me and continued to look at the computer. The spectre that I would have to start all over again not just explaining my story, but telling people what antibiotics I was supposed to have and for how long, started to rise up again. The receptionist started making phone calls. I was ordered to go and wait in Room 372. It wasn't very polite. There was no reassurance that everything would be okay, that the antibiotics would be found, or that she'd sort it out. It wasn't, as it turned out, a big problem, or indeed, an unusual problem, but I had seen before how small problems quickly got out of control at this hospital.

I didn't know what else to do, so I phoned Ankie Smeets. She could explain my history to them. According to Smeets, she could see all the information from Henriette about the antibiotics, the dose, the duration, and about my medical history in the system. So why couldn't the administrator in Emma see it? Smeets contacted Emma, told them what they needed to know, and the antibiotics

Deny, dismiss, dehumanise

were ordered. It took about half an hour, but they arrived, and although my name and date of birth were handwritten rather than printed on the label, they were correct.

The remainder of the week passed smoothly. The receptionist became friendly and every single one of the nurses was professional and caring. I arrived, received antibiotics and left – just like it's supposed to happen in a hospital. Twice during the week, my cannula stopped working and I was brought to the anaesthetists. The nurse waited with me. But Emma isn't open at weekends, so I would have to return to Henriette to get my antibiotics on Saturday and Sunday. On Friday, one of the Emma nurses walked with me to Henriette to remind them that I would again be going to them for IV antibiotics at the weekend. The Emma nurse had ordered the weekend doses from the pharmacy and brought them to Henriette. Everything was in order. Henriette was expecting me at around 14:00, and I knew Paul was on duty.

On Saturday 21 May, Peter and I arrived in Henriette at 14:20. I asked for Paul. Lia (whom I hadn't met before) said he was working "on the other side" and that she was to look after my antibiotics. As planned, she brought us into a quiet room. Then Lia went away and Madelein took over. She removed the bandage and found that the cannula was no longer working. We were given tea and told that she'd call someone to give me a new cannula.

We waited. And then we waited some more. One-and-a-half hours later, I still had the old cannula in my arm and no one was available to insert a new one. A patient was wheeled into the room we were waiting in. She was desperately ill. Staff were talking really loudly to her as though she were deaf. Her family – who were wondering what Peter and I were doing sitting at the table at the end of their mother's bed – were speaking to her in normal voices, which she had no trouble hearing.

Just before 16:00, still with the old cannula dangling from my arm, I went to reception to see if I could find Madelein, whom

I hadn't seen for nearly an hour. Some nurses I didn't know were gathered at the desk. I told them I had been waiting since 14:20 for someone to put a new cannula in my arm. I asked them to please find someone who could do this, or at least tell me how long I was going to have to wait. Was it another ten minutes or could I still be here in two hours' time? Nobody was interested. I asked them to find Madelein. Nobody could find her.

The nurses went away leaving me alone at reception. I could feel the panic and stress that I had been trying hard to control all afternoon rising up. I didn't want to go back into the room where the seriously ill woman was being tended by her family. It was wrong that Peter and I, total strangers, were hanging around their mother's bedside. My legs were shaky and I felt weak, worn out and desperate, so I just slid down to the floor in the corridor at reception, put my head in my arms and gave up. Some time later, one of the nurses fetched Madelein. I asked her had she read my patient notes.

"No", she replied impatiently. "I haven't read your notes. You're not my patient."

Again, I was in a situation where I was in trouble and no one knew anything about my medical history. I couldn't handle it. I just put my head back into my arms to block it all out. Madelein went away and left me there sitting on the floor. The other nurses took their cue from her and walked around me.

I don't know how long more I was there. Probably another fifteen minutes. I became aware of someone beside me speaking to me in Dutch. I looked up. I didn't know her and was just going to close my eyes again when I saw Paul over to my left. He did a double-take. He came over and with the help of the nurse who had been talking to me they persuaded me to go to the nurses' station. The other nurse was Pleun. I told Paul I had been waiting for my antibiotics since 14:20, but everyone was too busy to give me a new cannula. Pleun started making phone calls.

Deny, dismiss, dehumanise

Within five minutes someone was available to insert a new cannula and was already on her way to the ward. I asked Paul to stay with me for a few minutes because he was the only person I trusted. He and Pleun brought me to Room 340, which was quiet. Paul took out the old cannula, which had been dangling loosely from my arm for over two hours. Pleun stayed. I realized from watching her facial expressions and body language that she was a good and kind person. We had a little trouble at first communicating in English, but it didn't matter. We understood each other well enough. Pleun told me that she knew my story and was very upset by what had happened. I asked her if she would stay with me once Paul went home. It was after 16:30 by now and I knew his shift had ended. She agreed. I felt safe with her.

I eventually left Henriette that day at 17:40, almost three-and-a-half hours after I had arrived. If Paul and Pleun had not found me sitting on the floor in reception, I don't know how long I would have had to wait before I got my overdue antibiotics. Madelein and the other nurses had been waiting for the next shift to take over at 16:30. Then I would be someone else's problem. All they had to do was to keep their heads down, pretend they didn't know what was wrong, and let the evening shift take on the task of finding someone to insert a cannula.

If I had had any doubts before about whether to take Hoevenaar's advice about making a complaint, I was crystal clear now about what I should do. Although Smeets had always been considerate and helpful, I decided to go straight to the independent klachtencommissie this time. All Dutch hospitals are obliged by law to operate an independent complaints process. It's administered by someone in the hospital, but the members of the committee are doctors from outside as well as from inside. Each hospital klachtencommissie is headed by a judge from the Dutch high court. In my mind, it was going to take the wisdom of a high court judge to put the Bronovo wards back to rights.

21 | May and June 2016 … Westeinde Hospital, The Hague and UMC, Utrecht

The reasonable man adapts himself to the world; the unreasonable one persists to adapt the world to himself. Therefore, all progress depends on the unreasonable man.
George Bernard Shaw

So it was that I found myself in the summer of 2016 bruised in different ways after my encounters in two hospitals in two cities – and those were apart from the ongoing friction with UMCU. In each of the hospitals, AMC, Bronovo and UMCU, the causes for concern differed greatly. For all the chaos that reigned in the Bronovo wards, and for all the inadequate care I had received, no one there had ever said a mean word to me about not speaking Dutch. In AMC, intolerance of my lack of Dutch had been aired loudly and regularly across many areas of the hospital, and in a variety of ways – but in the main, the care had been good. In the case of UMC Utrecht, I was fighting bitterly with the hospital leaders about transparency and respect for damaged patients, but the nurses could not have been kinder. I was both intrigued and dismayed by the vast differences in patient experience I had been

Deny, dismiss, dehumanise

exposed to from hospital to hospital, and from department to department within hospitals.

On 25 May, I was about to add another hospital to my list of "Dutch hospitals I have known". It was time to replace the JJ-stent that had been keeping my left ureter open since January. Van Houten and I both agreed that this should take place in Westeinde Hospital in the centre of The Hague. Unlike Bronovo, which is located in The Hague's well-heeled northern suburbs, near the embassies, the International Criminal Court, the international tribunals, and the wealthy town of Wassenaar, Westeinde is in the heart of the city centre's poorer neighbourhoods.

With much difficulty, I had managed to get a printout of the nursing notes Willem had entered into my file on 13 May.[20] It was apparent by the response I got when I asked for access to my nursing notes that staff didn't like the idea of giving them to me. They suggested they were confidential, and didn't think I would be allowed to see them. Then I could see them but not make a copy. It had been another struggle, but eventually Van Houten told them that I was entitled to my own medical information and to hand over a printout. Acutely aware that I was being admitted to yet another hospital where no one knew my medical history, I felt that Willem's notes would help to explain everything anyone needed to know about me.

And they worked like a dream. On the tenth floor of Westeinde hospital, Peter and I were greeted by a nurse called Dinie. She started a very professional admissions process, explaining that she was still technically a student as she wouldn't graduate until July. She was thorough and kind. I gave her a copy of Willem's notes, saying that I had had a bit of a rocky time since 2013, and the printout might explain the consequences better than I could. She read the short summary carefully.

---

20   See Appendix 6 for a translation of Willem's nursing notes. The story in the notes is not absolutely accurate, but it's there or thereabouts.

"It is really important that we have this information", she began, echoing the words of every nurse and doctor who had ever heard my medical history. "I will put this in your file and make sure that everyone who treats you is aware of it. I will discuss it with the senior nurse and I'm sure we can also arrange that just one nurse from each shift will look after you and that you will be allowed to stay in a room on your own if at all possible."

Dinie was as good as her word. She prepared me for surgery that afternoon and went with me to the theatre. She showed everyone in pre-op the notes and didn't leave until she had handed me over to someone I trusted. In theatre, an anaesthetist Peter and I had met when we visited Westeinde a few days previously had also kept his promise and ensured he was there. Van Houten came in before I was put under, and between him and the kindly anaesthetist, I didn't feel too terrified. Everyone was aware of my situation. Even my glasses were allowed to stay on until they had knocked me out.

When I came to, my glasses were back on my nose. Small kindnesses such as this make such a difference, not just because I could see what was going on around me, but because it told me that I was being regarded as a human being. So much of what happens in hospitals is driven by system and processes that the patients too become "processed" – or worse, are seen as being impediments to the smooth-running of the hospital conveyor belt.

Van Houten had Peter at my bedside almost as soon as I came round. Lots of people were milling past, some stopping to check the machines I was hooked up to. A woman in scrubs stopped, sat by the bed and started speaking to us.

"I'm sorry", I interrupted her. "I don't speak Dutch."

"Oh, you don't speak Dutch?" she asked.

We both shook our heads. There were a few seconds of silence.

"How long have you lived here?" she asked, not looking up

from what she was doing with my IV.

"Not long", I lied, figuring that should end the discussion.

"How long?" asked the woman, looking up.

"Not long", I repeated more slowly.

"But how long?" she persisted. "Is it like, ten or twenty years or something?"

Neither Peter nor I answered, letting her words hang in the air.

Eventually, I broke the silence. "Maybe if I get better I'll be able to return to my own country", I answered.

The woman left. Damage done. The poison she left behind was eventually dispelled by the arrival of Dinie to bring me back to my room. What was she doing still on duty? Surely her shift had ended? It had, but she wanted to hand me over to the nurse on the evening shift. More kindness. I don't remember the evening nurse's name, but she was caring too. And that night, I needed all the care I could get.

Within an hour of getting back to my room, the pain started. I had developed a sudden and powerful infection. I received IV antibiotics immediately to prevent sepsis from setting in.

So I spent a few extra days in Westeinde looking out at the view over the city from my tenth-floor room. The agreement I had made with Dinie on the first day was honoured throughout my stay. Every nurse who looked after me was careful, kindly and professional, and I left on Saturday afternoon, armed with oral antibiotics, and feeling what all patients should feel when they walk out of a hospital: that they have been treated with respect and compassion by a team of highly skilled professionals.

★★★★★★★★

While I was skipping from AMC to Bronovo to Westeinde, news of another medical calamity hit the headlines. The radio programme, *Argos*, revealed that the family of young man who had died a preventable death in Tergooi Hospital in Hilversum in 2014 had been obliged to sign a gagging clause before the hospital would pay compensation. The dead patient's mother had signed an agreement that she would not discuss what had happened to her son with the media, would not report the doctors she believed were responsible to the *tuchtcollege*, and would not initiate legal proceedings against the hospital. In return, the hospital agreed to pay the mother compensation for the death of her son, which was caused by an undiagnosed infection of the pericardium. The hospital did not report the incident to the IGZ, although the law required them to do so. Reports in the media at the time indicated that less than half of the serious harm cases that should be reported to the inspectorate by hospitals were being reported.

When she received the compensation, the young man's mother donated it to a hockey foundation in memory of her son, who had been a promising player before his untimely death. She then contacted the media and told them how her healthy, sporty 21-year-old child had died a totally preventable death at Tergooi. She also made sure that the media heard about the gagging clause that Tergooi had insisted she sign.

I was in awe. I remembered all too keenly what it felt like to be asked to take part in such a degrading little pact and to be offered money in exchange for silence. While my heart bled for the woman who had lost her son, I applauded her courage. It's no easy thing to have been put through such a loss, followed by the humiliation of a hospital persuading you to be silent about what they did. But to then treat the settlement agreement with the contempt it deserved was phenomenal. This woman was my hero.

Her act threw the whole subject of hospital gagging clauses back into the public domain. Again, Health Minister Edith Schippers spoke out strongly against them, and again she considered banning them. She explained, not for the first time, that it was completely contrary to the public good to have calamities and medical errors covered up and hidden from the profession and the appropriate authorities. She also said that she felt such clauses had no place in agreements between hospitals and their patients – a sentiment I agreed with wholeheartedly. To get an idea of how prevalent such practices were, she called on patients and families who had signed gagging clauses to come forward. She wanted to see what patients were being asked to sign, and who was asking them.

I decided to tell Schippers' department the story of our gagging clauses. But I contacted UMCU first. Albert Vermaas, UMCU's head of legal affairs wrote back to me. I had read that Vermaas was, according to a profile in the UMCU magazine, *Uniek*,[21] the hospital's contact for dealings with the IGZ. I couldn't understand that. Healthcare protocols and standards and seriously harmed patients are, surely, the business of doctors. The IGZ is a *medical* inspectorate. Why then is the designated contact person at the hospital a lawyer? It seems firmly entrenched in the ethos of this hospital that lawyers are in charge of communication with damaged patients, and also with the IGZ.

Vermaas wrote to me in April 2016, "The Health inspectorate have asked the UMC Utrecht to send them the settlement agreement which our institute and our insurer closed with you and Mr Cluskey in November last year. According to the law the UMC Utrecht has to comply with that request. The Health inspectorate will examine the contents of the agreement according to the wishes of our parliament and minister of Health." I chuckled. I bet Vermaas was happy that Peter and I had stuck doggedly to our determination never to sign their gagging clauses. I was pretty sure that he wouldn't mention anything of the first, second, third and fourth drafts of UMCU's gagging clauses when replying to the IGZ.

---

21   See Appendix 7 for the *Uniek* profile of Albert Vermaas.

I hadn't had any contact with the IGZ since my phonecall to them in the summer of 2014 to tell them what had happened to me at UMCU. They had promised that someone would call me back, but I had never received a call. This time, I would persist until someone took me seriously. And so I did. I was put on to one of the inspectors, Mrs Majidah Shadid. She explained something to me that no one had explained before, and which I found quite hard to believe.

She explained: "The relationship between the IGZ and the hospitals in the Netherlands is based on trust. The hospitals themselves are responsible for the quality of care they provide, and how that's delivered."

I was astonished – but it explained a lot. I had assumed that the IGZ performed a function similar to the Care Quality Commission in the United Kingdom, which monitors healthcare providers and investigates and intervenes where care is believed to have fallen below standard. But it was being explained to me that the IGZ had no brief to investigate or intervene – the hospitals themselves were the ones who carried out investigations, if they saw fit, and implemented improvements, if they saw fit.

Shadid made an arrangement for me to speak with one of the IGZ's senior inspectors, Dr Sandra Mulder, their medical specialist inspector.

I spoke to Mulder for over an hour on the phone on 6 June. She told me that there was no doubt in her mind that when they became aware of the incident that concerned me in 2013, UMCU should have reported it to the IGZ immediately.

"What are you going to do about the fact that they didn't?" I asked her.

"I agree that hospitals that don't report major incidents should be punished", she told me. "There needs to be consequences. Since late 2013, a law has been in place that says that hospitals that don't report when they should will be punished. They will be fined, and that fine will be published."

But in my case, that wouldn't happen because the law came into force only after my calamity was discovered. The IGZ simply trusted that UMCU would do the right thing. So not only had UMCU betrayed the trust of their patient, they had betrayed the trust of the IGZ. But there was nothing the IGZ could do about that now. UMCU had, in July 2015, more than two years after the calamity was discovered, and at our insistence, finally reported it to the IGZ. The IGZ had closed the case the same month. They were happy that UMCU had learned from their mistakes.

But judging by way they continued to behave towards me, I couldn't see that they'd learned much.

I asked Mulder about the IGZ's decision to close my case. "The health inspectorate closed my case based solely on the paltry information it had received from the hospital, without ever contacting the patient to see whether what the hospital was telling you was true", I put to her. "You trusted UMCU so much that you didn't see any need to contact the patient. How do you know that what they told you is an honest read of the situation?" I asked her.

"From the IGZ point of view, one of the most important aims of doing an investigation is that you want the institution involved to learn from events", she explained. "If you really want to learn and improve patient care, it makes more sense to do the investigation yourself instead of sourcing it out to someone else."

I didn't agree. No investigation *had* actually been carried out, so how did that improve patient care and impart valuable lessons? I believed that Huub Van der Vaart had learned a lot, and, more recently, so had Arie Franx. But while the lessons they learned were valuable to them personally and professionally, that was where the learning ended. UMCU, as an institution, knew little and had learned even less.

I put it to Mulder that UMCU, and probably other hospitals too, were running rings around the inspectorate. I told her that from my dealings with the hospital leadership and the lawyers they had behaved like corporate high-flyers rather than like academics or doctors who had a responsibility to their patients. "They have no humility", I said. "They are behaving as though they are accountable to nobody – not the IGZ, and not their patients".

"They are responsible to their patients", answered Mulder. "That is the bottom line. Hospitals are responsible to their patients for their quality and delivery of care."

I reminded her that that was not the way UMCU had behaved with me. After they had damaged me, they pushed me away over and over again, denying me support, refusing to discuss what had happened, refusing to investigate, and allowing contact only through their lawyers. I told her: "When you damage a patient, it's not a legal issue, it's a care issue."

"I totally agree", answered Mulder. "When a hospital reports a calamity to us, we always ask if the patient has been involved, and how. You should have been heard by the hospital. You should have been informed of the investigation and involved. And then you should have been told what they found."

She was still referring to an investigation that had never taken place and so had no findings. She was regarding the SAFER report that UMCU had sent to the IGZ when they reported my calamity to them as being an investigation report. But surely she knew that a SAFER was a predictive analysis and if she had looked at it, she would have seen that my case was barely mentioned in passing.

We moved on to the various iterations of gagging clauses that UMCU had presented to us in November 2015 before they would make a financial settlement. I told her of the trauma Peter and I had undergone as clause after clause was sent to us.

"The inspectorate has UMCU under very sharp scrutiny", Mulder promised. "What you are telling me is very important to us. It all fits in with the picture we have of UMC Utrecht. It's important that this culture changes, that Margriet Schneider does learn from the things that Jan Kimpen has done wrong in the past."

Jan Kimpen, I reminded her, had moved to a prestigious job with Philips, and had been awarded a knighthood for his services to health.

✱✱✱✱✱✱✱✱✱

A few days after speaking to Mulder, I had an appointment to meet Schippers' advisors. The department was familiar with my name because my story in *NRC* had prompted a discussion in the *Tweede Kamer*, the Dutch parliament. They had also heard that I had spoken to Sandra Mulder at the IGZ – the inspectorate was part of the health ministry. I was to speak to one of the minister's advisors, Esther Veldhuis, who was attached to the department's curative care section, and her colleague, Wouter van de Sande. We met in the ministry on the afternoon of 9 June. Peter came with me but waited outside.

It took almost two hours for me to explain the details of what had happened to me since I was first treated in UMCU in 2011. No doubt I told them more than they wanted to know, but since no one else had taken the trouble to document any part of what had gone wrong in my case, I was keen that it would at least be on record in the ministry. I gave Veldhuis and Van de Sande the wording of the first gagging clause and a copy of the email where Frieda de Bruin, the loss adjuster, had sent the fourth draft to our lawyer, along with the emails where we were told that she had said there would be no settlement without a gagging clause. I wanted to make sure that the department would not just be told that "no gagging clause had been involved in the Cullen/ Cluskey settlement" – as though that were down to the goodness of UMCU rather than to our dogged determination.

I asked Schippers' advisors to ask the IGZ to reopen my

case, as no proper investigation had been carried out, and because I thought it was procedurally very high-handed to close a case dealing with serious harm to a patient without ever having contacted the patient concerned. I also asked them to inform the minister that a root-cause analysis of what had happened in 2011 would be much more appropriate than the SAFER report, which was only a predictive analysis of current protocols and had virtually nothing to do with my case.

The final matter I discussed was the suggestion Peter had made during the settlement process that UMCU would organize an annual bursary, or similar, which would be awarded to the staff member who made the best contribution on transparency and open disclosure. I told the ministry that I had written to Margriet Schneider reminding her that we had been told that UMCU would give "sympathetic consideration" to our proposal. I pointed out that seven months had now passed and we had heard nothing. I had written to Schneider: "I would be really interested to know what you have done to spread awareness in the hospital so that everyone, from junior doctors to department heads, will know what they are supposed to do in the event of a calamity befalling a patient at their hands." I had, as yet, received no reply.

I wasn't expecting the minister's advisors to really do anything much on my behalf. I was getting used to the officious and imperious distance that those who felt they were "my betters" adopted when dealing with me, although they all told me how much sympathy they felt. And when it came to it, of course, the minister didn't intervene.

All I could do was make sure that the relevant people in government had some idea of what was happening to patients in hospitals – and how they were being treated in the aftermath of serious harm. Nobody was speaking openly about patient experience. Nobody was making sure that investigations are carried out when patients are harmed. Nobody was making sure

Deny, dismiss, dehumanise

that patients are involved in investigations that concern them. Until that stopped, we would be forever stuck in the top-down model of healthcare where executives, lawyers and bureaucrats operated the system that suited them best, and patients would remain the voiceless majority.

22 | June and July 2016 … UMC, Utrecht

To be remembered after we are dead, is but poor recompense for being treated with contempt while we are living.
William Hazlitt

June and July were busy months. I had set a lot of balls rolling, and was wondering which would roll home. The first was an email from Margriet Schneider. I was pleasantly surprised to receive it within days of my conversations with the IGZ and the ministry. She had indeed given Peter's idea sympathetic consideration – and had come up with a plan. She mentioned that UMCU had been the "subject of significant media upheaval" since November. She wrote that, as a result of that upheaval, the hospital had "developed a recovery plan that also includes initiatives on increasing transparency as well as on increasing patient focus." She explained:

We will incorporate your ideas on open disclosure in our program on increasing transparency. We would like to organize a yearly symposium on open disclosure. The key note of this symposium will be the "Adrienne Cullen Lecture". Persons awarded for this lecture [will] have demonstrated extraordinary achievements on open disclosure in the past year.

Deny, dismiss, dehumanise

An annual symposium on issues such as duty of candour, open disclosure, transparency and a patient-centred approach to healthcare would really make a difference ... the first glimmers of hope flashed enticingly at me. Maybe these soulless behemoths of teaching hospitals *are* capable of change. Was I hearing the first inklings of a move towards treating patients as partners in their own healthcare? A new era of transparency beckoned instead of closed doors, silence and ... lawyers. I reread the email many times. They were going to do the right thing. Such is human vanity that people like to be remembered for something after their death. Given a choice, I'd like it to be a new daffodil, or a poem or a rocky headland overlooking the Atlantic – but an annual lecture that would remind UMCU that no patient, ever again, should be treated as I was in the aftermath of a calamity would do very nicely. I saw Schneider's idea as evidence that the hospital could change. And my position towards them softened ... cautiously.

The next email came from Esther Veldhuis, Schippers', advisor. This was more predictable. Although the minister wanted to thank me very much for "sharing my story" she wasn't in a position to intervene in any way. I wasn't surprised. I hadn't truly expected them to help. I knew better than to expect help. I believed that the health ministry, like the hospitals themselves, operated in a comfortable bubble into which the practical, economic, legal and physical nightmares faced by damaged patients rarely intruded. Dutch healthcare, ranked 17th in the international WHO ratings, is regarded as good. And in many ways it is. While it's well behind France, Italy, and other Mediterranean countries, it's on a par, points-wise at least, with Belgium, the UK, Ireland and Switzerland. But it also has an underside that people often don't see – and, as always, it's the most vulnerable patients who fall foul of it, and often the most dedicated and able staff members too. My aim was to shatter the complacency in the system and blow fresh air into the outdated and controlling leadership model I had faced in my encounters with hospital managers.

The next email to arrive was from Franx. He had been battling for some time to get clearance to send me a copy of the SAFER in English. I had first asked for it in December 2015 – and hey presto, here it was on 14 July 2016.[22] I opened it with great enthusiasm, which quickly faded when my fears were realized. I had thought that just maybe a professional translation would disclose findings that Google Translate had not made clear, but as I feared, there was zero information in the SAFER about my case. This was what the IGZ had accepted as sufficient evidence that UMCU had investigated the case and learned lessons from it.

Arie Franx was bracing himself for my reaction. He knew I would not be impressed. I wrote back to him the same day:

Dear Professor Franx,

Thanks for the translated SAFER report, which I have read through thoroughly several times.

I think you probably won't be surprised to hear that I am very unimpressed with it. I don't mean to be critical of those who went to the trouble of implementing a SAFER – at least they did something – but there is barely a single concrete conclusion or decision from beginning to end. Each of the "Areas for improvement" consists of open-ended questions, wish-list suggestions and calls to discuss issues. Nowhere does it actually say what decisions, if any, were taken and why. I am actually very surprised that a country's healthcare inspectorate would think this was an acceptable analysis of a problem, let alone evidence that steps have been taken to prevent a recurrence.

And speaking of recurrences, I have been assured by pretty much everybody at UMC Utrecht for the past three years that there was no case similar to mine, yet this report refers to other cases. It says: "Even though the incident took place during the transition from paper to electronic medical

---

22 You can find an English translation of the anonymized SAFER report on the website that accompanies this book.

records, recurrence is not inconceivable. Unfortunately, this has already been proven to be true, given similar reports in UMCU (see also SIRE report on PA [pathology] ophthalmology incident, September 2011)."

...

I'm also interested in the observation in 3, Working Method, that "in March 2014 an opinion on the incident was received from the PA department", who were "difficult to get in touch with". I'd like to know what was the opinion from the PA department ... and why they were difficult to get in touch with.

...

I'm horrified that the IGZ do not think it is necessary to investigate what caused a patient to be so severely harmed in a hospital that it will cost her her life. Maybe this is a cultural thing, but in other countries, when someone dies or is severely harmed, there's a proper investigation into why it happened, how it happened, who could have or should have prevented it, and only then does the focus shift to preventing it from happening to others.

...

Cheers,
Adrienne

We arranged to speak on the phone the following week. The nature of the communication between myself and Franx had started to change. As good as his word, he had been phoning me every few weeks as we had agreed at our meeting in December. At first, the tone of the conversations was a "duty phonecall" – he asked about my health, and I reminded him that I still hadn't received the SA-FER report. We were polite, but the conversations were guarded and stiff. He got an earful every time he phoned – when he asked about my health, either I had just had a rough time dealing with the language intolerance in AMC, or had been fighting to save my own life in the Bronovo wards. I made no secret of what I thought about UMCU's ongoing refusal to allow a root-cause analysis to be carried out on my case. It can't have been easy listening.

But recently, he had stopped keeping me at arm's length and started to engage with what I was saying about my experience as a patient, about the way hospitals often failed to respect their patients as functioning adults who were entitled to be involved in their own health decisions, and how that led to many of the problems patients experienced. He started to talk about a hospital in Sweden that had started to implement a different model and had made huge progress towards truly patient-centred care that moulded to the patient's complex needs rather than forcing patients to fit in with rigid and pre-defined systems and processes. I was interested in what he was saying, very interested, but even more, I was fascinated that he was talking to me about such matters. We started having more normal, information-sharing sorts of conversations. We found that, despite the friction between us, we wanted the same things. We both believed that patient experience is central to, not peripheral to, a properly functioning hospital in the 21st century. We had stopped being adversaries.

But being my ally was never going to be easy. I was a walking, talking reminder of what had happened in his hospital, in his department – and of how he had failed to limit the damage. And, despite my assertive energy, my seemingly tireless emails to hospital CEOs, government departments and health inspectorates, and my unstoppable determination to challenge the way I was being treated when that treatment was bad, I was still a woman heading towards an unpleasant and painful death. It's a brave person who extends the hand of friendship to someone like me. It was going to be a bumpy ride.

When the IGZ put UMCU under special measures, after my case and the cases in the *Zembla* broadcasts, the hospital started to tell its patients that if there was a calamity, UMCU would investigate it. They wanted to reassure patients. They were telling them that when something goes seriously wrong, they carry out a root-cause analysis, and write a report. If they now knew that this was the right thing to do, why would they still not carry an investigation into what happened to me? I agreed with them that as time has passed, many of the answers that we could have gleaned in 2013 might now be unavailable, but it is still possible, for a professional investigation team, to interview relevant parties, piece together the facts they had, and for a picture to emerge. Not even bothering to try this is wickedly remiss.

From any patient's point of view, the absence of an investigation and a report leaves them "hanging". When someone has been subjected to a medical calamity, they have a basic human need to find out what went wrong. It's part of making sense of their own story – and part of coming to terms with it. By pushing the incident aside on the grounds that it "happened too long ago", "things are different now", and "we won't learn anything from it", UMCU was denying me the opportunity to come to terms with what had occurred, and had condemned me to trying, ineptly, to carry out my own investigation. And I wasn't equipped to get answers, or probably even to ask the right questions. An impartial and experienced medical investigator would have the authority to demand answers. That, I would never be able to do.

My frustration with the SAFER report, UMCU and the IGZ deepened when I received the IGZ's formal reply on 28 July.[23] For all the understanding that we seem to have reached in our phone conversation, the follow-up letter from Sandra Mulder was impersonal, officious and guarded. She offered her sympathy on behalf of the inspectorate and acknowledged stiffly that my "experiences with the Dutch healthcare system have not met expectations". However, what the letter boiled down to was that the inspectorate was satisfied with the way UMCU had analysed my case and felt that the SAFER report was adequate in terms of investigating it. In addition, the IGZ didn't feel I should have been

---

23   See Appendix 8 for a copy of the letter from the health inspectorate.

contacted at any point before my case was closed by them – they don't, in the normal course of events, contact patients who have been involved in calamities. The letter went on to explain that the inspectorate would not take action against UMCU on the matter of the gagging clauses because there was no gagging clause in our final agreement. My case was now closed.

She ended by assuring me that all the information I had given her was very valuable and thanking me for my time. Although I was totally unaware of it when I spoke to her, Sandra Mulder was planning to leave the IGZ permanently and take up work elsewhere. She left at the end of August, a few weeks after the letter to me, and I had no further communication from the IGZ.

Deny, dismiss, dehumanise

23 | September 2016 … Bronovo Hospital, The Hague

We tell these stories because perhaps we know that not to listen, not to want to know, would lead you to indifference, and indifference is never an answer.
Elie Wiesel

In July 2016, I started learning Dutch. Now that Van der Velden had bought me some extra time by removing the metastases in March, I might live a little longer, so learning Dutch might be prudent. I knew from living in other countries and picking up languages along the way that it was not going to be possible for me to ever achieve a high standard. I was not a natural linguist; I was also almost 56 years old, and the days when I could hear something once and own it forever were long gone. I contacted a friend who runs a small school teaching Dutch to expats and asked her if she thought I was a lost cause. She assured me I wasn't, and so lessons began.

Peter and I had given the idea of moving away from the Netherlands a lot of thought. I was finding the constant barrage of disapproval over my lack of Dutch increasingly distressing, but to pack up my life when suffering from a terminal illness would be hard. So much had changed since 2013 – my career was gone, my activities had been curtailed, and a lot of my life was spent attending one practitioner or another to get help managing my cancer and its many consequences. It had taken time to build the support network I had – Van der Velden, the out-patient nurses at AMC who were truly kind and knew me, my GP, the local pharmacy, physiotherapists, psychologists, urologists, and so on. The thought of starting again from scratch was daunting, as was the prospect of packing everything we owned into boxes and moving abroad. We had moved house many times, and had no illusions about how stressful it would be, even if we were to return to Ireland, where we haven't lived since 2002. I had also built up a small network of friends here. This was now my home. There were also financial considerations. If we moved away, how would our respective incomes be affected? Not very well, we were advised, and getting health insurance could pose problems for me. So we decided to stay. I was determined not to let the intolerance of a minority of staff at AMC force me into leaving the country – a decision that would have been wrong for so many other reasons.

Deciding to stay had driven my determination to challenge UMCU's response to the errors they made – and my decision to challenge Bronovo for its poor care. I had never intended to live in the Netherlands for long, but it now looked probable that I would die here. The choice was, would I take whatever was dished out to me and patients like me, or would I object in the strongest possible terms? No prizes for guessing what I chose.

I wrote to Bronovo about what had happened to me on Henriette ward between 12 and 22 May telling them I wanted to make a complaint to their *klachtencommissie*.[24] The co-ordinator, Joke Luitwieler-Bosma, worked in the hospital, but the committee members, all medics, could be attached to any hospital, or none.

---

24   See the website that accompanies this book for the full text of the complaint made to Bronovo's *klachtencommissie*.

Deny, dismiss, dehumanise

The chairperson was a high court judge.

The co-ordinator invited Peter and me to come and see her so that she could explain the process to us in English. She said that an interpreter would be made available to us on the day of the hearing. There was a hiccup when Bronovo said they would be sending me all the written replies to my complaint in Dutch. I explained that this would mean I'd either never know what people had replied, or I'd have to employ a professional translator to translate the extensive and complex bundle of paperwork that the complaint had generated. This, I explained, would put the complaints process beyond the reach of their many English-speaking patients. In effect, it would mean that the "free" hospital complaints process was for Dutch patients only. They saw the point and agreed that the replies would be translated so that I could read and understand them.

And when the replies arrived, I was pleased that I'd asked for translations. The response from Henriette's manager, Manuela Lucas, and the nurses rubbished almost everything I had told the *klachtencommissie*. According to their replies, what had happened on 12 May when I was admitted to Henriette was that I had been, "extremely angry and upset when I had been admitted and had refused to be placed in Room 314". I had, "protested against a multiple occupancy room" and was "emotional and difficult to approach". As a result of my "refusal" to be placed in this room, I was "offered Room 340 shortly afterwards" and was "offered [my] own nurse, Berta van Os".

This was very far from the reality of that afternoon.

The replies continued, "Mrs. Cullen was admitted with UTI [urinary tract infection] on 12 May ...". She was "started on AB [antibiotics] immediately, and released home on 15 May. Nothing unusual up to this point."

I couldn't believe what I was reading. Nothing unusual! Even at this stage, the manager of the ward doesn't know that I was admitted with urosepsis – a condition which had been life-threatening for me on several previous occasions, as it had been on that afternoon.

The replies didn't mention that I had spent two-and-a-half hours in the bedlam of Room 314 – although they did acknowledge that "The set-up of Room 314 is less suitable for four beds as well as visitors for all of the patients. We are considering a different set-up for this room.". Nor did the replies from Lucas mention that I was not given any antibiotics for well over three hours after admission, or that I had been given nothing to reduce my fever for two-and-a-half hours. She didn't acknowledge my complaint that no one had measured any of my vital signs (temperature, blood pressure and blood-oxygen levels) or used a bladder scan – although she did admit that "the flexitime associate [agency nurse] who admitted Mrs Cullen, Mrs [Ilse] Werff, did not take down her medical history. This was reported to the flexitime bureau".

There was no indication from Lucas's replies that she was aware that I had a five-month old JJ-stent keeping my ureter open, and had hydronephrosis and pyelonephritis. Nor was there any acknowledgement that I was retaining urine and should have been catheterized on admission. Rather, the extensive replies painted a picture of a patient who was not particularly ill but who was difficult to communicate with, angry for no particular reason, and behaving badly because she didn't have her own room. To then allege that I had been moved immediately to a room on my own and "given my own nurse" was a gross distortion of the facts.

Of course I had wanted a private room – most patients do. But at no stage when I was in Room 314 did I ask for a private room. All I had asked for was paracetamol, antibiotics, and a catheter to treat my urosepsis, and for someone to look at my medical history – none of which I got for hours after admission, and which I probably wouldn't have got at all if Peter and I hadn't asked for them repeatedly. The noise in the room was outrageous and was totally unsuitable for any patient, let alone a patient with sepsis and PTSD.

The events of the following day, 13 May, where none of the nurses had any idea who I was, what I was doing on the ward or what my treatment plan was were glossed over, although there was an admission that "Lack of communication, improper handoff, and lack of familiarity with medical history appear to be common threads in this case. Two of these items are part of a plan of improvement for the department under supervision of a core team, quality coach and Care Manager."

The fact that there had been no one to speak to Peter on 13 May about what was happening was also glossed over. Bronovo's "cluster manager", Anja van Wel, in her answer, was critical of the helpful woman in whose office Peter ended up, saying that she was unfamiliar with the procedures in the hospital and that there was always an on-call care manager available to talk to patients or relatives. With regard to the apparent disinterest of the CEO's office in what was happening, no comment was made. Van Wel did however undertake that there would in future always be someone on duty in the administrative offices who would know how to contact a care manager and/or the complaints officer.

With regard to the fiasco on Saturday, 21 May – where I spent nearly three-and-a-half hours in Henriette as an outpatient waiting for someone to insert a functioning cannula and administer antibiotics – there was a letter from the nurses on shift that afternoon and evening to their manager describing what had happened:

Before Saturday, 21 May at 14:00, we made sure everything was ready for her so that Mrs. Cullen could be treated as soon as she arrived. However, after she arrived, the Venflon turned out not to be functional and had to be replaced ... so we explained that we were going to find somebody to insert the needle ... We informed Mrs Cullen of this delay immediately. After about 15 minutes, Mrs Cullen was extremely angry that nobody had arrived yet, and insisted that somebody come immediately because she did not think she ought to be made to wait ...

The nurses had told Lucas that Peter and I had become angry after waiting 15 minutes – again, the story was that the patient and her family were badly behaved and the nurses were doing a good job. The letter read like it had been written by a group of schoolchildren, lying to their teacher to cover each other's backs. It was conduct unbecoming of a team of healthcare professionals.

The replies from Henriette also included a series of emails between Lucas, Van Houten and some of the nurses on various issues related to my complaint. Jessica, the nurse I had approached for a copy of my nursing notes, wrote to Van Houten. She was puzzled, and wondering was there something wrong with me psychologically. She wrote: "Mrs Cullen was eager to obtain her medical files, and approached several nurses on different occasions. She seemed to be particularly focused on discovering what had happened to her. Are you aware of her prior history? It appears to be related to her behaviour." Obviously, all the efforts Peter and I had made to communicate my medical history and my diagnosis of PTSD still hadn't filtered through to anyone on Henriette.

Van Houten explained the situation to her clearly and succinctly in his reply: "The patient is suffering from PTSD following a serious medical error. See file. As a result, she is quick to distrust. Unfortunately, her distrust appears to have been justified on occasion, so that her suspicions were magnified."

Jessica's response to this was to get back to Lucas right away and suggest that the complaint be closed. She felt that the fact that she had now rumbled me as a certified lunatic justified all her reservations – and indicated that no further attention needed to be paid to anything I said.

She wrote to Lucas: "I received the [above] email from Doctor Van Houten in response. It looks like a closed case to me.

Do you want me to take any other steps?"

This, more than anything else, made me realize the depth of the problem I was dealing with. Here was a senior nurse who felt that a complaint from a patient with PTSD should be dropped, simply because she had PTSD. How could a relatively young, totally qualified nurse in the 21st century have such a benighted attitude to the psychological aspects of patient care? Rather than seeing that my PTSD had heightened the distress caused by the shocking care I had received on Henriette, she decided that I was the cause of everything that had happened on the ward, and she didn't need to take any further steps to see if the complaint was valid or not. It is also interesting that she seemed to think that asking for my medical file was a symptom of a psychological condition. She was particularly puzzled that I had, "approached several nurses on different occasions" asking for my notes. It didn't occur to her that had I got the notes from the first nurse, I wouldn't have needed to ask any additional nurses. Is requesting medical records so peculiar that staff see it as an indication of psychological instability? My fear was that the members of the Bronovo *klachtencommissie* would share Jessica's view.

****

The *klachtencommissie* hearing in September took place in Bronovo's windowless boardroom around a long conference table. As well as the judge, there were three committee members present, all doctors. The head of Emma had come along with two of her nurses who had looked after me while I was visiting them daily for antibiotics. I was surprised they were there. Although Emma had been mentioned in the complaint, it was only in reference to the fact that Henriette had failed to alert them that I would be coming to them daily. The complaint was never aimed at Emma. Manuela Lucas was there too. She had come alone. The "cluster manager", Anja van Wel, was indisposed and did not attend.

The interpreter at the hearing gave us headsets. She would translate what the *klachtencommissie* members were saying, and we would hear this through our headsets. With many years of radio and TV broadcasting behind him, Peter adapted quickly to this plan. I took a little longer, but within a few minutes I had got the hang of it.

Because of the distorted versions of events that had been depicted in the written replies to my complaint, I was little short of furious as I sat across the boardroom table from the *klachtencommissie* members. It took me all my willpower to keep Spitting Mad Adrienne silent and on a short leash. I had enough evidence to establish that my version of what had taken place was true, and that Henriette's replies were well out of order. All I needed to do was keep my cool and tell the truth. I focused on the interpreter's voice in my ears. Before long, I started to hear Henriette's shocking version of my story being conveyed. I interjected. I started describing again what had happened when I was admitted. The judge was brilliant. She had obviously read the detail of my complaint very carefully. She managed to successfully prevent me from undermining myself by jumping in every time Lucas spoke. Instead, she started to ask the best and most pertinent questions about the details of that afternoon. Every single detail was etched indelibly on my mind. I could answer accurately about whom I had spoken to, precisely when things had happened, exactly what had not happened – and so gave a clear, factual, truthful and chronological description of what had gone on. Lucas had no details. She had not been there and was relying on what her nurses had told her.

One of the doctors became interested in my timeline, and in how the events described by me differed from the descriptions offered by Lucas. He started to ask questions about whether I had had a UTI or urosepsis, like I claimed. I pointed him to my medical records, where it was written plainly. He started to quiz both Lucas and me about records from that afternoon indicating what time I had been admitted, what medical history had been taken, what time I had received medication and what the ward had been like at the time. Mostly, she wasn't able to answer. There was no record of me being given anything until after I was moved out of Room 314 just before five o'clock. He started to get visibly annoyed, although he never raised his voice. I could hear the translation of what he was saying from Petra and I watched his face. I knew he believed me. He could see that a dangerously ill patient had been allowed to languish on a chaotic hospital ward for hours without treatment, without anyone knowing how ill she was, and without anyone taking notice of her husband's attempts to impart her medical history. As a medic, he was very displeased, and completely understood why I had attempted to take over the management of my treatment myself by asking for my antibiotics, asking for my temperature to be measured, and asking for the bladder scan.

It was really useful that the nurses from Emma were there. Each time I was asked about my treatment on that ward, I was able to reply honestly that there had been no problem whatsoever, that the nurses had been professional and kind, that no single thing had been wrong over the seven days I had gone there for IV antibiotics – and Emma had had no problem with me either. I wasn't the patient from hell, demanding this, that and the other. I wasn't the badly behaved, unapproachable and overbearing person the Henriette nurses had described to Lucas.

After a pretty intense hour, we had covered almost every aspect of my stay on Henriette and my treatment as an out-patient there the following weekend. At this stage, even Lucas was acknowledging that I was telling them the truth and that I had been put in an unsafe and traumatic situation and that the version of events that her nurses had given her was obviously incorrect. I pointed out to her that her own nurses had sent her into a *klachtencommissie* hearing armed only with a pack of lies about their patient and a litany of childish excuses. I probably shouldn't have said that. It was harsh. But she nodded her head in acceptance.

The hearing was over and Peter and I walked outside first, chatting with the interpreter and thanking her for translating. I was aware of Manuela Lucas behind us. I didn't know what to do. I didn't know where to look or where to go. I suspected she wanted to throttle me. I had not gone easy on her, or on the nurses she was responsible for. They had painted a picture of me as an unpleasant lunatic, and I had defended myself vehemently.

She walked up to me.

"I'm sorry", she said, and extended her hand to me. I was stunned. I had got used to people never apologizing to me, no matter what. "Sorry" was a word I almost never heard. I stared at her, probably with my mouth open, for several long seconds before remembering my manners and taking her hand in mine.

"I'm really sorry that this happened", she tried again, still holding onto my hand.

"I can see you are", I stumbled, trying to find sensible words. "Thank you", I settled for. "I believe you."

"I really am sorry", she said again, and walked away from us towards her ward.

24 | September to December 2016 … AMC, Amsterdam and Bronovo Hospital, The Hague

Courage is … knowing you're licked before you begin but you begin anyway and you see it through no matter what. You rarely win, but sometimes you do.
Harper Lee, To Kill a Mockingbird

The findings of the *klachtencommissie* hearing came back in the autumn of 2016. For all the energy, passion and words that went into drafting the complaint, the findings were pared to the bare essentials. They made stark, rather sad reading.

Because of the complexity of my complaint, which had several elements to it, they had divided it into five sections, summarized them, and ruled on each point.

Point 1 *The admission [process] of 12 May, 2016 was not done correctly and took too long: no history was taken and the medication distribution in the form of necessary antibiotics began much too late.* *Complaint* **Sustained.**

Point 2 *There is doubt on the part of complainant whether the nurses at admission were aware of the urgency of the commencement of treatment due to the urosepsis suffered by the complainant.*
Complaint **Unsubstantiated**, *inasmuch as the medical expertise of the nurses is questioned, but* **Sustained** *(see under Point 1 above) insofar as the procedures that were followed are concerned.*

Point 3 *At and during the admission, her history was unknown to the caregivers concerned, such that complainant found it necessary (as far as was feasible given her condition) to take over the management of her treatment herself, resulting in her being unjustly viewed as a difficult patient.*
Complaint **Sustained.**

Point 4 *The transfer movements during the admission, from the department to outpatient treatment and among the caregivers concerned, were of insufficient quality due to the absence of mutual communication, supervision of the physicians and communication with the complainant and her partner. In addition, the registration for outpatient treatment and the transfer for this were also done incorrectly.*
Complaint **Sustained.**

Point 5 *On 21 May 2016, complainant had to wait a long time for the placement of a new Venflon [canula]. In addition, the room in which she had to wait was not suitable for that purpose.*
Complaint **Sustained.**

I read ruling after ruling. I delved into the details. I was amazed. They believed me! The *klachtencommissie* at Bronovo knew I had been telling the truth about everything that had happened on Henriette. The stress caused by the months of explaining and arguing fell away, and the whole sorry saga became worthwhile. If I have succeeded in protecting even one other patient from

Deny, dismiss, dehumanise

being put through what I went through, then it was worth every minute of the distress, and every last drop of energy I had spent.

A member of the hospital board, Dr Renée Barge, wrote to me a month or so later thanking me for bringing the matter to their attention.[25] She listed the new procedures, supervision plans, structures and training programmes that had arisen from the five points the *klachtencommissie* pulled from my complaint. She didn't, of course, apologize, but acknowledged: "your experiences with our hospital have been poor", and promised that my complaint would "certainly contribute to the improvement of the quality of care in our hospital".

I really hoped she meant it. I hope it did make a difference, and that it continues to. But when I close my eyes and let Flexitime-associate Ilse Werff enter my memory … and the angry nurse who wanted to take Peter outside … and Madelein, who had declared I was "not her patient" and so had left me sitting on the floor … I struggled to let hope triumph over experience.

---

25 The Bronovo *Klachtencommissie* ruling and follow-up letter can be found on the website that accompanies this book.

25 | October and November 2016 … UMC, Utrecht

… it is worth noting that nothing is harder to take in hand, more perilous to conduct, or more uncertain in its success, than to take the lead in the introduction of a new order of things.
Niccolò Machiavelli

Something else had been brewing in the autumn of 2016 while I was busy with Bronovo. I got a WhatsApp from Arie Franx on 6 October:

… UMCU is preparing the first symposium on open disclosure, including the lecture they want to name after you. I am convinced that intentions are sincere. The organizers have suggested it would be most appropriate to tell your story in the first edition of this meeting. They have asked me to explore if you, Professor Van der Vaart and I would be prepared to be present. I think this is challenging for all three of us, but also a chance. If you come, so will I. I have not asked Prof. Van der Vaart yet but will do so tonight …

Could it be true that UMCU was ready to adopt a professional and grown-up approach to open disclosure after serious harm?

Were they willing to address what had happened in 2011, how they had failed us again in 2013 by having no serious-harm protocol, and how they had aggravated matters further in 2015 by allowing their lawyers to drive the compensation process and try to impose a gagging clause? I was determined to repay their move towards openness and transparency with fair-mindedness and conciliation. Sure, I would tell the truth with no holds barred, but the important thing was that the Adrienne Cullen Lecture would do its job and herald a new era of openness and compassion for patients, families and doctors caught up in serious harm events.

A few weeks later, Van der Vaart, Franx and I met at a hotel across the motorway from the hospital. The organizer of UMCU's transparency programme, Professor Nine Knoers, would join us later in the morning. All three of us were approaching the matter enthusiastically, but cautiously. Van der Vaart was the person who was risking most, and Franx and I wanted to know could we speak openly without compromising him. I had visions of TV crews camped at the end of his driveway. I knew enough about journalism to worry that Van der Vaart could end up being scapegoated and blamed for everything. Of course, I wished he had made a note of what he sent to the lab in April 2011, and that he had noticed that my results were missing. But I had long since forgiven him for his part in my calamity. His human error was only part of the story. Other factors, such as attitudes in the pathology department to handling cancer diagnoses and the absence of set protocols for dealing with them, along with the ethos in the hospital and the apparent lack of extra safety measures, hospital-wide, to protect patient data during the massive migration to electronic files were too complex to make great news. It was much easier to look for someone to pin the blame on.

Curiously though, what Van der Vaart was most worried about was that the symposium would not be truly open – that it would be limited to a UMCU-only audience, and the board would stay silent. He had already spoken plainly and openly about what had happened to two different audiences at UMCU. He saw no point in doing the same again. An outside audience was a requirement as was a response from the board.

I was impressed. This was brave. Here I was, worried about protecting him from critical exposure, but he was more worried about the lecture not being open enough. We were all concerned that the board thought it was fine for staff and patients to be "open", but that the same rules didn't apply to them – certainly not if there were to be outsiders at the lecture.

At this point that Nine Knoers arrived. She was Professor of Genetics at UMCU, and had been chosen to manage the move towards transparency, which had been demanded by the IGZ. She was a good choice. She is empathic, insightful and a born diplomat. I liked her immediately. Franx explained what we had been discussing and the conclusion we had come to: we would all gladly take part in her symposium and deliver the first Adrienne Cullen Lecture, as long as all three of us were on the platform together; the audience was open to other hospitals, the public and the media; and the board needed to acknowledge its role in the calamity and its aftermath.

"I agree completely", Knoers said. "I'm meeting Margriet Schneider this afternoon, and I'll tell her what we've discussed and what we've agreed."

"Do you think she'll give her approval?" I asked.

"If not, I'll resign," said Knoers, winning my admiration forever.

Knoers' view was that it would not be possible to hold an "Adrienne Cullen Lecture" without explaining why the lecture was so called. In order to explain, it would be necessary to tell the Adrienne Cullen story.

"And why would anyone other than you tell the Adrienne Cullen story?" she asked.

Deny, dismiss, dehumanise

"I think that when Professor Schneider promised me that there would be an annual Adrienne Cullen Lecture, she might have been thinking it would be a memorial lecture", I explained, trying to put this awkward matter delicately. "She might have thought – because it was what we believed last year – that I would be dead before the symposium would happen. I don't think she visualized me alive and kicking and taking part."

All three looked at me in astonishment. This obviously hadn't occurred to them. Still, a promise was a promise. And I had it in writing. Would the CEO honour her promise? Nine Knoers was going to do her best to make sure she did.

Regardless of whether Knoers would succeed in persuading Schneider to do the decent thing, I was really happy that this meeting had taken place. Although I had been in regular contact with both Van der Vaart and Franx, this was the first time I'd felt we really understood each other. I sensed that both men – and now Knoers too – wanted to do the right thing. I had felt for some time that the only way I could redeem some of the damage caused by the calamity was to make something positive happen that wouldn't have happened had the calamity not occurred. It's probably a form of vanity, but if my death meant that UMCU, and maybe other hospitals too, would find a new way of dealing with serious harm and a new openness, well then it wouldn't be all bad. That morning, in the hotel room, I believe that the others saw what I was trying to achieve.

Arie Franx had something on his mind. He spoke, hesitating and very serious.

"Do you remember last summer, during the compensation issue when we were supposed to talk on the phone, and I sent you an app ... about only being able to talk to you about health questions?" he asked me.

I nodded. I remembered well. It had hurt.

"That was the lowest point in my career as a doctor", he said quietly. "I am ashamed that I let that happen. I will never again let anyone from a hospital board tell me what I can, or cannot, talk to a patient about. I will not allow this to happen ever again."

This was the second time Franx had surprised me at a meeting by telling me a truth I wasn't expecting. At the best of times, it takes guts to acknowledge failure. In this context, to admit that he had been pushed to act in a way that made him ashamed of himself was deeply moving. I wanted to tell him it was okay now, that I understood, but I couldn't find the words.

I wanted to know more detail, but the truth of it was that when the hospital heard he was planning to talk to me, they told him that he could only answer questions I asked related to medical or psychological help. He was instructed not to discuss any aspect of the compensation issue – that was the business of the lawyers.

"I spent so much of that holiday on my phone that my wife threatened to throw it overboard", Franx added, unintentionally lightening the atmosphere and making me smile. Yet it made me realize again how far the fallout of the calamity had spread. It was affecting the lives and holidays of people I had never met.

I was told something else at that meeting too. Franx said that in 2015, when things had been bad with my health, he and Van der Vaart had written a letter to the board. They told them that they felt that they had been kept in the dark about the compensation issue and that policy had been made without consulting them or listening to their advice as my doctors, and that they had been discouraged from having any contact with me except to discuss healthcare.

"We felt ignored and that we had allowed UMCU to make us abandon our professional ethical principles of transparency, and honesty to patients, always", said Franx. "To me, this was an obstacle to trust and collaboration. Huub and I were hoping we could restore this damage together. We hand-delivered a letter saying these things to Professor Schneider's office. We were listened to, but there was never any reply or follow-up from the board."

Their letter, like my own correspondence to the board, fell into a black hole.

26 | December 2016 to April 2017 ... UMC, Utrecht and AMC, Amsterdam

[S]he who fights, can lose. [S]he who doesn't fight, has already lost.
Bertolt Brecht

Christmas had come again. And I was still here. I knew better though than to annoy the gods by becoming complacent. There was little chance of that anyway because my CEA levels had started to climb again – just a shade higher than normal at first. In July, they had been 6 (fractionally higher than the 5 normal), but by October, they had hopped to 12 – still not very worrying, but there's only ever one reason why my CEA levels rise, and that's because another tumour is growing somewhere. Remembering how traumatic Christmas 2015 had been and my 2016 New Year in Bronovo, I decided to wait until January for investigations. It made sense to me, and Van der Velden agreed. If you start ordering PET-CTs and MRIs while tumours are tiny, they can be too hard to detect. So Peter and I had Christmas "off" – in the sense that we were determined to keep away from hospitals at all costs.

And it turned out to be a very peaceful Christmas. I was

feeling quite well. The second JJ-stent had been removed in July, and Van Houten had put me on a long-term, low-dose antibiotic. The result was that six months had passed without any recurrences of urosepsis – or even the tiniest UTI. My body was pleased with itself. I was comfortable and I had started exercising gently on the treadmill and on my bike to rebuild my fitness levels, such as they were. I was eating a disgustingly healthy diet with as much organic fruit and vegetables as possible. Even my shampoo was from the worthiest of organic suppliers.

Over Christmas, I spoke to Nine Knoers on the phone. The board wouldn't agree to Van der Vaart, Franx and me giving a joint lecture where we would all openly discuss what had gone wrong and describe the damage it had caused, in its various ways, to all of us. They weren't, Nine explained, "ready". In my experience, those holding power are never "ready" for any change that involves ceding that power.

"Did you resign?" I asked her, both wishing she had (because that's what the board deserved), and hoping she hadn't.

"I'm considering it", she replied. "I'm going to take some time over the holiday to see if I can still be associated with the transparency programme."

"If you resign, probably nothing will ever change", I said, starting to realize that Knoers was undoubtedly the best person in UMCU to lead the hospital towards openness and transparency and away from the rigid hierarchical structure where the board and lawyers were on top and the patients at the bottom.

Knoers had her own demanding career as a professor of genetics. The hospital's transparency programme threatened to take over much of her time for the foreseeable future – did she need this, especially if it was going to turn into an ongoing struggle against the board? But to walk away ... would that be the right thing to do? I wasn't any help. Spitting Mad Adrienne wanted her to resign with a flourish along with all of her team because the board wouldn't let them exercise their own judgement. A slightly more mature aspect of my personality knew that with Knoers at the helm, we stood a fighting chance of achieving a genuinely more transparent UMCU. I locked Spitting Mad Adrienne in her kennel and started trying to persuade Knoers to stay and fight.

I talked to Arie Franx and exchanged emails with Huub Van der Vaart. We were all very disappointed, but none of us was really surprised. We were relieved in the New Year to discover that Knoers had not resigned, or not yet anyway. She would go to the board again to try to make them understand. That didn't go well. With the original date of 8 February, 2017 now a non-runner, Knoers suggested April.

****

Back at AMC the latest bloods were back. Since October, my CEA had jumped from 12 to 39 and Van der Velden ordered a PET-CT. He had sort of got used to me throwing him googlies, but my latest results had a wackier spin than normal – even my normal. I had two new metastases. Meet Tumour 4 and Tumour 5. Tumour 4 was in the fairly predictable location of the abdominal wall, and it was about 2cm in size. Depressing, but not strange. Tumour 5, though, was already over 6cm long and 2cm in diameter – and it was in my upper left thigh, on the inside, where it becomes the groin. That was what was weird. In his entire career, Van der Velden had never seen cervical cancer metastasize in the leg. And being a gynaecologist, legs were not his area.

"The tumour is in the adductor brevis muscle in your upper leg", he explained. "My feeling is that it is operable, but we need to consult an orthopaedic oncologist."

"And the smaller tumour?" I asked.

"That one I can almost certainly remove", he said.

The orthopaedic oncologist, Dr Otto van Hove, agreed that

surgery was an option. He and Van der Velden would operate together. They'd make one long incision from just under my belly button, down my lower abdomen, across my pubis to the groin and 6 or 7 centimetres down my left leg. I took a deep breath. His sketch looked like a map of the River Nile.

"Not two small incisions, then?" I asked. Apparently, that wasn't possible. There wouldn't be enough space for the two surgeons to work together in this relatively tight space if they made two separate incisions. This was going to be a humdinger of a scar.

Surgery was scheduled for 5 April. With trepidation, I checked into the gynaecology ward the previous afternoon. Thirteen months had passed since my last stay there, and I was dismayed to find that the arrangements that had been made with the head nurse in 2016 had all been forgotten. But I had come prepared. I had brought Willem's famous nursing notes, along with a very good letter from my new psychologist explaining about my medical history, my PTSD, my previous unpleasant experiences at the hospital and the fact that I was terrified. With some additional encouragement from Van der Velden, the nurse looking after my admission, Britt, switched me to a room on my own, and relaxed the rules to allow Peter to come and go outside normal visiting hours. She also agreed to come with me to the theatre the following morning and to stay until I was knocked out. I was very conscious that I was returning to the place where I had encountered Sonja the previous year. I was terrified she would be involved in my care, or that I'd encounter her when I was too ill to do anything about it. Van der Velden had anticipated this and had spoken to the anaesthetists. I would be looked after by other people, and I would be kept in a private recovery bay away from where the incident had occurred.

With all this special care, I was reassured that I'd be okay. Anaesthetics wanted things to work out, and Britt would be with me the whole time. Van der Velden promised that he himself would be there when I woke up, and that Peter would be allowed in immediately afterwards. It was a deal. I was feeling strong. My psychologist had started me on EMDR treatment for complex and multiple traumas. We hadn't been sure it would work, because the majority of PTSD patients have been traumatized by one traumatic event, whereas my situation was that each time I was readmitted to hospital, and each time I encountered staff hostile to me because I couldn't speak Dutch, or I didn't get safe and competent care, I became traumatized anew. It was a bit like putting a soldier with PTSD back into battle again and again. But the EMDR had started to work, and I was unpicking some of the pain that had been caused in the past.

I was second on the surgery list. The nurses had me up, showered and clad in a blue surgical gown and fishnet knickers by 07:00. Transport came, and Britt joined the procession down to the first floor. They wheeled me through the double automatic doors right beside the bay where I had been parked during the "Ah! Hah! She doesn't understand!" incident. But then we turned sharp right, away from the bay and into a private cubicle. The friendly giraffes and monkeys painted on the walls gave the game away that these cubicles were usually kept for children. I didn't mind. Anything that was going to make this easier was fine by me. And anyway, I'd brought my own babysitter. To make her sterile for theatre, Britt was struggling into a dark blue onesie, complete with hood and feet.

"I'm just like a Tellytubby!" she laughed pulling up the zip to her throat. And she was. Dressed like this, she blended in well with the pre-school theme. I was glad she was there.

The anaesthetist, Evert de Haan, chatted away in English to put me at my ease. His assistant draped hot sheets over me to keep me warm as we all advanced together towards the theatre. There were two women already there looking at a wall-mounted screen

Deny, dismiss, dehumanise

or light box. I recognized one of them as the gynaecology intern I'd met with Van der Velden the previous afternoon. I smiled at her, pleased to see another friendly face. The woman with her also turned around when she heard us come in.

"Oh, you're speaking English!" she remarked, surprised. "Do you not speak Dutch?"

Everyone froze. I tried to keep calm – after all, she had just asked a question.

"No", I replied. "I'm sorry, I don't."

"How am I going to communicate with you?" she asked. "I think this is going to be a problem."

Still no one said a word or moved a muscle. The anaesthetist and his assistant were behind me. Britt was to my right. I stole a glance. She was staring at the woman with her eyes wide and her mouth open. Obviously, no one else was going to do or say anything, so I replied again.

"I don't think it'll be a problem", I answered her, trying my best to keep my voice steady. "Usually, we manage, and there are lots of people here today who can help." I indicated Britt and the anaesthetist, who were both still struck dumb. I thought that had done the trick, as the woman said nothing more. My bed was pushed alongside the operating table and the anaesthetist asked me to slide onto it. I did, and managed to keep the gappy surgical gown covering the important places in the process. I forced myself not to get upset at this hostile welcome. I was trying to focus on what I was doing and blanking out the latest member of the language police. I uttered a furious, "thanks a bunch!" in my mind to Britt and the anaesthetist for their timely and professional interventions.

No sooner was I on the operating table than the woman returned.

"But do you understand any Dutch at all?" she persisted. "If I say something to you, will you understand me or not?"

I'd had enough. Who was this person? She hadn't bothered to introduce herself and she obviously had a good command of English because her questions were totally fluent. I stifled every smart answer that Spitting Mad Adrienne wanted to hurl at her. Still no one else in the room was lifting a finger to help. Britt and the intern knew my history, and I suspected the anaesthetist had a fair idea too. Why did they think it was appropriate to let me deal with this ongoing onslaught on my own? Tears were a hair's breadth away. Keeping my voice as low and steady as I could, I turned to her.

"Look", I said. "If I *could* speak Dutch, we'd already be having this conversation in Dutch."

I didn't entirely succeed in keeping the anguish out of my voice. The woman looked taken aback. I think this was the first inkling she'd had that there might have been something wrong with her welcoming technique. I turned my head away and tried not to dwell on what had just happened. But it was pretty hard not to think that if I had been a Dutch patient, would she have greeted me with something like "Hello, my name is blah-blah and I'm going to look after you during your surgery today." How could anyone working in an operating theatre, with vulnerable, seriously ill patients, think that how she had approached me, from the moment I entered the room, even vaguely resembled an acceptable way to behave? The fact that neither Britt nor De Haan, who was the senior person in the theatre, had seen fit to stop her was something I couldn't bear to think about. I concentrated on what De Haan was saying to me about antibiotics, and on the assistant, who was putting a BP cuff on my arm.

Less than a minute later, the woman was beside me again. This time, the intern was right alongside her, shoulder-to-shoulder. The woman's face was very red.

"I'd just like to say", she began. "The important thing is that we are all here for you."

Deny, dismiss, dehumanise

So someone had eventually said something to her. I guessed it was the intern.

"That's good to know", I answered. "Thank you." I was being more gracious than I felt. She had totally smashed the flimsy shell of security I had tried to build around myself. I really didn't get it. AMC was full of patients who couldn't speak Dutch. Peter and I regularly heard English spoken in the cafeterias, the outpatient clinics, the hospital supermarket and on the wards. Why was she reacting as though this was something unique? And who on earth was she? She wasn't either of my surgeons, and she wasn't the anaesthetist. Was she a theatre nurse? Another intern? Why was the fact that she felt she couldn't communicate with me so important? Pretty soon, I'd be out cold, and no one would have to worry about communicating with me in any language.

I tried my best to blank her from my mind and concentrate on getting through the surgery. Van der Velden came in. I didn't mention what had happened – not a good idea to upset one's surgeon just before surgery, and anyway, I'd dealt with it ... for the moment. Van Hove, the orthopaedic surgeon, turned up too. Just a quick "hello" before disappearing again into the anteroom. The anaesthetist had found a vein in my left hand. Shortly after, I was in blissful oblivion where what languages I spoke mattered to no one.

While I was out cold, both tumours were removed. A worried Peter had to wait over four hours for news. Tumour 4 posed a few problems as it had started to adhere itself to my bladder. But it was removed intact and my bladder wasn't compromised. Tumour 5 was bigger than the scans had shown. Van Hove removed it, along with most of my adductor brevis muscle, part of one of the other adductor muscles and a thin slice of my pubic bone. They had warned me that I would have difficulty walking for a while, maybe even permanently. Peter had hired a pair of crutches from our local pharmacy, and they were already propped up behind the door in my room in H5 Zuid. I visualized Kerry Weaver from *ER*, Dr Greg House or Walter White Junior in *Breaking Bad*. I wasn't gone on the idea, but it was a small price to pay for the successful removal of two more tumours.

27 | April to August 2017 ... AMC, Amsterdam

April to August 2017
AMC Amsterdam

I firmly believe it is not just about common courtesy, but it runs much deeper. Introductions are about making a human connection between one human being who is suffering and vulnerable, and another human being who wishes to help. They begin therapeutic relationships and can instantly build trust in difficult circumstances.
Kate Granger[26]

My fears that my surgery would cause me to miss the first UMCU symposium on openness and transparency were quickly allayed. Nine Knoers wrote to say that the event had been pushed back again. She had spoken to

---

26 Kate Granger MBE, who died in 2016 was a campaigner for better patient care. While hospitalized with post-operative sepsis, she noticed that many staff looking after her did not introduce themselves before treating her. To Kate, a consultant geriatrician as well as a cancer patient, it felt incredibly wrong that such a basic step in communication was missing, hence the launch of the highly successful, "Hello, my name is ..." campaign in the United Kingdom. https://hellomynameis.org.uk/

Schneider about it in February, but she hadn't yet received a reply; the hospital was, she said, very preoccupied with the demands of the IGZ.

Three weeks or so had passed since the surgery on 5 April, and I was starting to feel better. I hadn't forgotten about the incident in the operating theatre, but I'd been curious to see whether anyone would contact me about it. They didn't, so on 25 April, I wrote to the hospital's complaints officer, Cornelis Gaal. I told him what had happened, and asked him to inform the surgical department. He promised he would send my letter to the management of the ward concerned.

★★★★★★★★★

Meanwhile, in London, Arie Franx was attending the 2017 International Forum on Quality and Safety in Healthcare, an annual event organized jointly by the US-based Institute for Healthcare Improvement (IHI) and the British Medical Journal (BMJ). He sent me enthusiastic WhatsApps showing slides from the presentations he was attending:

One declared: "Patient Safety Advocates and Healthcare Staff – A Shared Challenge". It had a picture beside it showing Sisyphus pushing his stone up the mountain. That made me smile.

The next slide was even better. "Patients as Teachers", it proclaimed, "Where's the Patient's Voice in Health Professional Education?"

"You would have liked to attend this conference", Franx texted. There were apparently patients there too, not just medics. I texted back that I was thinking of writing a book about everything that had happened to me since 2013. He was immediately supportive.

"That story can be extremely powerful", he texted back.

"Want to help?"

"I would be honoured to help you with the book".
That was 28 April 2017. I started writing that day.

****

I had a telephone appointment with Van der Velden. The pathology results were back. It wasn't good news. The margins were not clear in either of the sites from where the tumours had been removed. It was very likely that tumours would recur in both areas.

"How likely?" I asked. The answer was that it was 80% to 90% certain that cancer would recur in my leg and in my abdominal wall.

"How quickly?" was my next question. That was harder to answer. We decided to monitor my CEA and CA-125 levels more frequently, starting right now, in early May, to establish a baseline. I was to go for another blood test in mid-June.

I was still going to Dutch lessons every week, and filling notebooks with my attempts to write coherent sentences with the right prepositions and verb forms, "*Niels is bijna klaar met zijn werk.* (Niels is nearly finished his work)" I wrote, and, "*Waarom gaat hij vanavond op bezoek bij zijn ouders?* (Why is he going to visit his parents this evening?)". I was still struggling through the beginners' level textbook, and it wasn't getting any easier – although I'd noticed that I understood a little of what people were saying to me. Not enough though to be sure of the details or to formulate a reply.

The book, this book, had started to take up a good deal of my time. Once I began to write it all down, I had the sensation that it was already written somewhere in my subconscious, and all I had to do was dictate it to myself. The chapters started flowing out of me. In one way, it was cathartic; in another, the writing was making me relive a lot of the painful events.

As I relived it, I was amazed at how much had happened, and how entrenched attitudes were in the hospitals. UMCU was behaving as though I were the Antichrist, and looked set to postpone the Adrienne Cullen Lecture until I was long dead rather than let me cross their threshold and speak honestly about what had happened there. AMC was determined to turn its face away from any suggestion that the hospital might be systematically failing its non-Dutch-speaking patients, and so allowing the widespread bullying that some staff are meting out to them.

Talking to other patients, Dutch and expats, I heard over and over that many felt let down by their hospitals. Often, even when the treatment itself was good, the attitude to patients left them dispirited and humiliated. I heard so many personal stories: a friend was given a breast implant that was inexplicably a size too big, causing much discomfort when her own skin was stretched over it; a hospital A&E tried to send an elderly neighbour home with laxatives and an enema even though her husband and daughter told them they suspected she'd had a stroke (they were right); a bed-bound patient was handed a scissors with the comment, "cut it off" when she asked the nurses to help her wash her hair after being bed-bound for a week; a breast cancer patient, who had been disease-free for almost five years was told over the phone on Christmas Eve that she had a metastasis on her liver, she was home alone at the time; an ex-Navy veteran needed a knee operation, but the surgeon operated on the wrong knee, leaving him permanently in a wheelchair; an elderly woman who developed an infection at the site of her IV was accused by the nurse of causing it herself; a patient with advanced dementia was brought to A&E by her daughter and was disrespected and treated unkindly by all the staff except the ambulance crew. All these stories, and many more, were told to me by my Dutch neighbours, colleagues and friends. Other ex-pats had had experiences similar to mine. A friend who needed a sperm count tried his best to speak Dutch on the phone to the clinic. He started to struggle and asked if he could speak English. The clinic hung up. His partner, who is

Deny, dismiss, dehumanise

Dutch, phoned back and was told that the line had unexpectedly been cut off, "sorry". An English friend was taken to hospital with an acute asthma attack. He had forgotten his insurance card and the hospital refused to treat him. Another ex-pat, a very young man, needed surgery and was asked by a nurse did they not have hospitals in his country.

In none of the above cases did the patient or the family complain (apart from the Dutch partner of the man with asthma who kicked up a fuss until someone helped). A psychologist friend of Peter's told him that over the years she had been practising, she'd had hundreds of patients traumatized by their hospital experiences. Patients are able to deal with the illnesses and pain that are necessary parts of living and dying. What we cannot come to terms with is the frequent lack of empathy we face, the lack of respect for us as people and the way the systems-driven healthcare pushes us along a treatment conveyor belt that prioritises protocol and process over need, compassion and listening.

Many people working in healthcare see what's happening. Many feel that it's wrong. Mostly they decide, "this is the way it is and there's nothing I can do about it". And that's where staff burnout begins.

★★★★★★★★★

Mid-June came. Blood test time... and it made me wonder why I'd heard nothing back from Cornelis Gaal, AMC's complaints officer. I sent another email asking if he had been in contact with the surgical department after he received my email seven weeks earlier. He replied that he had indeed contacted them: "I apologize for the fact that you still have not received a reaction ... The manager of the operation centre and the anaesthetist concerned are preparing a reaction. I have contacted them and have insisted on sending it to you very soon."

I thanked him for his efforts on my behalf, and headed to AMC for the blood tests.

A week later, I got an email from Evert de Haan, the anaesthetist who had been with me in theatre that day. I took a deep breath before opening the email. My greatest fear was that he'd deny that any such incident had occurred, or would try to persuade me that the fault lay with me for misunderstanding hospital staff's friendly questions. I opened the email.

Dear Mrs. Cullen,

First I would like to express my apologies for the delay in answering your complaint.

In your complaint, you stated that again you were confronted with a staff member who inappropriately reacted on the fact you don't speak and understand Dutch language.

Present at the incident in theatre, I remember that other members of the surgical team, including myself, immediately have corrected this staff member. Unfortunately for you this was again an unpleasant experience on a tense moment, right before surgery.

After your complaint, we've discussed the incident with other members of the operating staff and stressed the importance of being hospitable to all patients, especially vulnerable patients. This includes refraining from remarks about knowledge of the Dutch language, particularly because the use of English is no problem for any member of the surgical team. Only when patient safety is endangered, Dutch is mandatory to ensure proper and immediate patient care.

I hope the unpleasant experience didn't have any influence on your recovery and trust in the AMC and staff can somewhat be restored.

Sincerely,

Well, at least he wasn't denying that it had happened. That's a start. And at least my complaint provoked them into actually talking about the incident – but it depressed me that it took a written complaint, three weeks after the incident, to provoke them into looking at their own actions and behaviour towards a patient. I would have thought that such an incident would have been discussed thoroughly and critically immediately afterwards.

I wrote back on 26 June. I told him that I took heart from the fact that my complaint had prompted them, albeit belatedly, to discuss the matter. I asked him why, if "the use of English is no problem for any member of the surgical team", was such a fuss made of the fact that I couldn't speak Dutch.

I took issue with his memory of what had happened and his assertion that "other members of the surgical team, including myself, immediately have corrected this staff member". That didn't happen. Everyone in the theatre stayed silent the first time I was asked did I not speak Dutch; amazingly, no one intervened when the unknown woman asked me how she was going to communicate with me and declared that it was going to be a problem; and still no one intervened when she approached me for the third time asking, "But do you not understand any Dutch? If I say something to you, will you understand it or not?" In what way was this "immediately correcting" the staff member? From where I was sitting on the operating table, what happened was that everyone watched while I dealt with the woman three separate times until it became clear that I was on the verge of tears. Whatever steps were eventually taken to "correct" her came way too late.

I asked for the opportunity to speak to them about the matter as sending reminders and waiting eight weeks to receive any reply whatsoever from them didn't make for a very spontaneous dialogue, and I was still at a loss to understand why it had happened. But I heard no more from them.

✴✴✴✴✴✴✴✴✴

A few days later, the CEA and CA-125 results were back. They were still rising. I'd been aware for a week or so that Tumour 5, the one in my left leg and groin, was starting to make its presence felt again. This was the one that had worried me most because the previous tumour in that area had grown very quickly at the end of 2016. I went for an ultrasound of the leg, groin and lower abdomen.

On 24 July, we took the train to Amsterdam and talked to Van der Velden. He told us that the ultrasound showed two "suspicious areas". Meet Tumour 6, already seven-and-a-half centimetres long in the left leg and groin, and a less clear Tumour 7, on the abdominal wall. He said he had spoken to Professor Lucas Stalpers in radiotherapy – I remembered him from 2013 – who believed he could treat the leg tumour with radiotherapy and hyperthermia.

"I thought I couldn't have radiotherapy a second time?" I said.

Apparently, because much of Tumour 6 was outside the area that had been irradiated in 2013, they believed they could treat this tumour with radiotherapy. The addition of hyperthermia – heating up the tumour – would make the radiotherapy more effective. Another PET-CT was not needed at this stage. Van der Velden felt the size of Tumour 6 made treating it asap the highest priority, regardless of what might be happening elsewhere in my body.

We met Stalpers on 3 August. He was as I remembered him, a few years younger than us, kindly, a little pensive and very engaged with us. We spent more than half-an-hour with him. He told us he believed that the radiotherapy with hyperthermia that Van der Velden had discussed with us was the way to go. Unlike Van der Velden though, he *did* want to see what was going on elsewhere, so there and then, he arranged another PET-CT. He was concerned about two areas in the abdomen – the spot Van der Velden had alerted us to, and another area in the lower abdomen where the ultrasound had found uneven tissue.

Deny, dismiss, dehumanise

"They can do the PET-CT on the morning of the 9th of August", he said. "I start my holidays that day, but we can look at the results together and make a plan before I leave." This was kind, and we appreciated his efforts to put everything in place.

He was as good as his word. When we turned up at the radiotherapy department an hour or so after the PET-CT, Stalpers was waiting for us.

"I can already see the CT on my computer, but not the PET", he said. "I want to go upstairs to take a look at it and I'll be right back down. Can you wait for me?"

Of course we could wait. He was going to discuss the results with the nuclear medicine expert. We appreciated the trouble he was going to. Twenty minutes later, he was back, and he led us into one of the department's consulting rooms. We gathered around the screen.

"There are two problem areas", he began. "The one in the leg that we already know about, and another here", he said, pointing to his own throat.

"My thyroid?" I asked, totally surprised. This I hadn't been expecting.

"Yes, probably the thyroid."

"What about the abdomen?" asked Peter.

"The abdomen is clean."

"Clean?", I asked. "What about the tumour on the abdominal wall that the ultrasound showed?"

"That's surgical scarring", Stalpers explained. "Neither area we were concerned about in the abdomen is suspicious on the PET-CT."

This was wonderful news – except for the bit about the thyroid. A metastasis in the thyroid was very left-field.

"We'll do an ultrasound of the thyroid," said Stalpers. "What's lighting up there could be a tumour, a lymph node or brown fat."

I had never heard of brown fat, but I was immediately in

favour of admitting to any quantities of it. Whatever it was, it was better than a tumour. But the main problem was still Tumour 6, in the left leg. According to the CT scan, it was now around 12 centimetres long and three wide. I wasn't surprised. I had been in pain there for several weeks. Stalpers proposed 23 sessions of 2Gy of radiotherapy over five weeks, with weekly hyperthermia to make it more effective.

"If it turns out that the thyroid spot is not a tumour, I think I will increase that to 30 sessions of 2Gy", he said.

"So I will have radiotherapy every day for five or six weeks?" I had been hoping that this time, there wouldn't be the same gruelling schedule as I had faced in 2013. But I was out of luck. Stalpers explained what would happen. For the hyperthermia, a probe would be inserted into Tumour 6 on my first day of treatment. This would stay in situ for the duration. They would then heat the tumour once a week using microwaves, only stopping when the probe indicated that the tumour had reached 42 degrees centigrade.

"By how much do you hope to reduce the tumour in Adrienne's leg?" asked Peter.

"The aim is to shrink it completely."

We were both pleased. Perhaps seeing our optimistic faces, Stalpers issued a warning.

"I have to discuss the side effects with you", he said.

Well, I didn't need to be told that everything comes with a price.

"It is probable that you will get lymphoedema in your left leg."

I nodded and told him I already suffered from lymphoedema. The new radiotherapy would make this worse.

"You will also probably suffer, for a time, with urethritis," he said." That's inflammation of the urethra."

Another complaint area I was no stranger to.

"And the radiation will cause bone pain. And that is likely to be ongoing."

"Which bone?" I asked. "My pubic bone?"

"Yes."

"How bad will it be?"

"You will always be conscious of it."

Well, if that was the price, then that's what I'd pay. It would be a bargain if he was going to shrink the aggressive Tumour 6 into oblivion and buy me some more quality time. I was busy; I had a book to finish. I took a deep breath and nodded my agreement. I was to start my first treatment on Monday, 21 August, and I would be called for an ultrasound of the thyroid the following week. Stalpers would be on holiday for three weeks, but his student, Dr Ineke Erelman, would look after me until his return.

We drove home. Every time I found myself spooked about the insertion of the probe into my tumour, or overcome at the thought of another five or six weeks of daily commuting up and down to Amsterdam, I reminded myself that my abdomen was "clean".

28 | August 2017 to January 2018 … AMC and AvL, Amsterdam

We have two options, medically and emotionally: give up, or Fight Like Hell.
Lance Armstrong

The good news didn't last long. A week later, the official PET-CT report was in. Although it was compiled by the same expert that Stalpers had consulted with upstairs on the day of the scan, the official result painted a different picture – or leastways, it was being interpreted differently. Van der Velden told me that he had discussed the matter with the tumour board and the agreement now was that I should not be given the radical treatment that was aimed at totally shrinking Tumour 6. Instead, the tumour board recommended a milder, palliative treatment of just ten radiotherapy sessions of 3Gy and no hyperthermia. The reason was that in addition to Tumour 6, the PET-CT report indicated that I had three additional tumours, two in the abdomen and one in the thyroid. Patients with four metastases are not candidates for radical radiotherapy with hyperthermia.

I wasn't happy. Nor was Peter. Stalpers had been crystal clear.

The abdomen was "clean", and the thyroid "tumour" was likely to be brown fat. I wasn't prepared to throw away my one and only shot at shrinking the large and painful Tumour 6 on the basis of metastases whose very existence was debatable. Arguments that the "overwhelming likelihood" was that they were metastases weren't entirely convincing me. At no point in my medical history had "likely" scenarios featured very prominently. A missed cancer diagnosis was unlikely. A mucinous adenocarcinoma was unlikely. A metastasis in my ovary was one-in-a-hundred. That the same ovary pressing against a ureter where a kidney stone happened to be trying to descend was almost unbelievable. And Tumour 6 deciding to show up in the leg – Van der Velden had never seen or come across another instance of this, so that wasn't a likely scenario either. My body wasn't prone to doing what was expected, and I didn't see why it would start now.

I started to research. There is only one recorded instance ever of an adenocarcinoma metastasizing in the thyroid gland. Either mine was the second instance in international medical history... or it was brown fat. The alleged tumours in the abdomen had originally been interpreted by nuclear medicine experts as scarring from past surgeries and uneven tissue. I preferred those interpretations. A lymph gland high in my abdomen near the diaphragm, was harder to argue away as it was reported to have grown from 8mm in April to 18mm in August. But it was not causing me any trouble, while the tumour in my groin was growing aggressively. Unless we treated that radically while I had the chance, I was sure it would be my downfall.

I wanted to talk to another radiotherapist. No one was available. I asked again, and again, and eventually Ineke Erelman, the resident looking after me in Stalpers' absence, was free to come and talk to us. Whatever her own opinion was on the matter, Erelman was not in a position to argue with the hospital's tumour board. Only a consultant could do that. She promised she'd talk to her interim supervisor about me. I went home and started writing down questions. In my experience, doctors like to think of communication with patients being based on a framework of questions-and-answers – patients had questions, doctors answered them.

On Monday, 21 August, I presented myself at AMC's radiotherapy department for my first palliative radiotherapy treatment as recommended by the tumour board – a course of treatment I was convinced was wrong for me. Before going to the radiotherapy suite, we spoke again with Erelman, who had another senior doctor, Dr Hendrik Bauer with her. I remembered Bauer from 2013, when I had found him honest and clear. He wasn't Erelman's supervisor, but he was the only senior doctor she could find that Monday morning. He was happy to take a look at our list of questions.

His answers gave voice to my worst fears. The palliative radiotherapy I was due to start that morning would be expected to stop the growth of Tumour 6 for only four to six months. That meant that as soon as Christmas, Tumour 6 could be growing again.

"And what treatment options would be available to me then?" I asked.

"Chemotherapy", said Bauer, and Erelman nodded in agreement.

"But Adrienne has always been crystal clear that she doesn't want more chemotherapy", said Peter.

"It doesn't seem to offer much help to cervical cancer patients with metastases", I explained.

Bauer and Erelman nodded their understanding. They didn't disagree.

"I don't want this." I was adamant. "It isn't what I agreed to. I want the radiotherapy plan outlined by Professor Stalpers. I'm not convinced enough that I have three other metastases, and I'm absolutely not ready for mild, palliative radiotherapy!" I added, trying to look as alive as possible. Erelman promised to talk to her interim supervisor, Dr Simon van Borselen, during the week and arrange another consultation where Peter and I could talk to him and ask him our questions.

With a heavy heart and a feeling of despair, I headed towards the radiotherapy suite for my first session. It went without incident. The radiotherapy staff were as kind and as patient as I had remembered from 2013.

We met Van Borselen and Erelman at the end of my first week of radiotherapy. Van Borselen heard us out. It was plain that I wasn't happy to be undergoing a course of treatment that would buy me only a few months before aggressive Tumour 6 started growing again, probably just as rapidly as before.

"She only has one shot at this", Peter explained. "As we understand it, when this tumour starts to grow again, she can't have more radiotherapy, and the tumour is inoperable. It's vital that we get the right treatment now, while there's still a chance of stopping it in its tracks."

I had a couple of suggestions. "Is it still possible to extend the ten sessions of radiotherapy to the original 23 Stalpers suggested, and maybe target the tumour more closely to minimize the damage to surrounding tissue?" I asked. "And is it too late now for the hyperthermia?"

The answer on the hyperthermia was clear enough. That boat had sailed. It only made sense to begin the hyperthermia and the radiotherapy at the same time. But Erelman was enthusiastic about the idea of extending the radiotherapy sessions and targeting this additional radiation on a smaller area. It was along the lines of what she had been planning to suggest to us.

"But what will the tumour board say?" I asked. "I presume we have to get their agreement? Can I talk to them? I'm sure I could convince them that I'm not ready for mild palliative care."

I saw the ghost of a smile on Van Borselen's face and a flash of horror on Erelman's.

"We will talk to them about this on Monday", promised Van Borselen.

"But will they agree?", asked Peter.

"I think we can make a case", nodded Van Borselen. "We'll do our best."

The AMC gynaecology tumour board sits on Monday afternoons. On Tuesday morning, Peter and I were back with Erelman and Van Borselen. The tumour board had no problem with the new radiotherapy treatment plan. This plan, the third in as many weeks, would involve finishing the ten sessions of 3Gy I had already started and then adding a further seven consecutive sessions where the irradiated zone would be smaller and more focused on the tumour. There would be, as Van Borselen had indicated, no hyperthermia with this treatment plan.

I couldn't believe how happy I was to hear that I could have a more radical radiotherapy treatment. I knew there would be a price to pay in terms of side effects, but what was of much greater concern to me was what had happened over the past weeks at AMC. My confidence was shattered. I had been presented with three different radiotherapy plans by three separate doctors over three weeks – the first was a radical plan to shrink Tumour 6 completely, the second was a plan for mild palliative care that would stop Tumour 6 for a few months, and the third seemed like a compromise, reached only because I had protested in the most adamant manner. Attempts had been made to convince me that palliative care was most appropriate for me now and that quality of life was what mattered most. But quality of life had always mattered most. Right from the day in March 2015 when I heard that the cancer had recurred, I had been totally focused on quality of life and determined never to opt to stay alive at any cost. But where to strike that balance between treatment and quality of life was, I was sure, my call.

I asked to be referred to Marc van Beurden at Antoni van Leeuwenhoek (AvL) Hospital, the Netherlands' Cancer Institute, and walked away from AMC. I was devastated as I left AMC behind. Sure, I had had a troubled history with the hospital, but for all the bullying, unkindness and lack of compassion from certain quarters, Van der Velden and his team had saved my life more than once, and there had been kindness too, lots of it. I didn't want to lose sight of that.

The move to AvL was the best thing I ever did. Right from the moment Peter and I walked through the doors, we sensed the difference. It was like landing on another planet. It was full of light, colour and warmth. Someone was playing a piano near the restaurant. A wall of Post-its carried patients' feedback for the hospital and words of encouragement for others. We had lunch on the roof garden high above Amsterdam's busy western suburbs.

The meeting with Van Beurden went well, as did subsequent meetings with other doctors and nurses. I went, on my own, for an MRI, an ultrasound and to have blood taken. Staff were nice to me. No one made barbed comments about my lack of Dutch. At reception, staff looked up and smiled as we approached. It made the world of difference.

At first, I was afraid to trust that this hospital was truly different. I expected the next appointment to be with the person who would shatter the illusion, and for the bullying that I dreaded to resume. I expected the next doctor I'd meet to be offhand, unfamiliar with my history and forget what was discussed at our previous appointment. But here, doctors looked at your file to inform themselves about your history. They saw us as human beings and talked to us as equals. They were kind and professional and they communicated with each other about their patients. I was a long way away from feeling comfortable in any hospital, but for the first time since I became ill I felt that I was receiving highly advanced medical care from a hospital in a western European country in the twenty-first century.

The results from the imaging started to go well too. An ultrasound confirmed that there was nothing suspicious on my thyroid. An MRI of Tumour 6 showed that the radiotherapy had shrunk it somewhat to about 9.5cm, and a subsequent MRI a few months later showed that it was not growing, or not yet anyway. The same MRI reported that "there was nothing suspicious in the abdomen". I didn't know what to make of that. The two alleged tumours that the PET-CT had found in my abdomen in August were not visible in an MRI a few months later. I asked them to look again with reference to the PET-CT. Same result. A highly sensitive MRI showed that there were no tumours visible anywhere in my abdomen. But I knew enough about the inexactitudes of imaging to not let my hopes run too high. If there were tumours there, I'd know about them soon enough.

29 | October to December 2017

In my country, the Netherlands, research showed that 1.6% of patients admitted to hospitals in 2011/2012 suffered a form of potentially preventable harm. That amounts to 70 patients each day, of whom 2-3 die as a result of the preventable harm. Every day. Day in, day out.
Ian Leistikow, Senior Inspector at IGJ

While I was recovering from my radiotherapy, Margriet Schneider began to prey on my mind. Sixteen months had now passed since she had given a commitment to organize the Adrienne Cullen Lecture. The plan Huub van der Vaart, Arie Franx and I had suggested to Nine Knoers had been decisively scuppered by Schneider and the UMCU board nearly a year ago.

I kept in touch with Knoers, from time to time. She told me that she had spoken to Schneider several times during 2017. Schneider told Knoers that she remembered very clearly the promise she had made me and had been thinking about ways, other than the open lecture we wanted, of giving me the floor to tell my story. One of the alternatives was to invite me to speak during the yearly strategic meeting of UMCU's "top" 60 people in the autumn. I told Nine

I didn't see the point in speaking at yet another internal meeting, and when it came to it, this proposition was never made to me. In mid-September when Knoers contacted me again, she felt embarrassed that the Open Disclosure Symposium and Adrienne Cullen Lecture that had been promised had never materialized. She said that she strongly believed that my story "would give the UMCU and its professionals and leaders a great chance to learn from their mistakes".

A few weeks after my contact with Knoers in September, I learned that she had resigned from UMCU to take up a position in another teaching hospital in February 2018. What a loss! Not just from my point of view, but for the hospital to lose a professor of her calibre and ability was shocking. Knoers is a high flyer. She was head of UMCU's department of medical genetics and held the chair of its biomedical genetics division. She also chaired the Dutch Society of Clinical Genetics from 2007 to January 2015 and was a member of the Dutch Health Council. She is internationally renowned as, among many other things, editor of the international scientific journal *Nephron* and is vice-chair of the board of the ERA-EDTA Working group on Inherited Kidney Disorders. Now in her fifties, Knoers had been at UMCU since 2011. There's little doubt that her ongoing inability to get the board to agree to her proposals for introducing "meaningful transparency" to the hospital had played a large part in her decision to leave.

Knoers' imminent departure spurred me into action. On 13 October, I wrote to Schneider expressing my disappointment that no progress had been made on the symposium, and that the decision of the board not to allow the lecture that she herself had proposed was incomprehensible. I also pointed out that some people might think it was a rather cynical exercise to tell a terminally ill patient, who had suffered because the hospital had no "after-serious-harm" protocols in place, that she planned to organize a yearly event on the matter and put that patient's name on the keynote lecture – and then do no such thing.

I started to think of other options – Franx, Van der Vaart and I could hold our own symposium elsewhere; I could write this book faster and find a good publisher, or I could contact the media to tell them the story of the symposium promised by the hospital's CEO, and blocked by her own board.

So I was surprised when Arie Franx phoned me ten days later to tell me that the symposium was to go ahead. It would be organized by Professor Jan-Willem Lammers, director of quality and patient safety, and successor to Kit Roes. My first thoughts were that it was a trick, and that the hospital planned to hold some watered-down version of the symposium that would be attended by a small, hand-picked audience. But Franx assured me that we could hold the lecture exactly as we had proposed it to Knoers a year previously, and that it would be open to people outside UMCU, including the media.

"What's changed?" I asked. "Was it my email to Schneider? Had Knoers' frustrated resignation brought the board to its senses?"

Franx knew no more than I did. He suggested that we meet Jan-Willem Lammers to discuss how to proceed.

And so I found myself, on Friday, 17 November, back in the hotel across the motorway from UMCU. I tried to hide the fact that I couldn't quite forgive Jan-Willem Lammers for not being Nine Knoers, but I don't think I succeeded. I was suspicious of him. I still didn't believe that the hospital board, after adamantly refusing for a whole year to allow the symposium to take place, had suddenly seen the light. I questioned Lammers to see if I could discover what the catch was. I asked him why Schneider and the board had changed their minds. He didn't know either, it seemed. He assured me there was no catch, the symposium Van der Vaart, Franx and I had agreed on, where we would be on the podium together delivering the lecture to an open audience, would go ahead.

I wanted to make sure we were all organizing the same lecture, so I told Lammers and Franx some of what I would be talking about in the lecture. If lines were to be drawn or vetoes issued on mentioning certain subjects, I needed to know now. I would speak only if I were allowed to speak freely. Specifically, I wanted to make sure that Lammers knew about the gagging clauses that UMCU had pressured Peter and me to sign before they would pay any compensation for their medical negligence. Franx had been told that there were never any gagging clauses, and although he assured me that he believed me, I was furious that UMCU had told the doctor who was trying his best to support me that it was absolutely not the case that the hospital had tried to gag us to prevent the details of my story from being made public. I was determined that if the story were going to be told at this symposium, then it would be the whole story.

Lammers listened. He knew some of the story already, but the bit about the gagging clauses was, I sensed, new to him. He acknowledged that I wanted to discuss matters that the UMCU board would not find palatable. And the same went for Van der Vaart and Franx, they too had suffered as a result of the way the hospital had chosen to look the other way after serious harm had been caused. Lammers assured us that there would be no restrictions on what any of us wanted to say.

In his turn, Lammers started to explain the new system that UMCU had put in place over the past year. The hospital had, he said, learned from what had happened to me and now had a proper system for reporting harm, investigating it, compiling reports, and providing support for patients, their families and staff. They had, he said, sought external expertise on the matter from organizations in the Netherlands and abroad.

Indeed, the scenario he outlined was precisely what Peter and I had expected would happen in 2013, and what Professor Prue Vines had described in her letter in October 2015. Now, it seems, when harm is caused at UMCU, a specially trained, "independent" team from a different hospital department carries out a root-cause analysis, or SIRE. This team talks to everyone involved – including the patient and the patient's family. If the patient doesn't want to go back to the hospital to talk to the investigators, the team will meet them at home, or wherever the patient feels comfortable. At the end of the investigation, the team writes a report on its findings, copies of which are shared with the IGZ, the hospital board and all involved – including the patient. Throughout the process, the patient, family members and the doctors and nurses involved in the serious harm all receive specialist support. There were now, Lammers told me, 90 trained peer-support staff in UMCU. He didn't mention how many trained personnel there were to deal with traumatized patients and their families.

The main element of the plan that Lammers outlined that I wasn't convinced about was that the investigators were all UMCU employees. With the best will in the world, it's hard for medical staff to be truly independent when investigating their own colleagues. Hospitals are like villages, small communities where people know one another or are connected in any number of ways. It would be better if the investigative teams came from an outside organization or another hospital. It shouldn't be too difficult for the country's eight teaching hospitals to pool their SIRE investigators and provide more truly independent teams for one another.

I was in danger of feeling tearful listening to Lammers. If what he was saying was true, then it was a start, and it was happening as a direct consequence of what had happened to me – and because of Peter's determination, and mine, to hold them to account. If we had kept silent, as the hospital had expected us to, my medical negligence case would have gone no further than the hospital's legal affairs department.

But UMCU's new protocols put my own situation into stark and painful contrast. Still, no one at the hospital had gone to the trouble of carrying out any investigation into what had happened to my cancer diagnosis. According to Pathology Department Head, Paul Van Diest, he hadn't ever spoken to whoever handled my test results in the lab, he claimed he didn't know who it was who had made the fateful decisions not to contact my doctor and not to contact the tumour board. Nobody had spoken to the outside agency charged with co-ordinating the move from paper to electronic files to ask them what procedures they had been following and what supervision had been in place. Nobody had asked CEO, Jan Kimpen, what safety nets, if any, he had seen fit to put in place while the hospital had gone through the paper-to-electronic transition.

If UMCU is now aware of what it should be doing, why is it still refusing to do the right thing in my case? When no one tries to find out what happened to you after a life-ending error at a hospital, the message you hear is: "It doesn't really matter. You don't matter". If what happened to me mattered to UMCU, they'd find out what went wrong.

The other advantage that UMCU's new serious-harm protocols brought with them is that written records would exist of what happened to patients. In the past, including in my case, when patients were damaged by the hospital, there was often no trace anywhere in the hospital that anything had happened. There was still no record in UMCU that anything untoward ever happened to Adrienne Cullen while she was a patient. I'd have to make that record myself and make sure that it was never buried in the archives. This book would be the first part of that record, and the annual Adrienne Cullen Lecture would be the rest of it.

30 | December to April 2018

Never doubt that a small group of thoughtful committed citizens can change the world. Indeed, it's the only thing that ever has.
Margaret Meade

The day after Christmas I stopped being able to eat. We thought it was the result of too much rich food. Then we thought it was a virus. By the end of January, I had lost six kilos. I was admitted to AvL on 1 February and they discovered that I had two tumours blocking my small bowel in two separate places.

It looked at first as though surgery would not be an option. I was told they could put a tube directly into my stomach to nourish and hydrate me with a bag of food. I wasn't gone on the idea and started to think about contacting the euthanasia team I had met in 2015. Then, with more diagnostic screening, the picture changed and surgery was an option after all. The new tumours – Tumour 7 and Tumour 8 – were relatively high in the abdomen, in the mesentery around my small bowel, and so outside the previously irradiated areas. There was about a 15 per cent chance that my bowel would leak after surgery. But an 85 per cent chance of success sounded better to me than being fed bags of white liquid through a tube in my stomach for what remained of my life.

So off to the theatre we went. It was 8 February, 2018, Peter's 60th birthday. His present was that the complex surgery by the irrepressible Dr Christianne Lok was a success. Tumour 7 and Tumour 8 were successfully removed from two separate places and everything was looking good. Recovery was slow though. I spent three weeks in hospital. Starting to eat again took time and patience, as did getting back my strength.

And strength I surely needed. The First Annual Adrienne Cullen Lecture would take place at UMCU on Friday, 13 April, ironically, seven years to the day after I had undergone cryosurgery there and the ill-fated tissue sample had been sent to the lab and lost. I was weak, anaemic and barely able to walk. If I were going to stand in front of an auditorium full of people, I wanted to look strong. I needed more Spitting Mad Adrienne and less Patient Adrienne. I had nine weeks to get myself fit enough to deliver this desperately important lecture that had been promised and denied so many times since June 2016.

The lead-up to the lecture was fraught. I was pushing hard for it to be advertised beyond the walls of UMCU, and the wider medical public was declaring its intention to attend. Suddenly, the 120-seat auditorium was not big enough and a 270-seat auditorium was arranged. I wanted maximum media coverage to make sure our story was heard by the widest possible audience; UMCU favoured inviting certain "trusted media" only. I knew that was code for non-critical. Filming was not to be allowed. Reporters were told that "Mrs Cullen is not available for interview". The hospital suddenly became concerned that I was going to tell the details of the various iterations of the gagging clause. They were right. That's exactly what I was planning to do. I'd said so from the start.

I contacted the media and told them that I was, and always had been available. I spoke to NOS radio, *NRC*, *Algemene Dagblad*,

RTL, RTV, *Een Vandag*, *The Irish Times*, and several others. I contacted investigative journalist, Ton van der Ham, from *Zembla*. I told him an agreement had been reached with NOS and RTL that allowed them to film some wide shots of the lecture theatre and a few minutes of my speech. After fifteen minutes, the cameras would have to leave the room. Ton said that arrangement would suit him too, and I asked him to come along and to bring a cameraman.

The atmosphere before and during the lecture was tense and uneasy. Franx, Van der Vaart and I were, understandably, apprehensive. The organizers were anxious too. They didn't quite know what was going to happen – and they didn't trust me. Each of the main doors had a security man on it. Outside, security personnel watched who was coming and going. An Irish friend was stopped and questioned about who she was and asked for credentials before being allowed in. Another friend, who was taking notes while the lecture was underway, was questioned about what she was writing. The security guard tried to take her notebook away. Unbeknownst to me at the time, Van der Haam had arrived and had been refused entry. He was promised that I would give him an interview after the lecture, and he sat down near the entrance to wait.

At the front of the auditorium, Hans van Delden, UMCU's professor of medical ethics, who was chairing the lecture, was warning those in attendance not to film or record any part of the lecture or to post anything from it on social media. The hospital had refused to allow its own communications department to record it for teaching purposes. The reason for this was, I was told, that Professor Van der Vaart didn't want to be filmed. Not so. Van der Vaart had been crystal clear in a meeting just before the lecture that he was in favour of it being filmed and used for training.

In the front row of the auditorium, Margriet Schneider sat alongside Ronnie van Diemen, head of the Dutch Healthcare

Inspectorate (IGZ). Beside them sat Kevin Kelly, Irish Ambassador to the Netherlands, who had been a huge support to Peter and me since he arrived in The Hague in 2016. In the row behind sat UMCU's head of legal affairs, Albert Vermaas, and other members of UMCU's executive and supervisory boards. The rest of the audience consisted of division and department heads, senior medics from the Netherlands' seven other university hospitals, patients, doctors, nurses and final-year medical students. Nothing like this lecture had ever taken place before in a Dutch hospital, or anywhere else in the world, for that matter. Nobody knew what to expect.

Van der Vaart spoke first. Then I spoke. Then Arie Franx. We took it in turns to unfold the events of the past five years and tell of the unbearable consequences they had had for all three of us. Franx and Van der Vaart concentrated on their own shortcomings (too much so, in my view). I concentrated on the more serious shortcomings of UMCU as an institution and on how shamefully it had behaved towards Peter and me. The audience was appalled at the extent of UMCU's failures. Someone gasped as I recounted my meeting with Jan Kimpen in 2015 when he had asked pointedly if I trusted him to consider my position and come back to me – and then never saw him or heard from him again. There were more gasps as I displayed the text of the gagging clause that prevented Peter and me from speaking about my treatment at UMCU, what had happened, or about the settlement agreement. There was audible amazement when I said that no inquiry had ever been carried out into what had gone wrong in my case and that I was probably going to die without knowing precisely what had happened, and with those responsible (apart from Van der Vaart) never being held to account. People were getting upset. They could see the human misery that had been caused solely in the interest of preserving the hospital's reputation and the standing of its leaders.

Deny, dismiss, dehumanise

In the front row, Margriet Schneider listened. At the end of the lecture, she said nothing to explain her hospital's role in the fiasco we had just revealed. She shook my hand, thanked me, took credit for organizing the lecture, and left the room.

Outside, UMCU security guards had bundled Ton van der Ham into a room and called the police. He had, they said, been filming people, including patients, leaving the auditorium. Van der Ham said he had approached the first people he saw leaving the auditorium to ask if the lecture was finished. He was still waiting for his interview. His cameraman was sitting away from the auditorium doors, and the camera was turned off. The police came and Van der Ham, a journalist doing his job, was arrested and kept in custody for several hours. Of course, he was never charged with anything. There would be no interview with me that day.

UMCU was no doubt glad when the lecture was over. They had, they felt, limited the damage to those who had attended on the day. The fact that there was no recording was a big plus for them. All they needed to do now was to keep their heads down and wait for it all to blow over.

I had a different plan. The latest imaging showed that the cancer had spread to my lungs, my liver and my pancreas. My left ureter was partly blocked again and the mesentery around my small bowel from where Tumour 7 and Tumour 8 had been removed in February showed recurrence. Tumour 6 in my groin had also started to grow again and I had tumour nodes coming through my skin.

I went on holiday. I spent a few days in a hotel by the sea in Ireland, finishing this book and planning my next move. Only Peter knew where I was. I wrote another email to Margriet Schneider and Jan-Willem Lammers and said it was my final request for an inquiry to be carried out into what happened in 2011. I told them I was tired of having only an anecdotal and incomplete version of events, where professors Franx and Van der Vaart believed that the changeover from paper to electronic files had been central, but Professor Jan Kimpen, CEO at the time, denied categorically that this had played any role at all. I told them it was unacceptable that I was floundering around still searching for answers. I pointed out that, only as a result of my persistence, UMCU now carried out independent investigations into serious-harm events because it now suddenly believed it was the right thing to do. So why was it still not the right thing to do in my case? I concluded by asking them if they were still unwilling to investigate, and, if so, I asked them to explain to me in writing why:

I got my answer the next day. Lammers replied and appeared to be agreeing … with me:

We also feel it is inappropriate that we did not do a thorough investigation at the time of discovery of this very serious incident, which is so harmful to you, your husband and your relatives. After the lecture I have had several discussions both within and outside the UMC Utrecht whether we should initiate an investigation several years after this has happened. Most opinions were against it, mainly because necessary steps have been taken to very much reduce the chance that such a mistake happens again. However, it is, as you clearly mention in your email, not correct not to do so.

I reread it several times, just to make sure I wasn't misunderstanding. UMCU was going to carry out an independent investigation into what happened to my results in 2011. I would, finally, be given answers. All I needed now was to stay alive long enough for the inquiry to conclude.

****

Deny, dismiss, dehumanise

The End

Having developed serious complications just before Christmas, Adrienne Cullen died by euthanasia at the Netherlands Cancer Institute in Amsterdam on Monday, December 31, 2018, at 10.15 am.

This was exactly three weeks, to the day, after she was conferred with an Honorary Doctorate in Laws from the National University of Ireland at her alma mater, University College Cork (UCC).

She'd been especially moved by a speech by the President of UCC, Professor Patrick O'Shea, which ended simply with the words: "Adrienne, welcome home ..."

Afterword

When asked by Adrienne if I would be prepared to write the afterword for her book I hesitated for a moment. After all I am the doctor who is responsible for missing her diagnosis and, by doing so, greatly reducing her chance of survival. In fact, she will not be cured from her cervical cancer and that hurts. Every day.

However, Adrienne, in her own particular persistent way of getting things done, convinced me that the message she is sending by publishing her story is not complete without me writing this afterword. Writing the afterword is completely in line with the red line that runs throughout this book: in the case of medical errors, doctors and hospitals should team up with the patient to minimize the harm done and regain trust. Trust itself is one of the key elements in restoring the doctor–patient relationship, and maybe moving towards forgiveness. Not helping or allowing the patient to regain trust by not using open and honest communication is not only wrong, but in fact creates extra unnecessary wounds. Peter, Adrienne's husband, describes this lack of open disclosure and reaching out as "killing Adrienne twice".

Patients like Adrienne spend a lot of time living between hope and fear. The one thing they don't need is to spend their energy

Deny, dismiss, dehumanise

fighting anything else but the disease itself. And when that fighting is done, regardless of the outcome, they should be able to spend their time enjoying life. Adrienne in particular loves her husband, Peter, her garden and Georgie the cat, of whom she wrote to me several times with great humour. In her book, Adrienne vividly describes the hurt she experiences knowing she has to leave all she loves behind. She uses it as a tool to point out to hospital board members that she is not just patient X with registration number Y, but a human being who is entitled to be treated with a human touch. Isn't the one most important adage for doctors of medicine the concept that you should treat your patient in the way you would like to be treated yourself? Certainly, I would not want to be neglected, talked to through lawyers, and kept unaware of what happened to me in a hospital and by a doctor I put my trust in.

When reading the book, I am quite sure that at certain moments you were thinking, "this cannot be truly happening". Is the Adrienne Cullen story fact or fiction? Unfortunately, it is fact. Both Adrienne and I, on several occasions, and each for our own reasons, wished it was all a bad dream. But it isn't. Medical errors do occur and will occur. There's no doubt about that, regardless of the effort we put into preventive measures. But why are we, doctors and hospital representatives, performing so poorly in apologizing for the harm we do? By our poor performance, we are making the harm even worse. This is contradictory to primum non nocere (first, do no harm), part of the Hippocratic oath that medical graduates swear to in many countries. Doing no harm not only means refraining from unnecessary interventions, which is the usual way it is perceived by doctors, but it also means that we should not sidestep necessary interventions – like offering a full apology and explanation after medical errors are made.

So what's happening? Why is it so difficult to acknowledge medical errors and apologize? Is it the fear of losing face to your colleagues, the realization that you have failed, fear of legal consequences, fear of disciplinary measures, fear of public hanging on social media? All these factors, and maybe more, may be involved. When anxiety really kicks in, it will negatively affect rational thinking and behaviour. It is frightening news that up to fifty percent of medical doctors and trainees have signs of depression. The direct consequence of this is that they will perform less accurately and will be prone to make even more mistakes. In the case of severe medical errors, some call doctors the "second victim", although the term "victim" is somewhat misplaced next to the real victim, the patient. Fortunately, many hospitals have now installed some type of peer support. In peer support, trained colleagues reach out to the doctor involved. They offer help by listening to the story and giving basic advice for the next steps to be taken. Although this support helps, the most important opportunity is often overlooked or not used: the help that the patient or relatives can offer. This may sound weird, expecting support from someone you have done, sometimes fatal, harm to. Certainly, it is not about directly asking for support from the patient. That would be very inappropriate. But by keeping communication open and honest, in a sincere way and not just for the record, many will be surprised by the understanding and humanity the patient or relative will show towards the doctor or hospital. This open disclosure and apology is the most powerful tool in restoring trust and diminishing anxiety for both parties. Adrienne did this in my case. She asked, after getting over her initial shock, how I was coping. Of course, being an old-fashioned doctor, I denied having any sleepless nights, anxiety or fear of repercussions. She did not argue, but intuitively knew that just her asking was enough to help me.

Back to Adrienne and her story. If things had not gone so terribly wrong, with so many missed opportunities, this book would never have been written. If the many mistakes in her treatment and care, at all levels, had not been made, they would never have been made public in the way they are now. And as a consequence, all the opportunities that other healthcare providers now have to learn from them would not have existed. To realize this is bitter. It was a dirty job, but only Adrienne could do it. It is time to clean up the system when things go wrong. Colleagues and hospital officials: I rely on you not to waste the lessons from the Adrienne Cullen story.

Adrienne, say hi to Touchwood when and wherever you meet.

Professor Huub van der Vaart
Utrecht, 28 December, 2018

Appendices and the pages that reference them

Appendix 1 (Prue's letter; 7ᵗʰ or 10ᵗʰ October 2015) p.101

Appendix 2 (1ˢᵗ draft of the settlement agreement with gagging clause Number 1; early November 2015) p.111

Appendix 3 (Letter from Horstman with gagging clause Number 4; on the 8ᵗʰ or 9ᵗʰ November 2015) p. 114

Appendix 4 (UMCU press release about me) p.121

Appendix 5 (My email to Levi and his reply; March 2016?) p.175

Appendix 6 (Willem's nursing notes) p. 217

Appendix 7 (*Uniek* profile of Vermass describing him as the hospital's "contactperson" for the IGZ; also online resource) p.221

Appendix 8 (The IGZ's written reply) p. 233

Online resources
- The SAFER report
- The complaint to Bronovo Klachtencommissie
- Bronovo ruling and Letter from Renée Barge
- My presentation given at UMCU on 13 April, 2018

Deny, dismiss, dehumanise

THE UNIVERSITY OF
NEW SOUTH WALES

FACULTY OF LAW

PRUE VINES
PROFESSOR
DIRECTOR OF FIRST YEAR STUDIES
CO-DIRECTOR, PRIVATE LAW
RESEARCH&POLICY GROUP
School of Law

7th October 2015

Supervisory and Executive Boards of UMC Utrecht
Raad van Bestuur / Raad van Toezicht
Huispost D 01.343
Postbus 85500
3508 GA Utrecht

Dear Sirs/Mesdames,

Mrs Adrienne Cullen, patient

This letter concerns Mrs Adrienne Cullen, who was a patient of UMCU from approximately February 2011 to 2013 and who, because of a failure to follow up on a pathology test lost the chance of recovery from cervical cancer. I understand this case is well known to you and that the hospital has admitted liability.

Mrs Cullen has sought compensation for her own losses and those of her husband and is represented by August Van of Beer Advocaten of Amsterdam.

First I must apologise that I cannot write this letter in Dutch.

I am writing this letter in my capacity as an academic. My expertise is in the area of tort law or delict, with particular emphasis on the impact of compensation systems on individuals and apologies on propensity to sue. I am a Professor of Law at the University of New South Wales, Australia, co-director of the Private Law Research and Policy Group at the Faculty of Law there. I am also Visiting Professor at the University of Strathclyde Law School, Scotland and have recently spent six weeks as Visiting Professor at the Vrije University Amsterdam at the Centre for Comprehensive Law in the Private Law Department of the Faculty of Law. I am the author of many publications in the area of tort law and compensation, including co-editor of the well-known treatise, *Fleming's the Law of Torts*, now in its 10th edition. This treatise covers the common law of torts in Australia, Canada, USA, UK and New Zealand. It should also be noted that Scottish law and Netherlands law share Roman Law roots and the law of delict is similar in both countries. More detail about my publications may be found at www.law.unsw.edu.au/staff/VinesP.

SYDNEY 2052 AUSTRALIA
Email: p.vines@unsw.edu.au
Telephone: +61 (2) 9385 2236
Facsimile: +61 (2) 9385 1175

Location: Law Building Rm 216
Enter Anzac Parade Gate, Kensington

I am familiar with Mrs Cullen's history. What I wish to do in this letter is set out some results of research which might encourage you to deal with her more directly and to deal better with future patients who have suffered from medical adverse events including medical negligence in your hospital.

That Mrs Cullen's treatment was flawed was known to someone in the hospital from the moment when it was realised that there had been no follow up to a reported malignancy. Dr Van der Vaart did the right thing and reported this to her in April 2013 and investigated. But the hospital appears to have had no system for dealing with the fact that there had been an adverse event other than the individual initiatives of doctors and staff. (Of course I recognise that I have only been informed from the plaintiff's side, but the hospital has admitted liability. This follows from that. I also acknowledge that the investigation or audit that took place in the pathology department was an example of a good system in place). From the time that knowledge of the original problem existed the hospital should have had a system in place to acknowledge the problem, apologise to Mrs Cullen and support her through the investigation and subsequent treatment. This demonstrably did not happen. How that support operated should have been discussed with her and met her needs. If that had happened, although it might not have prevented Mrs Cullen from dying it might have reduced her suffering considerably

There is considerable research and there are systems in place in Britain, the USA and Australia - these are the systems with which I am most familiar- which facilitate the disclosure of such events in hospitals. In Australia there is a public system of Open Disclosure run by the Australian Commission on Safety and Quality in Health Care (see http://www.safetyandquality.gov.au/our-work/open-disclosure/implementing-the-oopen-disclosure-framework/open-disclosure-resources-for-clinicians-and -health-care-providers). In the UK the duty of candour (*Health and Social Care Act 2008 (Regulated Activities) Regulations 2014, Regulation 20*) and the Serious Incident Framework (NHS England Patient Safety Domain, *Serious Incident Framework*, 2015: <www.england.nhs.uk/wp-content/uploads/2015/04/serious-incidnt-framwrk-upd/pdf> are similar to the Australian Open Disclosure Process. In the USA individual hospitals run incident disclosure systems. I also believe there has been a pilot program at the Amsterdam University Hospital. What may be of interest to you is that there is evidence that such systems not only meet patients' needs in many respects, they also often result in reduced costs to the hospital because patients are happier, sue less and settle cases earlier. (See, for example, R Boothman et al, 'A Better Approach to Medical Malpractice Claims ? the University of Michigan Experience' (2009) 2 *Journal of Health Science Life Law 25-29*).

To explain how the Australian system is supposed to work I set out the steps briefly here:
    1. Patient is told of the incident (preferably within 24 hours) if they don't know already and a meeting is set up to include patient, family, carers and staff involved in the incident.
    2. Apology is given.
    3. Factual explanation. This has to be done in a way which ensures the patient understands.
    4. Patient and family are given the opportunity to respond to the explanations, contribute their knowledge and ask more questions.
    5. Patient is encouraged to talk about the personal effect of the incident on them.
    6. A plan is agreed on and recorded about what patient and family hope to get from the process, what questions need to be answered. A copy of this is given to each person and filed in the appropriate place.
    7. There is a pledge to feed back to the patient and family any information about any further reviews or investigations into the incident and their results, anything further that happens in the proposed process and the expected timeframe for these processes.
    8. An offer of support is made including reimbursement of out of pocket expenses, assurances of follow-up care, clear statements of who will be responsible for ongoing care, contact details of person(s) responsible; and information about how to take the matter further, including complaint and legal processes.

9. Support for patients, family and carer and for staff is given so that they can engage in the open disclosure process.
10. Other health organisations may be involved in the process if the incident arose from more than one service.

The Open Disclosure process is therapeutic and also offers a path to the review of system faults to prevent them being repeated.

This is the ideal process, and obviously it may not always be perfectly followed. However in the case of Mrs Cullen there was an enormous deviation from the principles outlined here. Mrs Cullen had no contact from the hospital explaining, apologising or acknowledging the event at all until after legal proceedings had been initiated. She had no meeting about the event with anyone from the hospital apart from Dr Van der Vaart until 18 months after the problem was reported to her. What was required, given that the issue was her death from medical negligence, was a meeting with Dr van der Vaart and other members of the hospital including pathology which gave her the opportunity to hear and be heard about the catastrophic nature of this event to her and how the hospital was going to respond to her needs from then on. Because this didn't happen Mrs Cullen was set adrift by the hospital and not until she had a lawyer did she get a second opinion. In my discussion with Mrs Cullen she said, 'if we had been taken in hand in any way we would not have contacted the lawyers.' Be that as it may, when an apology came after the meeting with Professor Franx and Professor Roes it was far too late, although still welcome.

Mrs Cullen is now concerned about what will happen to her husband after she dies. She is the major breadwinner of their household, and her illness has severely impacted on her earnings and her death will obviously end her earning capacity. Her husband will be left, a foreigner in the Netherlands (which brings its own issues), but where he and his wife had settled and had their economic life. He will have lost not only his breadwinner but his life partner and all that that involves. If he is forced to return to Ireland or the UK he may have to deal with housing issues which are not part of life in the Netherlands (renting in Ireland or the UK is much more onerous for the tenant and has many fewer guarantees, for example). Negotiations about compensation are proceeding.

In writing this letter to you I wish to point out that Mrs Cullen has not only been injured by medical negligence, she has suffered further because the hospital in my view did not adequately carry out its responsibilities. This ought to be recognised in her compensation.

I have set out some of the research about examples of better practice which you may wish to consider if you have not already and I would be happy to discuss this further or to point you to academics in the Netherlands who are working in this area.

Yours sincerely,

Prue E Vines

PROFESSOR PRUE VINES

VASTSTELLINGSOVEREENKOMST

ONDERGETEKENDEN

1. mevrouw A.M. Cullen, geboren 9 november 1960, en haar echtgenoot de heer P. Cluskey, geboren 8 februari 1958, wonende aan de Veurseweg 200, 2252 AG Voorschoten (hierna te noemen Cullen/Cluskey)

    en

2. Universitair Medisch Centrum Utrecht gevestigd te Utrecht, rechtsgeldig vertegenwoordigd door mr. A.M. Vermaas, Hoofd Juridische zaken Raad van Bestuur (hierna te noemen UMCU),

IN AANMERKING NEMENDE:

dat op 13 april 2011 bij mevrouw Cullen een endocervix curretage is verricht;

dat de uitslag van dit onderzoek niet door de behandelend gynaecoloog is gezien/opgevraagd;

dat dit op 4 april 2013 aan het licht is gekomen;

dat mevrouw Cullen in mei 2013 is behandeld in verband met cervixcarcinoom;

dat inmiddels sprake is van recidief carcinoom waarvoor een curatieve behandeling niet meer mogelijk is;

dat UMCU bij deze gebeurtenis betrokken is;

dat UMCU in dezen optreedt als de aangesproken partij;

dat Cullen/Cluskey zich daarom met UMCU inlaten en daarmee akkoord gaan;

dat UMCU aansprakelijkheid heeft erkend voor de gevolgen van het missen van de uitslag van de endocervix curretage;

dat UMCU en Cullen/Cluskey zijn overeengekomen de schade op basis van artikel 6:107 BW en 6:1018 BW minnelijk te regelen.

Schadenummer: AJV/IM/D-14-003947/Cullen, A./UMC14.12248/EH/eh   Paraaf: 1

Rev 12.07

VERKLAREN TE ZIJN OVEREENGEKOMEN ALS VOLGT:

Artikel 1
Partijen stellen het totale beloop van de door Cullen/Cluskey uit hoofde van de hierboven omschreven gebeurtenis geleden en nog te lijden (im)materiële schade zoals bedoeld in artikel 6:107 BW en 6:108 BW in volledige overeenstemming en bindend ten opzichte van ieder wie de schade van Cullen/Cluskey mocht aangaan, naar wederzijdse redelijkheid en billijkheid vast op een bedrag van € 545.000,-- (zegge: vijfhonderdvijfenveertigduizend euro) op welk bedrag reeds bij wijze van voorschot € 45.000,-- (zegge: vijfenveertigduizend euro) is voldaan zodat nog als slotbetaling een bedrag van € 500.000,-- (zegge: vijfhonderdduizend euro) resteert. Dit bedrag zal worden overgemaakt op

bankrekening ....

ten name van ....

Artikel 2
Cullen/Cluskey verklaren tegenover de hiervoor bedoelde uitkering finale en voorbehoudloze kwijting te verlenen aan UMCU en de bij UMCU werkzame medische specialisten en/of verplegend personeel.

Cullen/Cluskey bevestigen dat zij na bedoelde betaling niets meer terzake de bedoelde gebeurtenis van UMCU te vorderen zal hebben.

Artikel 3
Beide partijen verklaren, ieder voor zichzelf, alle goede en kwade kansen en gevolgen van de onderhavige minnelijke regeling te aanvaarden en deswege uitdrukkelijk afstand te doen van ieder beroep op toekomstige of reeds ingetreden aan hen al of niet bekende feiten of omstandigheden te ener of te anderer zijde, welke ook, die anders invloed zouden kunnen hebben op de omvang van de aansprakelijkheid of op de omvang van de door de gebeurtenis veroorzaakte schade.

Artikel 4
Partijen verklaren met de ondertekening van deze overeenkomst geen ruchtbaarheid meer te geven aan deze zaak en/of het verloop van de medische behandeling. Zij zullen in elk geval niet proactief of zelfstandig media, waaronder in ieder geval wordt begrepen de schrijvende pers, radio, televisie en/of internet(fora), benaderen en spreken af dat zij over deze zaak, de medische behandeling, de overeengekomen regeling, deze vaststellingsovereenkomst en/of de wijze waarop deze tot stand is gekomen aan derden, al dan niet onder eigen naam of via derden, geen informatie zullen geven.

Voor wat betreft de reeds bestaande contacten met de media zullen Cullen/Cluskey via hun advocaat tegenover de betreffende media verklaren dat in goed overleg met het ziekenhuis een minnelijke regeling is getroffen.

Artikel 5
De kosten buiten rechte (ex artikel 6:96 BW) maken geen onderdeel uit van deze overeenkomst en zullen separaat tussen partijen worden geregeld.

Aldus in tweevoud opgemaakt en getekend

Schadenummer: AJV/IM/D-14-003947/Cullen, A./UMC14.12248/EH/eh   Paraaf: 2

Rev 12.07

Voorschoten, ... - .... - 2015   Utrecht, ... - .... - 2015

A.M. Cullen   Universitair Medisch Centrum Utrecht

P. Cluskey

Schadenummer: AJV/IM/D-14-003947/Cullen, A./UMC14.12248/EH/eh   Paraaf: 3

Rev 12.07

FW: SPOED: mw A. Cullen

August Van <van@beeradvocaten.nl>   9 Nov 2015, 22:06
to me

Dutch

English

Translate message

Turn off for: Dutch

Hi Adrienne,

Here's a little birthday present from the UMCU:

- They are prepared to let me spend an extra five hours to help you after the settlement (I didn't yet get to ask them to compensate you for Petra's hours; that's not a problem; my hourly rate is € 300,- excluding VAT; if we don't use that, the UMCU will not have a problem to spend it on Petra)
- They think your idea to set up a 'Cullen-Vines Open Disclosure Award' sympathetic and they will take it into consideration
- They will provide a tax garantee, i.e. they will pay taxes for you if the Belastingdienst will consider your compensation as income. The result of that is that the compensation is net, not gross

The only matter that remains is the gagging clause. The UMCU has proposed a different clause from the one we drafted earlier today. Their greatest fear is not that you will talk to the press, but that you will be negative about the UMCU in the press. So they changed the wording. You are now allowed to talk to the press (or publish a book), but only if you confine yourselves to the facts and refrain from negative statements about the UMCU, Marketform (the insurer), the doctors that treated you at the UMCU, your treatment, the handling of this claim and the settlement negotations.

The UMCU seems to think that a fact is a fact. I think that leaves a lot of room for discussion, and therefore a lot of room for you to manoeuvre. Are you okay with the clause proposed by the UMCU just now? For a full version, see the email below (use Google translate).

Well, that was it. Hope to hear from you soon. I'll be at the Uni tomorrow, but I can be reached by telephone (06-   ). I have a student between 10 and 11. But otherwise I will be free (correcting papers).

Bests again

August

Van: Els Horstman
Verzonden: maandag 9 november 2015 20:03
Aan: August Van
CC: 'Vermaas, A.M.';Unit C
Onderwerp: SPOED: mw A. Cullen
Urgentie: Hoog

Beste August,

De door je cliënten voorgestelde geheimhoudingsclausule richt zich op de Nederlandse media en het onthullen van feiten. Zoals ik al eerder aangaf gaat het UMCU niet zozeer om onthullen van feiten, wel om stoppen met negatieve uitingen in de Nederlandse media en daarbuiten.

Namens UMCUtrecht stel ik voor de volgende formulering te gebruiken: "Partijen verklaren met de ondertekening van deze overeenkomst dat zij over deze zaak niet proactief media zullen benaderen, waaronder in ieder geval wordt begrepen de schrijvende pers, radio, televisie en/of internet(fora)/social media. Als er contacten met media zijn, beperken Cullen/Cluskey zich tot de feiten en onthouden zij zich van negatieve uitlatingen over UMCUtrecht, Marketform, concrete behandelaars, werkprocessen, claimbehandeling en de regeling. Als Cullen/Cluskey over gaan tot een zelfstandige publicatie, bijvoorbeeld in de vorm van een boek, geldt dezelfde voorwaarde (alleen feiten en geen negatieve uitlatingen)."

Deze formulering staat contact met het Ierse radiostation en de eventuele publicatie van een boek niet in de weg, op voorwaarde dat niet kwaad gesproken wordt over UMCUtrecht etc..

Wat betreft de overige voorwaarden. Een belastinggarantie zal worden afgegeven en UMCUtrecht streeft naar een regeling nog deze week. Wat betreft je extra kosten na realiseren van deze regeling stel ik voor artikel 5 van de vso als volgt aan te passen: De kosten buiten rechte (ex artikel 6:96 BW) maken geen onderdeel uit van deze overeenkomst en zullen separaat tussen partijen worden geregeld. Voor het geval Cullen/Cluskey na het tot stand komen van deze regeling nog een beroep op hun advocaat doen, zal UMCUtrecht deze kosten tot maximaal 5 uur vergoeden.

Tenslotte de "Cullen-Vines Open-Disclosure Award", UMCUtrecht zal dit (sympathieke) idee meenemen bij de besluitvorming in het kader van het beleid "open en transparant over fouten".

In bijlage tref je de aangepaste vaststellingsovereenkomst en belastinggarantie aan. Graag verneem ik op zo kort mogelijke termijn of je cliënten hiermee kunnen instemmen. In het bevestigende geval verzoek ik je de stukken met spoed te laten vertalen zodat de zaak uiterlijk aan het einde van de week kan worden afgerond.

Ik wacht je berichten af.

Hartelijke groet,
Els Horstman
Van Kouterik Personenschade

Van: August Van [mailto:van@beeradvocaten.nl]
Verzonden: maandag 9 november 2015 14:55
Aan: Els Horstman
Onderwerp: Adrienne Cullen
Urgentie: Hoog

Best Els,

Inmiddels heb ik overleg gehad met Adrienne Cullen en haar echtgenoot over de inhoud van de geheimhoudingsclausule. Onderstaande versie is door beiden akkoord bevonden:

By signing this contract, Cullen/Cluskey agree that they will not proactively seek out any Dutch newspaper, TV station or radio programme with the intention of divulging the facts of this case, information about the medical negligence, information about this settlement or the negotiations leading up to it. (This undertaking does not apply to media already contacted and informed before this agreement was proposed.)
Nor will Cullen/Cluskey use any social media, such a Twitter, Facebook or LinkedIn, to disclose any of the facts and/or information described above.

De achterliggende gedachten voor deze alternatieve formulering zijn, zoals ik je al eerder berichtte, dat Adrienne in Ierland wil deelnemen aan een radio-interview waarin met name het aspect van de euthanasie aan de orde zal komen. Ook wil ze eventueel een boek kunnen schrijven over haar ervaringen. Als dat laatste voor het UMCU een zwaarwegend punt is, zouden we daar eventueel nog naar moeten kijken. Nu valt dat buiten het bereik van de geheimhoudingsclausule.

Ik ben de komende dagen telefonisch redelijk goed bereikbaar, hoewel ik niet steeds op kantoor zal zijn. Daarom geef ik je mijn mobiele nummer: 06-

Wat de verdere afwikkeling betreft, zijn er wat ons betreft nog een paar details die we moeten regelen:
- Adrienne wil graag een belastinggarantie;
- Adrienne wil graag dat de definitieve versie van de vaststellingsovereenkomst en de belastinggarantie voor haar worden vertaald in het Engels, voordat zij ze tekent; ik kan dat eventueel op korte termijn laten verzorgen;
- Adrienne wil graag dat de zaak volledig is afgewikkeld en de betalingen zijn verricht op uiterlijk 20 november; in hoeverre dat haalbaar is, zal natuurlijk ook van haar zelf afhangen;
- Adrienne heeft aangegeven dat zij in de toekomst wellicht nog een beroep op mij zal willen doen. De aanleiding daarvoor vormen de problemen die zij heeft gehad rond het contact met de Levenseindekliniek. Wellicht kunnen we afspreken dat ik - indien nodig - nog een beperkt aantal uren mag besteden aan afronding van de zaak. Die zal ik dan alleen in rekening brengen als dat echt noodzakelijk is. Ik denk dan aan maximaal 5 uren.

Tot slot heeft Adrienne geopperd dat het UMCU een beurs of een jaarlijkse prijs in het leven roept voor degene die het beste artikel heeft geschreven over het onderwerp 'open disclosure'. Ze schreef mij daarover het volgende:

As a goodwill gesture and a sign of their commitment to transparency, we would like the UMCU to offer an annual bursary/scholarship/award for the doctor who produces the best written paper on the subject of how hospitals should handle the situation when a patient is seriously harmed as a result of hospital/medical care, focusing on the issue of open disclosure.

The award should be open to junior doctors (graduates but still in the first stages of their medical careers) in any department.

The value of the award should be 5000 euros, an amount which can be revised every five years.

The award should be called the "Cullen-Vines Open-Disclosure Award".

Dit laatste is geen 'harde' eis maar een goed bedoeld voorstel (althans, zo vat ik dat op). Wellicht kan het UMCU daar iets mee gezien de recente negatieve publiciteit die dit heeft teweeggebracht. Ik laat dat graag aan jou en het UMCU over.

Ik hoop dat we dit snel kunnen oplossen, ik hoor graag hoe jullie hier tegenover staan.

Hartelijke groet,

August Van
advocaat

UMC Utrecht press release translated

1. Hospital response:

More than two years ago we found out in the gynaecology department that we missed a result of a tissue biopsy. The result is that the diagnosis of cancer was made later with fatal consequences for the patient and her family. The attending physician did not see the result of the biopsy, and did not take into account that he would not receive an alert from the laboratory. It is very sad for everyone involved and we live intensely with Mrs and her loved ones.

Prof. dr. Dr Margriet Schneider (Chairman of the Executive Board): "It is terrible what happened to Mrs Cullen. It is indefensible that everything has taken so long and that Mrs Cullen has not received any support from the hospital. Our first priority is to care for our patients and support them, especially if something goes wrong unexpectedly. Mrs Cullen's story shows that we have failed.

That must be really different. We will take this course of affairs into the research that has recently been announced. It is extremely brave of Mrs Cullen that she speaks so frankly about her experiences. She can be assured that we are picking up the glove. "

Naturally, the responsible specialist has contacted the patient to discuss the consequences and to guide her. Despite the efforts of the specialist and others from the hospital, we have to conclude that the patient feels insufficiently informed and involved. We sincerely regret this. We have failed here.

We reported this incident to the IGZ two years late. That should not have happened. We will include this aspect in the investigation that the board of directors announced two weeks ago.

The error (missing the tissue biopsy) was investigated in 2014: the improvement suggestions that emerged from this study were implemented in the work process.

For example, our processes and procedures around worrying results of diagnostic investigations have been tightened up, both on the part of employees and systems. Shortly after this incident, a fully digital patient file was taken into use. The digital system is equipped with automatic alerts to clinicians for new diagnostic results. For example, it must be ensured that a diagnosis can not linger anywhere in the organization and that it is properly communicated to the patient. From February this year, UMC Utrecht patients have full access to their medical records. In this way they can immediately view all reporting and results in their own file. To learn broadly from this error, this incident and the points for improvement in a hospital-wide setting with medical professionals are mutually shared.

The financial settlement with the insurer has taken too long for the patient. UMC Utrecht counts this itself. The hospital will do its utmost to speed up the handling of these procedures.

ACADEMIC MEDICAL CENTER
UNIVERSITY OF AMSTERDAM

Mrs A. Cullen
via e-mail

Board of Directors

Prof. M.M. Levi, MD PhD, chairman & dean

e-mail: m.m.levi@amc.uva.nl

8-2-2016

Dear Mrs Cullen,

Thank you for your e-mail of last week. I apologize for the delay in answering you, but it took me a few days to sort things out.

I really feel very sorry that you have encountered another unpleasant situation on the telephone with the AMC. After your initial complaint we have taken a couple of actions which I thought would take care that this would not happen again.

Over the last months the situation of non-Dutch speaking patients was extensively discussed in our plenary staff meeting. From that, a consensual policy was formulated that we would offer all patients a translator (directly or by phone) for contacts within the hospital requiring communication with doctors or nurses. Obviously, for most patients speaking English this would not be required as most doctors and nurses have sufficient language skills to do without a translator, nevertheless for some co-workers this would still be an option. Regarding administrative co-workers, people answering the phone, or other hospital employees, we all agreed that if they were not able to communicate in English, they should ask for help from a colleague that is capable of speaking in English and transfer the patient to that person. This policy was included in our regular training of these co-workers, specifically in the out-patient clinic and in the supporting departments, such as radiology and laboratory.

We also discussed whether we would find it appropriate to ask a patient why he/she did not speak Dutch. While many of us believed this question was just intended friendly and possibly out of curiosity and many of us also thought Dutch is such an erratic language that it is not strange at all if someone with another mother's tongue would choose not to speak it (this is more or less the same type of response we discussed when you visited me), we agreed that it might be better to abstain from this question as it apparently evokes a negative feeling from the patient (as you explained). Also this policy was implemented in our regular training program. All these policies will be published on our internal website as official AMC policies.

Returning to your specific complaint regarding your phone call of last week: Your very specific information helped me to trace the call and what happened. I remember I have asked you to do this and I am grateful for your information. I spoke to the operator who answered your call. Her story is that she did understand that you wanted to speak in English, she did understand what you wanted, but was not able to answer you in proper English and wanted to transfer you to a colleague who could do so. However, when completing the transfer, the line was interrupted. I am not sure what happened but she convinced me that she did not actively hung up on you.

Academic Medical Center E2-126, Meibergdreef 9, 1105 AZ Amsterdam, the Netherlands

Just as a sign I take your comments seriously, I did a small project with a group of master students that I am supervising as a mentor. I asked them in November and January to phone to the AMC on different times and speak English to the operators, policlinic attendants, and radiology department with various questions. I am happy to say that no one reported irregular behavior. Having heard your complaint, I will ask them to do this again next month.

Lastly, I will also be a bit frank to you regarding a specific issue, as I know from our previous encounter that you appreciate truthfulness and openness. I hope you will not mind me doing so. I am certainly aware of and have maximal understanding for the difficult position you are in and I am fully convinced that everybody in our hospital will really do their best to help you to the very best of their potential. Having said this and once again emphasizing that we strongly feel that we need to be as hospitable as possible to speakers of all foreign languages and try to do our utmost to feel them confortable in our hospital, I have to say that I must take exception to your use of words like "offensive behavior", "mistreatment", "abuse" or "bullying". That is certainly not what our staff is doing, for which I can vouch personally, and the use of these words certainly do not relate or contribute to the friendly and helpful atmosphere we want to create for our patients.

I hope my response to you answers your complaint satisfactorily but please do not hesitate if you want an additional response. Also, I would really like to encourage you to report to me if negative incidents occur to you during your treatment in our hospital.

I will copy Dr. van der Velden to this letter as you mentioned him in your letter to me and I am happy to hear that you speak so positively about his care for you.

With kind regards,
Sincerely,

Prof. Marcel Levi, chairman and dean

cc.- Dr. J. van der Velden, gynaecologist-oncologist AMC

Appendix 6

Mw is in 2010 in het UMC geweest waar een tumor is gezien, de gegevens zijn echter kwijtgeraakt en na 2 jaar bleek dat mw een gemetastaseerd cervixcarcinoom met verschillende metastasen had.

Er is mw en dhr verteld dat als er in 2010 goed actie was geweest het met een kleine ingreep verholpen had kunnen zijn. Nu heeft mw radiotherapie en chemotherapie gehad en is mw terminaal.

Bij elke opname blijkt dat vpk niet goed op de hoogte zijn van de situatie en dat hier pas verandering in komt als er een "Crisis" onstaat, aldus mw.

Mw word ook snel emotioneel en kan het niet aan om steeds weer tegen iedereen het hele verhaal te moeten vertellen.

Door deze traumatische ervaring heeft mw moeite om mensen te vertrouwen en kan het psychisch niet aan om op een meerpersoonkamer te liggen.

Mw dus onder geen beding verplaatsen naar een andere kamer!!

- *Met mevrouw afgesproken dat mevrouw een eenpersoonkamer krijgt*
- *Met mevrouw de afspraak gemaakt dat er elke dienst een vaste vpk krijgt*
- *Met mevrouw de afspraak gemaakt dat na elke dienst haar situatie wordt overgedragen*
- *Met mevrouw afgesproken dat niemand die niet bekend is met haar geschiedenis voor haar zou zorgen.*

Mevrouw Cullen was at UMC Utrecht in 2010 where a tumour was seen, the data was lost, however, and only after 2 years, was she told that she had cervical cancer with multiple metastases.

There, she and her husband were told that prompt action at the start could have saved her and the cancer could have been totally cured with minor surgery. The patient has had radiotherapy and chemotherapy and is terminal.

Every time she ends up in hospital, it becomes apparent that nurses are not well aware of the situation and that they only become aware of what is wrong when a "crisis", arises she says.

The patient becomes emotional very quickly and doesn't want to have to keep telling the whole story to everybody.

Because of these traumatic experiences she has difficulty trusting people and it can be psychologically difficult for her to be placed in a multiple-occupancy bedroom.

This patient thus should not be moved under any circumstances to another room!!

It was agreed with the patient that she gets a single room.
It was agreed with the patient that she will have a fixed nurse looking after her on each shift.
It was agreed with the patient that each shift will transfer information about her to the next shift.
It was agreed that no one who was not familiar with her history should be looking after her.

Hoofd Juridische Zaken

Albert Vermaas is Hoofd Juridisch-bestuurlijke zaken. Hij verdedigt de juridische belangen van het UMC Utrecht, is contactpersoon voor de Inspectie voor de Gezondheidszorg, beoordeelt contracten en adviseert medewerkers bij vragen zoals: 'Mag dat?'

Maandag Mijn papadag. Isabelle is bijna twee, Nikki bijna drie jaar. We ontbijten samen, doen spelletjes en ik serveer fruithapjes. Ze willen op de 'pommel'. Sinds kort staat er een schommel bij ons in de tuin, en ze zijn er niet af te slaan. Ik zeg dat de schommel nat is, maar ze nemen geen genoegen met mijn antwoord: 'Pommel droogmaken!' Na de middagboterham gaan ze slapen. Ik maak van de gelegenheid gebruik om offertes voor een collectieve ongevallenverzekering door te nemen. Het UMC Utrecht heeft zo'n verzekering nog niet, want als een medewerker tijdens woon-werkverkeer van de fiets valt, is het UMC Utrecht wettelijk gezien niet verantwoordelijk voor letselschade. Maar de huidige jurisprudentie neigt meer en meer naar uitdijende aansprakelijkheid voor de werkgever. Ik heb drie offertes mee naar huis genomen om met elkaar te vergelijken. Ik let bijvoorbeeld op dubbelingen; zijn onderdelen in de polis al gedekt binnen een van onze andere verzekeringen? Ook vind ik het belangrijk dat de verzekering geldt voor inleenkrachten. Bijvoorbeeld voor een chirurg van buiten die een dag komt opereren; hij struikelt over een tas en breekt zijn pols. Om half zeven komt mijn partner Jan Harm thuis. We eten met z'n vieren stamppot met koude makreel. Klein als de kinderen zijn, ze eten altijd elk een hele vis! Zo lekker vinden ze het.

Dinsdag Vandaag heeft Jan Harm zijn papadag. Ik ontbijt in mijn eentje, Jan Harm en de kinderen slapen nog. Om kwart over zeven rijd ik vanuit Vinkeveen met de auto naar Utrecht. Ik haal koffie en neem de post en mailtjes door. Veel vragen over contracten en verzoeken om juridisch advies. Iemand wil weten of een wilsonbekwame patiënt met een verstandelijke beperking beenmergdonor mag zijn voor zijn ernstig zieke broer. Een ander wil een driejarig patiëntje een antibioticakuur geven, maar vader wil in tegenstelling tot moeder geen toestemming geven. Ook post van een medisch specialist die ik heb bijgestaan in een tuchtzaak. Hij heeft de zaak gewonnen en stuurt als dank een fles wijn. Men realiseert zich onvoldoende hoeveel een tuchtklacht met een individuele beroepsbeoefenaar kan doen. Deze man was zeer opgelucht. Om negen uur begint het wekelijkse teamoverleg. We bespreken binnengekomen juridische vragen en relevante gepubliceerde jurisprudentie. Die specifieke casuïstiek geeft invulling aan de algemene kaders van de wet, en het is voor ons erg interessant om te weten wat het oordeel van de rechter is geweest. 's Middags heb ik in de Utrechtse binnenstad een bespreking bij de Nederlandse Kankerregistratie. Ik maak namens de NFU deel uit van een commissie die toezicht houdt op hun activiteiten. Ze verzamelen gegevens van alle patiënten met kanker, zodat er zicht is op

epidemiologische ontwikkelingen. Om zes uur wil ik de parkeergarage onder Hoog Catharijne uitrijden, maar het staat potdicht vanwege de 50+ beurs. Ik mis het eten met de kinderen. Jammer, want doorgaans zijn ze maar drie avonden per week bij ons.

Woensdag 's Ochtends een kennismakingsgesprek met de nieuwe officier van justitie van het arrondissement Utrecht en Flevoland die belast is met medische zaken. Ik hecht aan een goede onderlinge band, want niet zelden hebben we met elkaar te maken als de politie hier opsporingsactiviteiten wil verrichten. Ze willen bijvoorbeeld een bloedtest doen als iemand vermoedelijk onder invloed heeft gereden. Of ze hebben verdachte bloedsporen gevonden en willen weten wie er vannacht op de Spoedeisende Hulp is binnengebracht. Vaak weigeren we. Want wij zijn hulpverleners en geheimhouders, geen opsporingsbeambten.
's Middags beoordeel ik enkele nieuwe contracten, en heb ik een afspraak met de directeur van dochteronderneming Unovate. Het bedrijf exploiteert nieuwe zorgconcepten die in het UMC Utrecht zijn ontwikkeld. Hij heeft een vraag over een stressmeter die hartslag, bloeddruk en zweetafscheiding registreert. De software is bedoeld voor medewerkers van bijvoorbeeld Spoedeisende Hulp of operatiekamers. Het helpt hen te

48 Uniek   Tekst: Rintje Duursma Foto's: Edwin Walvisch

Dagboek

▶ trainen om ook in stressvolle situaties rustig te blijven. Hoe kunnen we het apparaatje op juridisch verantwoorde wijze op de markt brengen of ter beschikking stellen aan anderen? Doen we dat als fabrikant zodat we er winst uit kunnen halen? Dan neemt het UMC Utrecht een nieuwe rol aan die niet onze *core business* is. De vraag is of we dat willen. Als ik thuiskom, is Nikki weer terug naar haar moeder, maar Isabelle is nog bij ons. Haar moeder is strafrechtadvocaat, en is de hele week in Boedapest voor een mensenhandelzaak. Om acht uur ga ik tennissen voor de clubkampioenschappen.

Donderdag
Medewerkers moeten incidenten met geringe schade altijd veilig kunnen melden. Ze brengen de patiënt op de hoogte, en doen vervolgens officieel een MIP-melding (Meldingen Incidenten Patiëntenzorg). Dit heeft geen gevolgen voor hun positie. Vanochtend heb ik een afspraak met twee vertegenwoordigers van De Letselschade Raad. Zij hebben een nieuwe code opgesteld (GOMA-code: Gedragscode Openheid Medische Incidenten) die helpt de afwikkeling van letselschade te verbeteren. Een voetnoot bij die code wekt de suggestie dat

medewerkers verplicht kunnen worden om in bijzijn van de advocaat een getuigenverklaring af te leggen. Ik ben namens de NFU faliekant tegen. Want wat blijft er over van veilig melden als er een proces-verbaal wordt opgemaakt? De voetnoot heeft afgelopen jaar tot een aantal onderlinge discussies en debatten geleid. Uiteindelijk heb ik de raad weten te overtuigen en vanochtend hoor ik dat de toelichting wordt aangepast. Daar ben ik erg blij mee! 's Middags heb ik de wekelijkse staflunch. Alle stafleden worden dan door de Raad van Bestuur op de hoogte gebracht van nieuws en ontwikkelingen. Om twee uur schuif ik aan bij een interdepartementaal overleg met de directeur Informatievoorziening & Financiën van het UMC Utrecht. De drie ministeries – waarvan er twee subsidies geven – willen weten hoe wij het geld besteden. Ze verlangen – terecht of onterecht – steeds vaker transparantie van ons. 's Avonds eten we met z'n drieën. Als Isabelle in bed ligt, ga ik tennissen. Ik verlies glansrijk, net als gisteren.

Vrijdag
Ik breng Isabelle met de auto naar crèche. Om negen uur ga ik in gesprek met de onderzoeksleider van

Pontes Medical, een samenwerkingsverband met twee andere academische ziekenhuizen voor ontwikkeling van nieuwe medische technologieën. Utrecht heeft een hielsensor ontworpen die de druk op een been meet. De sensor heet Feedb@ck en kan helpen bij trainingsschema's na een botbreuk. Voor een CE-keurmerk moet onderzocht worden of het instrument werkelijk aan de kwaliteitseisen voldoet. De onderzoeksleider wil weten bij wie de studie gemeld moet worden en welke verzekering hij moet afsluiten voor het geval proefpersonen schade ondervinden. 's Middags een werklunch met de notaris. We praten onder meer over de juridische gevolgen van een hypotheek die we hebben genomen op onze gebouwen. Daarna een overleg met voorzitter Raad van Bestuur Jan Kimpen over onder meer de contacten met de Inspectie voor de Gezondheidszorg. We bespreken ook de klacht van een leerling van het ROC die op een klinische afdeling geen stage mag lopen omdat ze weigert mannen een hand te geven. Ze beschuldigt ons van discriminatie. Jan Kimpen en ik zijn dezelfde mening toegedaan; als ze ons geen hand geeft, zitten wij daar niet zo mee. Maar we willen voorkomen dat patiënten zich moeten schikken naar het gedrag van stagiaires waarbij ze zich wellicht ongemakkelijk voelen. Al onze patiënten behoren op correcte en eenduidige wijze bejegend te worden. Zorg is immers heel persoonlijk en vertrouwelijk. Aan het eind van de dag haal ik Isabelle op van de crèche. Morgen gaan we samen naar mijn moeder in Nijmegen. Dat is voor allebei een feest. ▪

'Men realiseert zich onvoldoende hoeveel een tuchtklacht met een individuele beroepsbeoefenaar kan doen'

50 Uniek

Health Care Inspectorate
Ministry of Health, Welfare and Sport

> Postal address P. O. Box 2518 6401 DA Heerlen The Netherlands

Per e-mail verzonden
Cullenadrienne@gmail.com
Mw. A. M. Cullen

Stadsplateau 1
Utrecht
P. O. Box 2518
6401 DA Heerlen
The Netherlands
T +31 88 120 50 00
F +31 88 120 50 01
www.igz.nl

Information with
Meldpunt IGZ
meldpunt@igz.nl

Our reference
2016-1314097/ 1016527-
M1026437/SM/am

Date   July 28, 2016
Subject   M1016527 en M1026437

Dear Ms. Cullen,

With this letter the Dutch Health Care Inspectorate (hereafter: inspectorate) acknowledges the information you have provided the inspectorate with. This information was provided to the inspectorate by telephone and by e-mail.

In addition to your report to the inspectorate, the Ministry of Health, Welfare and Sport has invited you on behalf of its Minister, Ms. Edith Schippers, to share your experiences with them. The inspectorate has been informed by the ministry of the major points addressed in this conversation.

First, I wish to offer my sympathy, on behalf of the inspectorate. Your experiences with the Dutch health care system have not met expectations.

This letter is the formal response of the inspectorate to your information.
Furthermore, with this letter, the inspectorate aims to clarify its position, actions, and also its limitations.
Firstly, this letter addresses the original adverse event, i.e. the failed diagnosis of cervical cancer.
Secondly, it addresses the issue of the 'gagging clause', and the more general aspects.

In the Dutch health care system health care providers are responsible for quality of care.
As explained to you over the telephone, according to Dutch law, hospitals are responsible for the (quality of) care they deliver. By the same law, it is mandatory for hospitals to report sentinel events to the inspectorate and to conduct internal investigations concerning these sentinel events. The inspectorate assesses whether the health care provider has analysed the event thoroughly and whether the health care provider is able to implement appropriate measures to improve quality and safety of care.

Failed diagnosis
The UMC Utrecht has reported to the inspectorate that your treatment of cervical cancer was delayed for two years because the result of the pathology analysis did not reach the physician who was treating you.

Page 1 of 3

Based on Dutch law, the inspectorate has asked the hospital to conduct an analysis of the event. After receipt of this report, the inspectorate has assessed it. The inspectorate concluded that the hospital had analyzed what had happened satisfactory, and had taken measures to prevent reoccurrence of similar events. In this judgement, the inspectorate has taken into account, that the original events took place several years earlier.

The inspectorate had also taken notice of the way the hospital has involved you, after events became known. It is regular policy of the inspectorate to contact patients only when they report to the inspectorate. As you had not reported to the inspectorate yourself at that time, the inspectorate had not contacted you in 2015.

The inspectorate has closed these proceedings in July 2015.

In our latest conversation, on July 15th 2016, you stated that you would very much appreciate a personal conversation with the head of the Pathology Department of UMC Utrecht. We agreed the inspectorate would ask the UMC Utrecht to consider your request. On July 28th 2016 this point was addressed in a meeting between UMC Utrecht and the inspectorate. UMC Utrecht indicated they had already taken action in this matter.

General aspects and 'gagging clause'

Regarding your contract with UMC Utrecht, the inspectorate, after consulting its legal department, responds as follows:

The Minister of Health, Ms. Schippers, has made an announcement in Parliament. She considers civil law contracts between health care providers, for instance hospitals, and patients (or their families), in which they must agree to remain silent, 'highly undesirable'.

On April 25th 2016, UMC Utrecht has provided the inspectorate with the contract as signed by you and your husband.

In light of this statement by the Minister of Health the inspectorate has specifically assessed this contract, taking into account the information you provided regarding this arrangement.

The contract specifically states *'regarding future press and media contacts, ... Cullen/Cluskey are free to disclose the facts of the case and the impact it has had on their lives'*.

As I explained to you by telephone, the inspectorate will not take action toward UMC Utrecht regarding this specific contract, as signed by you, as there is no 'gagging clause' in the contract as signed so the inspectorate has neither cause nor competence to take any further action.

You have told both the inspectorate and the ministry of how the agreement was reached, and the difficulties you and your husband experienced during this process. These, more general points, the inspectorate will take into account in her ongoing enhanced supervision of the UMC Utrecht. As I explained, in light of other causes, at present the hospital is more intensely supervised by the inspectorate.

When we spoke, you elaborated on your continuing experiences with the Dutch healthcare system. You still experience difficulties and misunderstandings, especially since neither you nor your husband speak Dutch. You have asked if the inspectorate or ministry can be helpful in this matter, more specifically you asked if someone could assist you when you visit caregivers. I have explained to you that, however much we sympathise, neither the inspectorate, nor the ministry is in a position to do so.

In conclusion

I thank you, on behalf of the inspectorate, for all the time and energy you put into this matter.

You have made poignantly clear, how important it is to inform and involve patients, in 'regular' healthcare, but even more so when something unexpected happens or things don't go as foreseen.

As I pointed out, all information you provided the inspectorate and the ministry with, is valuable and important. The inspectorate will close your file. Your information will be added to our file of UMC Utrecht and UMC Utrecht will receive a copy of this letter.

I am very much aware of the ordeal you and your husband are going through. My thoughts are with you both.

Yours sincerely,

Ms. S.M. Mulder
Voorzitter Meldingen Overleg
Medisch Specialistische Zorg

cc. prof.dr. M.M.E. Schneider, Raad van Bestuur, UMC Utrecht

DENY, DISMISS, DEHUMANISE –
What happened when I went to hospital
© 2019 Adrienne Cullen

ISBN13: 978-90-6523-223-6
Als e-boek PDF met ISBN13: 978-90-6523-273-1
NUR: 402,860,870,897

1st edition, April 2019

Editing: Helen Burke, Eleanor McNicholas
Graphic design: Eugenie van Dam van Isselt
Cover design: TenU – Den Haag
Cover photo: © Sudok1 | Dreamstime.com

More information
🌐 www.uitgeverijvanbrug.nl
ⓕ www.facebook.com/uitgeverijvanbrug
ⓧ @vanbrugboeken
🟢 +31(0)653950054

Adrienne has described her experiences in this book as accurately as possible. Many of the names used have been altered for privacy reasons. The names of a small number of people have not been changed, because they can be revoked at any time in connection with their (then) position.

9 789065 232236